THE COMPREHENSION AND MISCOMPREHENSION OF PRINT COMMUNICATIONS:
An Investigation of Mass Media Magazines

JACOB JACOBY, Ph.D.

*Merchants Council Professor of
Retail Management & Consumer Behavior*

New York University

WAYNE D. HOYER, Ph.D.

Associate Professor of Marketing

University of Texas at Austin

Routledge
Taylor & Francis Group
New York   London

First published by Lawrence Erlbaum Associates, Inc., Publishers
10 Industrial Avenue
Mahwah, New Jersey 07430

Transferred to digital printing 2010 by Routledge

Routledge

270 Madison Avenue
New York, NY 10016

2 Park Square, Milton Park
Abingdon, Oxon OX14 4RN, UK

Library of Congress Cataloging in Publication Data

Jacoby, Jacob.
    The comprehension and miscomprehension of print
communications.

    "February 1987."
    Bibliography: p.
    Includes index.
    1. Advertising, Magazine.   2. Advertising, Fraudulent.
I. Hoyer, Wayne D.   II. Advertising Educational Foundation
(New York, N.Y.)   III. Title.
HF6107.J32   1987   659.13'2   87-1366
ISBN 0-8058-0087-5
ISBN 0-8058-0143-X (pbk)

10   9   8   7   6   5   4   3   2   1

To Jon, who in a very palpable and characteristically supportive way, facilitated the completion of this monograph.

J.J.

To my parents, Lou and Doris, and to Shirley for her support.

W.D.H.

Contents

Chapter 5. Conclusions, Implications, and Future Directions

---

*An attempt was made to include all 54 non-advertising test communications and their corresponding quizzes in Appendix I. As a number of authors and/or publications denied our request for permission to reproduce, only about half of these communications have been included.

Acknowledgments

Any project of this scope necessarily involves the contributions of many individuals. The authors would like to acknowledge with appreciation the roles played by a number of significant others in bringing this project to fruition.

First and foremost are the members of the ad hoc Academic and Industry Review Committees of The Advertising Educational Foundation — the groups that oversaw the planning and implementation of the project from start to finish. The Industry Review Committee consists of its Chair, Joseph Plummer (Executive Vice President, Young & Rubicam Inc.), Rena Bartos (Senior Vice President, J. Walter Thompson Company), John Fiedler (formerly Senior Vice President, Ted Bates Worldwide, Inc.), Arthur J. Kover (Senior Vice President, Cunningham & Walsh, Inc.), and Marilyn Bockman (Senior Vice President, American Association of Advertising Agencies) as an ex officio member. The Academic Review Committee consists of Jacob Cohen (Professor of Psychology, New York University), Stephen A. Greyser (Professor of Business Administration, Harvard University), and Benjamin Lipstein (formerly Professor of Marketing, New York University). It was both a pleasure and a genuine learning experience interacting with these individuals and responding to their questions and comments. The substantial assistance provided by Rena Bartos and Jacob Cohen warrant special mention.

Our deepest thanks go to Alfred J. Seaman (Chairman of The Advertising Educational Foundation, Inc.) and the many sponsoring organizations whose financial contributions to The AEF made this study possible. The AEF commitment to publish the results regardless of the outcome, and their strict "hands off" policy in regard to the execution of the project, reflect professionalism of the highest order and could well serve as a model for other industry-sponsored investigations in the public policy arena. Thanks are also due Paula Alex (Vice President, Advertising Educational Foundation) for her efforts in disseminating the results of this report.

As the project evolved a number of others also made significant contributions. These included Marvin M. Gropp (Vice President, Director of Research) at the Magazine Publishers Association and Laurence R. Stoddard, Jr. (Senior Vice President, Director of Communications Information Services) and his staff at Young & Rubicam, Inc. Also noteworthy were the comments of colleagues on various portions of this project. These include Professors Mark I. Alpert (Department of Marketing, University of Texas at Austin), James J. Jaccard (Department of Psychology, S.U.N.Y.— Albany), Jerry Olson (Department of Marketing, Pennsylvania State University), and Mr. David G. Mick (Department of Marketing, Indiana University.

The planning stages also involved meetings with nearly twenty staff members at the Federal Trade Commission and Food and Drug Administration. Especially helpful were the constructive criticisms provided by Dr. Gary Ford (consultant to the FTC) and Dr. Louis A. Morris (FDA) both at these meetings and in subsequent communications.

The project necessarily relied on a number of subcontractors. Professor Richard Maisel (Department of Sociology, New York University) is to be thanked for developing the respondent sampling plan and the intricate counterbalancing design for presenting the test communications across respondents.

Our second subcontractor was the Document Design Center, a subsidiary of the American Institutes for Research (Washington, D.C.). In particular, thanks are due to Dr. Janice Redish, its Director, and her staff for analyzing the linguistic and graphic features of our test communication (Dr. Veda Charrow) and evaluating and improving the comprehension/miscomprehension assessment quizzes (Dr. Dorothy Edwards).

Third, the efforts of Norman S. Passman (President), Ronald L. Silver (Vice President), Karen L. Bernal (Vice President), Elyse Gammer, and an army of other talented people at Guideline Research Corporation (New York), our field-work subcontractor, are also warmly acknowledged.

Our principal typist, Sara Pendley, is due a warm note of appreciation, as are Linda S. Nagel for the application of her editorial skills, Steven M. Weinberg for his technical assistance in the word processing of this manuscript and John T. Gray for his efforts in proofreading and index compilation.

Several present and former graduate students also made contributions throughout. These include Fliece Gates and Tammy Cornwell at the University of Texas at Austin, and Tracy Troutman (now at Warner-Lambert) and Ruth Gross at New York University.

A final note of thanks is due Leonard S. Matthews (President), Charles F. Adams (formerly Executive Vice President, Washington office), Marilyn Bockman (Senior Vice President), and the other staff members of the American Association of Advertising Agencies whose efforts facilitated the smooth execution of this project.

JACOB JACOBY

WAYNE P. HOYER

Foreword

As Chairman of the Advertising Educational Foundation, the sponsor of this study, I should like to make several comments concerning the importance and application of the findings. These comments are made from a practitioner's point of view or, to be more specific, practitioners who create the written work, publish it, and pay for it. That would include advertisers, advertising agencies and publishers, not necessarily in order of importance. I have been assured that Professors Jacoby and Hoyer have no significant disagreement with these comments:

1. There is always a tendency to expect research to bring forth some unexpected and illuminating discovery that will change forever people's ways of looking at things—a kind of minor version of $E = mc^2$. So far as we know at this moment, this study does not contain such a discovery.
2. What it does give us, however, is in many ways just as important and just as useful. It gives us a scale against which to measure our concepts and our expectations. Writers, publishers, advertisers, academicians, and regulators can all benefit from these findings. It gives them specific and reliable reference points for discussion and for assessing values. For example: to regulators, the study makes clear beyond debate that there is no such thing as "zero miscomprehension" in mass communications and that miscomprehension within certain ranges is to be expected in mass communications.

   To writers and visualizers, the study sets a range of expectations for comprehension and miscomprehension—pointing the finger of caution that even what seems the simplest of language can be misunderstood, but also calling forth their best efforts, because this benchmark study shows that some communications can be much more successful than others and there is usually room for improvement.

To advertisers, the study says that perhaps we often take comprehension too much for granted, being satisfied when consumers respond with something in the general area of our message, rather than in the precise area of what is meant.

To academicians, the study gives reliable reference points for thought and dialogue among themselves and the advertising and publishing communities. The material in the full report can be mined by scholars for many years, increasing their understanding and indicating the need for further investigations.

To regulators and legal analysts, the study indicates that implications and facts can be evaluated as roughly equal instruments of comprehension, since "inferences" are misunderstood at only a slightly higher level than are facts.

Once again, the study underlines what intuitive editors and writers have always known but have not always practiced: that words and ideas are fragile—*handle with care* if you hope to deliver them intact from one mind to another.

Although we have not attempted to compare directly the results of the TV miscomprehension study with the magazine comprehension/ miscomprehension study because of certain differences in methodology, nonetheless, the observation can be made that miscomprehension of the two are roughly of the same magnitude.

This makes us wonder how right or at least how comprehensive Marshall McLuhan was when he proclaimed that "the medium is the message." These two studies suggest that *people are the message,* or—more comprehensively— media, people, and the message are the message! In fact, comprehension is a linear sequence involving the message itself, the medium that carries it and the person who receives or doesn't receive the message intended by the sender.

Unless the message is clear and interesting, unless the medium delivers the message with fidelity, and unless the people are intellectually and emotionally equipped to process the message, the communicator must fall far short of his goal.

All of the above points in one direction—the further study of people— people as they relate to messages, rather than the other way around. What effects do various types of experience on the part of the viewer or reader have upon the correct comprehension of messages? What effect does culture—as distinguished from education—have on comprehension? How do intellectual and emotional prejudices (political, philosophical, or stylistic) affect reception and comprehension of messages? Scholars can make a list as long as your arm for further study and discussion.

The Advertising Educational Foundation began these studies with a statement of modesty about what we might accomplish. Some may say the need for modesty has been amply justified, but we hope that most—and the most thoughtful—will agree that we are progressing toward a greater knowledge of communications.

By defining and measuring the components, we are opening the way for ourselves and others to move the cause of good communications forward. Together, we may make important contributions toward attainment of one of democracy's greatest needs and brightest hopes: The comprehension of the vital issues of our lives and the information and understanding necessary to act upon them.

ALFRED J. SEAMAN

1 The Historical Context

AN IMPORTANT NOTE TO READERS

This volume was written with a number of diverse audiences in mind. Most broadly, these audiences fall into two categories: the practitioner and academic communities.[1]

At the risk of overgeneralizing, it seems fair to say that the writing styles of these two communities differ dramatically. Research reports written for practitioners tend to be relatively terse. Discussions of conceptual foundations and methodology generally are brief, with much detail relegated to technical appendices. The major emphasis in reports written for practitioner audiences tends to be on the findings and their implications.

In contrast, academic scholars are likely to discount the value of empirical findings unless they can evaluate thoroughly the conceptual foundations and research designs upon which they are based. Yet when prepared in proper academic style, discussions of conceptual foundations and research designs understandably seem arcane and abstruse to most practitioners.

Our solution to these conflicting demands is as follows. Chapter 1 closes with an abbreviated overview of the issues treated in considerably greater detail in Chapter 2 ("Conceptual Foundations") and Chapter 3

---

[1]The relevant practitioner community includes those engaged in some form of commercial activity involving advertising, marketing and/or the mass media. Another segment includes those occupying policy-making roles in government. The relevant academic domains consist of scholars in a variety of disciplines, including those doing research in advertising, artificial intelligence, communication, consumer behavior, education, educational psychology, cognitive psychology, social psychology, psycholinguistics, semiotics, sociolinguistics and marketing, among others.

("Methodology"). Practitioners who wish to pursue this material in depth may do so by reading these chapters. Those who find the brief version contained in this chapter sufficient may proceed from the end of this chapter directly to Chapter 4 ("Findings") and Chapter 5 ("Conclusions and Implications") without reading the academically oriented Chapters 2 and 3. This should facilitate communication with practitioners while avoiding any sacrifice of academic integrity.

INTRODUCTION

Communication is fundamental. It permeates virtually every institution and sphere of human endeavor. Without our ability to communicate with one another, life as we know it would be impossible.

While definitions vary in some respects, most authorities concur with Laswell's classic formulation of communication as a process involving "*who* says *what* in which *channel* to *whom* with what *effect.*"[2] The five core components of the communication process have been termed *source, message, media, receiver,* and *effect.* Each one of these components may be considered from a variety of perspectives and subdivided in a number of different ways.

The present investigation focuses on one type of medium and one type of effect. Specifically, attention is limited to the print mass media and, within that category, to the subvariety termed magazines. The effect studied is comprehension/miscomprehension.

Comprehension is defined as "the act of grasping with the intellect; understanding."[3] The present study examines the extent to which the essential meanings of print communications carried in mass media magazines are either comprehended or miscomprehended by readers of this medium. As will become clearer below, the term comprehension refers both to the process of achieving understanding and to one particular outcome of this process.

The present study represents a continuation of an earlier investigation that delved into the miscomprehension of televised communication.[4] This chapter describes the historical context that gave rise to both investigations, and outlines the major findings of the first study. The chapter then identifies the specific research questions to which the current

[2]Laswell, 1948, p. 37; italics added.
[3]Webster's, 1977, p. 232.
[4]See Jacoby, Hoyer, and Sheluga, 1980; Jacoby and Hoyer, 1982a.

project is directed. A concluding section provides an overview of the conceptual foundation and methodology to be discussed in detail in Chapters 2 and 3. Thus, the reader not particularly interested in these details can then skip directly to the findings and their implications (Chapters 4 and 5).

COMPREHENDING MASS MEDIA COMMUNICATION

The Evidence to 1978

A decade of consumer activism, beginning in the mid 1960's and continuing into the early 1970's, stimulated interest in whether consumers accurately comprehend the advertisements that they see, read, and hear. President John F. Kennedy's March 15, 1962 message to Congress is often cited as the beginning of the modern era of consumerism. This message articulated four basic consumer rights:

- The right to be informed
- The right to choice
- The right to safety
- The right to be heard (redress)

Subsequent emphasis on the right to be informed proceeded in two directions. On the one hand, it was argued that consumers needed more information than was being provided in order to be able to make "informed choices." This has led to the implementation of a number of information provision programs, including nutrition information on labeling, unit price information on shelf tags, freshness dating information on products, truth in lending information in contracts, and affirmative disclosure statements in advertising, to mention but a few.

The second major direction to emanate from the right to be informed has been a concern with insuring that the information that is being provided is not deceptive or misleading. Again, this focus directed consumer and regulator attention to the informational contents of package labeling, contracts, and advertising, to mention but a few relevant areas.

Regardless of whether the focus is on information disclosure or deceptive/misleading communications, the core issue concerns the consumer's comprehension/miscomprehension of these communications. If the information is not understood it will not have the appropriate effect.

Perhaps as a result of consumer and regulator interest, the mid 1970's also reflected greater advertiser interest in the subject of communication comprehension. Up to that time, advertisers had routinely gathered recall data.[5] However, little systematic attention had been devoted to assessing the extent to which the meanings inherent in the recalled information were accurately or inaccurately comprehended.

Academicians appeared similarly unconcerned. For example, the authoritative and extensive *Handbook of Communication* contained only three brief paragraphs devoted to the subject of comprehension/miscomprehension.[6] As another example, as of 1978, the scientific literature on television consisted of approximately 2,500 published items.[7] In a comprehensive review of this literature, Comstock et al. identified only a handful of studies devoted to comprehension/miscomprehension, all focusing on children. Not a single investigation employed adults as respondents.

While our own review of the behavioral science literature yielded a small number of seemingly relevant studies, closer examination revealed that the vast majority of these either involved personal rather than mass media communications,[8] addressed some effect other than comprehension,[9] or used specially constructed test communications that were far removed from those typically conveyed via the mass media.[10] Of the studies considered directly relevant, most were actually concerned with assessing memory rather than comprehension.[11] The principal findings of the remaining studies were that "reading a radio script is significantly more effective than listening to a radio dramatization for imparting information"[12] and that readers often extract erroneous meanings from print advertisements.[13] Unfortunately, these studies used small, atypical samples and therefore could not be relied on to serve either as a benchmark or as a basis for generalizing to the population at large. As a recent report from the National Research Council emphasizes: "A number of questions about cognition [specifically, comprehension, judgment, and recall] are impossible to answer without benchmark data from large, representative samples."[14]

---

[5]"Recall" may be defined as the extent to which certain components of the message, such as the brand name, can be remembered at later points in time.

[6]See McGuire, 1973, pp. 221–222.

[7]See Comstock et al., 1978.

[8]For example, comparing the comprehension that resulted from reading a message to in-person listening or watching someone deliver the same message, cf. Beighley, 1952; Corey, 1934; Fisher, Johnson et al., 1977; Harwood, 1951; King, 1968; Maier and Thurber, 1953; Sales et al., 1977.

[9]For example, attitudes or evaluations, cf. McGinnies, 1965; Worchel et al., 1975.

[10]As examples, Allen, 1967; Chaiken & Eagley, 1976; Williams, Paul, and Ogilvie, 1957; Young, 1953.

[11]Examples include Grass and Wallace, 1973; Katz, Adoni, and Parness, 1977; Wilson, 1974.

[12]Haugh, 1952, p. 493.

[13]Preston, 1967; Preston and Scharbach, 1971.

[14]Jabine et al., 1984, p. 6.

The state of affairs that existed as of 1977–78 could thus be described as follows. Little published evidence could be found that examined the existence, degree, correlates, and causes of mass media comprehension/miscomprehension. The existing evidence tended to be impressionistic and anecdotal, more in the nature of oral tradition than anything scientifically established. While it was acknowledged that mass media communication could be miscomprehended, the degree to which this occurred, and the circumstances surrounding its occurrence, were empirically neglected issues.

The Significance of the Issue

Despite the dearth of previous work on the subject, mass media comprehension is of more than trivial importance. Consider the following.

First, the functioning of a democracy is predicated upon, and presumes, an informed citizenry. Being informed requires acquiring and comprehending relevant information regarding the world and events around us. Since the overwhelming amount of this kind of information is now disseminated via the mass media, it becomes important to know whether and how well this information is comprehended. This is especially true in regard to television, which has progressively become the dominant source of news information.[15] Indeed, according to a Gallup Poll,[16] TV reports are the sole source of news information for a great segment of the American public.

Second, a considerable amount of mass media information, especially in the print media, is designed for informative or educational purposes. Consider the potential for serious threat to health and safety if the consumer misunderstands some essential label instruction on how to use a combustible petrochemical product, or the correct dosage of a potentially lethal self-administered drug.

Third, most theories and research on the persuasion process assume that satisfactory comprehension necessarily precedes and facilitates attitude and behavior change.[17] According to theory, without adequate comprehension there is likely to be little or no accurate persuasion. Yet this assumption has rarely been empirically examined. In those relatively few instances where it seems to have been examined, researchers have usually relied on measures of memory rather than comprehension, since it has been assumed that recall and recognition measures of retention provided satisfactory indications of comprehension.[18]

Yet *remembering* information and *comprehending* information are dif-

---

[15]Barrett and Sklar, 1980, p. 8; Comstock et al, 1978, p. 8.
[16]As reported in *Time* Magazine, July 6, 1981, p. 45.
[17]Eagly and Chaiken, 1984; McGuire, 1985; Mitchell, 1983.
[18]See the discussion of this issue by Eagly and Chaiken, 1984.

ferent and separate processes.[19] Since at least 1885, when Ebbinghaus published his classic studies on the learning of nonsense syllables, it has been clear that we can remember things we don't understand. A moment's reflection will also reveal that we can understand things that we can't later remember. This issue is discussed at greater length in Chapter 2.

Fourth, as discussed in greater detail near the end of Chapter 2, assumptions regarding comprehension bear upon a number of important public policy issues, including deceptive advertising, misleading advertising, and the regulatory imposition of corrective advertising and affirmative disclosure statements. For some, the fact that consumers derive an incorrect meaning from an advertisement is considered prima facie evidence that that ad was somehow deceptive or misleading. Others consider such a view unrealistic or, at the very least, simplistic. They contend that all forms of human communication are subject to miscomprehension and that at least some of the miscomprehension of commercial advertising is a function of this human tendency. Unfortunately, the dearth of empirical evidence made it impossible to identify the degree to which mass media communications were miscomprehended or, more to the point, whether advertising communications were more or less miscomprehended than their noncommercial counterparts.

Fifth, hundreds of millions of dollars are spent annually by advertisers trying to get their messages across to consumers. A fundamental question is: Are these messages understood by those target consumers?

THE AAAA "TV MISCOMPREHENSION" PROJECT: 1978–1980

It was in this context that the Educational Foundation of the American Association of Advertising Agencies commissioned[20] a basic research study into the issues surrounding the comprehension and miscomprehension of mass media communication. The initial study, which focused on televised mass media communications, addressed the following four research objectives:

1. To determine whether television viewers do, in fact, miscomprehend televised communications.
2. Assuming that some degree of miscomprehension was detected, to

---

[19]Ortony, 1978.

[20]The specifics of these efforts are detailed in pages 13–16 and 113–118 of the earlier monograph (Jacoby, Hoyer, & Sheluga, 1980).

determine whether there was a "normative range" of miscomprehension associated with communications broadcast over commercial television.

3. To determine whether advertising tended to be miscomprehended at a different rate than the program content that constitutes the major portion of commercially televised communication.
4. To determine whether viewers possessing certain demographic characteristics were more prone than others to miscomprehend televised communications.

Briefly, the initial study involved a quota sample of 2,700 individuals broadly representative of the United States population in terms of age (13 years and older), sex, income, education, and marital status. The respondents, all of whom reported viewing at least one hour of commercial television weekly, were shown two of 60 test communications that were drawn from network TV broadcasts of the preceding year. Comprehension/ miscomprehension was assessed via six-item true-false quizzes developed to assess the core meanings contained in each communication.

The resultant data base was quite large and the earlier monograph provides many detailed findings. Distilled in terms of the seminal research objectives, the principal findings were as follows.

A large proportion of the American television viewing audience tends to miscomprehend communications broadcast over commercial television. After exposure to two of the test communications, totalling 60 seconds of content, the vast majority (96.5%) of the 2700 respondents exhibited some degree of miscomprehension.

None of the 60 test communications were immune. Each and every communication was miscomprehended at least some of the time by some of the viewers.

The average amount of miscomprehension associated with the core meanings contained in each of the 60 test communications was 29.61%. In other words, approximately 30% of the core informational content contained within each communication was miscomprehended.

As a preliminary estimate, the typical range of miscomprehension was 29.5% plus or minus 6.5%. That is, typical TV communications seem to have their core content miscomprehended at anywhere from 23% to 36%.

Non-advertising communications were associated with higher levels of miscomprehension than were advertising communications. Excerpts of TV programs were miscomprehended at higher levels than were commercial advertisements for products, brands, or services. However, though statistically significant, these differences were small and practically trivial.

Although miscomprehension was significantly related to age and education, the magnitude of these differences was trivial. For practical purposes, no major demographic variables were associated with miscomprehension.

Miscomprehension seems to be widespread throughout the populace, occurring at all age, income, and education levels and to virtually the same degree.

Perhaps the chief significance of this initial study was to suggest that miscomprehension of televised communications might be more pervasive than many had imagined it to be.

THE COMPREHENSION OF
MASS MEDIA COMMUNICATION:
1980 TO THE PRESENT

The Broadcast Media

The monograph detailing the AAAA-sponsored investigation was published in 1980. At about the same time, reports began appearing which described related research conducted in Great Britain by two other teams of investigators.

The first stream was essentially concerned with "memory for," rather than "comprehension of," televised news programming. Here, Gunter and his colleagues found that:

1. news item recall can be adversely affected by the presence of pictorial items;[21]
2. verbal content is more potent than visual content;[22]
3. people seem to recall more from seeing the news at 9:30 in the morning than at 5:30 in the afternoon;[23]
4. introverts remember more than extroverts;[24]
5. the grouping together of related stories in order to make them more meaningful and memorable seems to have the adverse effect;[25]
6. items presented near the beginning or end of a newscast are better remembered;[26]
7. memory for news items likely involves a complex interaction of cognitive factors.[27]

---

[21]Gunter, 1980a, b.
[22]Gunter, 1981, Gunter, Jarrett, and Furnham, 1983.
[23]Gunter, Furnham and Jarrett, 1984; Gunter, Jarrett, and Furnham, 1983.
[24]Gunter, Furnham and Jarrett, 1984.
[25]Gunter, 1981.
[26]Gunter, 1981; Gunter, Clifford, and Berry, 1980.
[27]Gunter, Berry and Clifford, 1981.

Initiated by Robinson and extended by Davis and Sahin, the second stream of research also produced a number of reports.[28] A principal objective of this research was to assess comprehension of the main points of news stories presented on British Broadcasting Corporation (BBC) evening newscasts. Though the measures of comprehension were seriously confounded with memory, the findings are nonetheless quite dramatic. The unaided recall measure revealed an average accurate retention rate of *less* than 15%. When respondents were tested only four hours after viewing the news, the aided recall measure yielded an average accurate retention rate of only 27.7%. As had also been revealed in the AAAA study, Robinson et al. found no relationship between the accurate retention and either educational or occupational status. However, age was found to be correlated curvilinearly, with those in the 25–54 age bracket showing better retention than those above or below that bracket.

The year 1980 also witnessed a quasi-independent assessment of televised miscomprehension by Lipstein (1980). A member of the Industry Review Committee at the time the design and procedures of the AAAA study were finalized,[29] Lipstein used our procedures to develop quizzes for assessing comprehension of the advertising and program content of the popular CBS Sunday evening show "Sixty Minutes," and found average miscomprehension levels of approximately 30%.

The period immediately following publication of the AAAA miscomprehension study produced a series of exchanges between some who were critical of the study[30] and its authors.[31] These exchanges, as well as subsequent commentaries,[32] had a number of positive effects:

First, they helped clarify genuine issues and identify nonissues.

Second, those criticisms considered valid were incorporated into the planning of the present investigation.

Third, the exchanges helped stimulate additional research designed to address the questions raised or to extend knowledge into new areas.

Several subsequent studies involved a re-examination of the same AAAA data base. In one thoughtful study, Schmittlein and Morrison[33] estimated that the data presented by Jacoby, Hoyer, and Sheluga reflected an accurate comprehension rate of only 46%, not the 70% suggested by the original report. They further argued that if guessing constituted miscomprehension, then the remaining 54% could be viewed entirely as miscomprehension.

[28]Dyer and Robinson, 1980; Robinson, Davis, Sahin, and O'Toole, 1980; Robinson and Sahin, undated; Robinson et al., 1986; Sahin, Davis, & Robinson, 1981.

[29]See Jacoby, Hoyer, and Sheluga, 1980, p. 11.

[30]Mizerski, 1981, 1982; Ford and Yalch, 1982.

[31]Jacoby and Hoyer, 1981, 1982b.

[32]See Preston, 1983; Preston and Richards, 1986a, 1986b.

[33]Schmittlein and Morrison, 1983.

Alternatively, if guessing were not viewed as miscomprehension, then the average miscomprehension reflected by the AAAA data would be no higher than 19%. Partially as a consequence of their analysis, the measurement procedures of the present print investigation were modified so as effectively to minimize ambiguity due to guessing.

Another investigation[34] re-examined the AAAA data with an eye toward identifying message and receiver factors that might be causally related to miscomprehension. In addition to the earlier findings that age, education, and message complexity bore a slight relationship to miscomprehension, this study revealed that:

1. the presence of printed copy in a TV ad is associated with an increase in miscomprehension,
2. surprisingly, the presence of music seems to lower the rate of miscomprehension slightly.

Based upon the finding that the nine public affairs communications contained in the original set of 60 test communications had greater miscomprehension rates (of 26% to 50%) than did the remaining 51 communications, a third study[35] considered the relevant data from the original study in terms of the argument that democracy is or should be predicated upon an informed citizenry.

A fourth study[36] addressed the criticism that the miscomprehension levels found in the TV study were inflated due to the use of a true-false format. These authors found extremely small differences when comprehension was assessed via true-false as compared with multiple-choice quizzes, thereby suggesting that the findings of the earlier investigation were not biased by testing format.

The original investigation examined the direct impact of a single exposure. Accordingly, a fifth study[37] examined the impact of repetition on levels of comprehension. Different groups of respondents received either 1, 2, 3, 4, or 5 exposures to some of the communications from the original study before being tested. The findings revealed that additional exposures exerted only a minor and statistically insignificant impact on levels of miscomprehension.

The original study influenced the design and conduct of a number of other investigations, both in the U.S. and abroad. Research conducted in Germany[38] found that miscomprehension of the verbal content of 30-second

[34]Hoyer, Srivastava, and Jacoby, 1984.
[35]Hoyer and Jacoby, 1985.
[36]Gates and Hoyer, 1986.
[37]Alpert, Golden, and Hoyer 1983.
[38]Kuss, 1985; Haedrich and Kuss, 1986.

televised commercials drops dramatically as one goes from 7- and 8-year-olds (42%), through 9-year-olds (41%), 10-year-olds (36%), 11-year-olds (35%), and 12- to 13-year-olds (31%), to those aged 14 and older (26%). Miscomprehension of verbal content was found to be substantially greater than miscomprehension of pictorial content.

Jacoby, Troutman, and Whittler[39] examined factors associated with miscomprehension of the 1980 pre-election debate between incumbent President Jimmy Carter and candidate Ronald Reagan, finding a median miscomprehension rate of 23%.

Other relevant work has included a thoughtful piece on the comprehension of television news[40] and an edited collection of papers reviewing information processing research in advertising.[41]

The comprehension investigations mentioned thus far all focus exclusively on televised communication. The edited volume by Harris also contains a paper summarizing the findings of research on comprehension of simulated radio commercials.[42] Though the test circumstances generally involved introductory psychology students at a single midwestern university examined on specially constructed, inauthentic commercials regarding fictitious products, the methodological approach was relatively sophisticated. The basic and consistent finding emerging from this research is that respondents hearing an ad tend to make inferences regarding the advertised product, which they then believe to be true and to have been explicitly stated by the ad, even though such meanings neither were expressly contained in the communication nor could be logically derived from it.

The Print Media

Mass media other than television also exert considerable impact on the buying public. These include radio, newspapers, and magazines, in which advertisers purchase time or space so that their advertisements/commercials appear in the context of editorial or program material. They also include media totally under the control of a single advertiser, such as package labels and inserts, outdoor "billboard" advertising, matchbook covers, etc.

Little appears to have been published in the period since 1980 that focuses on the comprehension of authentic print mass media. Testing for purportedly misleading claims appearing in 10 magazine ads, one study found an average miscomprehension rate of 80%. Even after these claims were excised and the same ads were provided in "corrected" form, an

---

[39]Jacoby, Troutman, & Whittler, 1986.
[40]Woodall, Davis, and Sahin, 1983.
[41]Harris, 1983.
[42]Harris, Dubitsky, and Bruno, 1983.

independent group of respondents exhibited a 50% miscomprehension rate.[43]

Another investigation[44] tested comprehension of six statements developed by staff members at the Federal Trade Commission for insertion in selected analgesic advertising. These authors found "completely inaccurate" comprehension rates of approximately 35% and "partially inaccurate" comprehension rates of approximately 40%. In other words, approximately 75% of the respondents extracted an incorrect meaning from the FTC-proposed corrective advertising statements.

A 1982 study commissioned by the Magazine Publishers' Association found that, though no measures were taken of actual comprehension, magazine readers believe that they learn a great deal from reading magazines.[45]

Two studies attempted to compare print and televised communication. The first of these[46] used six of the 60 audio/video test communications from the original AAAA study, and also had these converted to tape-recorded (audio only) and typewritten print versions so as to represent radio and print communications. The same six-item true-false quiz was used to assess miscomprehension for all three versions. The data revealed lower miscomprehension rates for the print versions than for their televised or radio counterparts. The rates were 17% when respondents were given unlimited time to read the passage and 21% when given only 30 seconds of reading time (so as to correspond to the broadcast conditions), as compared with 25% for TV and 26% for audio only. It must be emphasized, however, that these print communications were unlike those generally found in the mass media, being only typescripts of the televised communication. They lacked the characteristics of most print communications, such as typesetting, different type sizes and styles, accompanying illustrations, color, etc. They were static representations of messages that had been designed to be conveyed in dynamic form.

The second cross-media comparison study was a large-scale investigation conducted by the Food and Drug Administration.[47] Television and magazine ads were professionally developed for two fictitious drug products and embedded in either a magazine or a TV show. Comprehension was assessed via quizzes that used a three-point true-false-don't know format. Although the miscomprehension rates did not differ by more than a few percentage points from those obtained in the cross-media study described

[43]Russo, Metcalf, and Stephens, 1981.

[44]Jacoby, Nelson, and Hoyer, 1982.

[45]See Opinion Research Corporation, undated.

[46]Jacoby, Hoyer, and Zimmer, 1983.

[47]Morris, Brinberg et al., in press.

in the paragraph above, this study found somewhat greater miscomprehension rates for the two magazine ads (20%) than for the two televised commercials (17%). Similarly, the average "don't know" response rate was higher for the magazine ad (36%) than for its television counterpart (28%). Unfortunately, the study was confined to one product category (drugs) and employed only two ads, both for hypothetical products. Research is needed that covers a more representative array of products and services and that uses authentic print communications.

It might be noted in passing that cross-media studies of memory reveal generally consistent results. With one exception,[48] print communications tend to be better recalled than audio-video or broadcast communications.[49]

In sum, as far as could be determined, until now there has been no broad-scale, nationally projectable investigation into the nature of comprehension and miscomprehension of real-world advertising and non-advertising print communications. The present study addresses this gap.

OBJECTIVES OF THE
PRINT COMPREHENSION/MISCOMPREHENSION
INVESTIGATION

The initial call for proposals issued by the AAAA Educational Foundation in the fall of 1977 clearly noted the Educational Foundation's intent to commission research into the comprehension/miscomprehension of all major mass media.[50] Practical considerations arising from the enormity of the task required that attention initially be limited to televised communication. Accordingly, this second project was undertaken to focus on the comprehension/miscomprehension of mass media print communication.

A literature review[51] revealed no published articles focusing specifically on the comprehension (as distinct from the recall) of authentic magazine communications. Researchers at both the Magazine Publishers Association[52] and the Newspaper Advertising Bureau of the American Newspaper Publishers Association[53] were then contacted to determine the status of relevant industry literature. None of those contacted could recall any directly relevant research published up to that point in time. A second set of calls made during November, 1985 reconfirmed these impressions. A

---

[48]Williams, Paul, and Ogilvie, 1957.
[49]Browne, 1978; Furnham and Gunter, 1985; Gunter, Furnham, and Gietson, 1984.
[50]See page 117 of Jacoby, Hoyer, and Sheluga, 1980.
[51]This review included examining each relevant item cited in Lipstein and McGuire, 1978.
[52]Marvin M. Gropp.
[53]Dr. Leo Bogart and Dr. B. Stuart Tolley.

broad-scale investigation into mass media print communication seemed long overdue.

The objectives of the present study include the same objectives as those articulated for the initial study on televised communication, along with the following additional objective:

1. *Comprehension:* To what extent do magazine readers understand what they read?[54]

The four objectives based upon those of the initial study are as follows:

2. *Miscomprehension:* To what extent do magazine readers misunderstand what they read?[55]
3. What is the "normative range" of miscomprehension of magazine content that might be expected from readers?
4. Do magazine advertisements and editorial communications elicit different levels of miscomprehension?
5. Are demographic characteristics of readers related to their magazine content miscomprehension?

Chapter 2 is devoted to conceptualizing and clarifying these five objectives so that they might be addressed empirically. Chapter 3 then specifies how these conceptualizations were implemented. Both chapters were written with an academic audience in mind, and contain considerable technical language. The essentials of these chapters are summarized below for those wishing to skip over this technical material and proceed directly from Chapter 1 to the findings (Chapter 4) and their implications (Chapter 5).

OVERVIEW OF CHAPTER 2: CONCEPTUAL FOUNDATIONS

The early sections of this chapter describe the nature of the sources, messages, media, and receivers employed in the present investigation.

---

[54]For reasons described below, attention was confined to general circulation magazine communications.

[55]As discussed in detail in Chapter 2, miscomprehension is not the precise opposite of comprehension.

Sources

For purposes of this study, no attention was paid to source identity.

Messages

In contrast, various aspects of the message were of great concern. The important points raised with respect to messages may be summarized as follows:

1. Attention was focused equally on advertising and editorial messages.
2. For both advertising and editorial messages, emphasis was placed on message content, not structure. That is, attention was concentrated on the *meanings* contained in and expressed by the messages, rather than on such factors as graphics, organization, etc.
3. Emphasis was placed on two types of meanings:
   a. *Asserted meanings (or "facts")*. These are defined as objectively verifiable meanings that are explicitly expressed in the message.
   b. *Implied meanings (or "inferences")*. These are defined as meanings that are not explicitly expressed in the message but that may be logically or pragmatically derived from the message.
4. Attention was limited to material content, that is, to meanings that pertain to some consequential aspect of the central focus of the communication. For example, given an ad in which a spokesperson described a product, the assessment focused on what the spokesperson said or implied about the product (material content), not on the color of the spokesperson's suit (immaterial content).

Media

Two broad categories of media were identified: interpersonal and mass. The latter was further subdivided into broadcast and print. Though the initial intent was to study both major varieties of print mass media (namely, newspapers and magazines), the substantial differences across these varieties coupled with the enormity of the project dictated that attention be devoted to only one of these. Faced with this necessity, the Academic and Industry Review Committee chose magazines.

Receivers

The population studied is defined as individuals aged 18 and older living in the 48 contiguous United States who claimed to be readers of mass media magazines.

Comprehension and Miscomprehension

The communication effects studied were comprehension and miscomprehension; most of Chapter 2 is devoted to considering these concepts in some detail.

The opening portion of this material reviews the literature in social psychology, advertising, and consumer behavior and indicates how the concept of comprehension plays a central role in all these domains.

Psycholinguistics and cognitive psychology are the academic domains in which most of the fundamental research on the subject of reading comprehension is done. Because it relies heavily on the scholarly literature in these domains, the remaining material in Chapter 2 is written in technical language and may be of only passing interest to some readers. The essential points made in this portion of Chapter 2 are as follows.

1. After being exposed to a communication, the receiver is likely to proceed through a series of mental and behavioral stages.
2. Comprehension is but one stage in this complex series. It is preceded by stages such as attention, and succeeded by stages such as attitudes, intention, and behavior formation.
3. Comprehension is a complex process in its own right, involving the dynamic interaction of numerous sub-processes and stages.
4. The scientific literature reflects two broad, mutually compatible perspectives on how comprehension is achieved.
   a. The first of these perspectives is termed *bottom-up processing.* It emphasizes how the mind begins to work with the detailed physical characteristics of the incoming information, organizing these into larger and larger units until meaning is achieved.
   b. The second of these perspectives is termed *top-down processing.* It emphasizes how the receiver uses *schemas,* a type of preexisting global mental structure, to interpret the incoming information.
5. Using these two perspectives as anchor points, a conceptualization is then derived that views comprehension as the result of two types of analyses. These are termed sensory analysis and semantic analysis.
   a. *Sensory analysis* represents the receiver's attention to features of letters, entire letters, then letter clusters.
   b. *Semantic analysis* involves the individual in arriving at isolated individual meanings, technically known as *morphemes.* These then become integrated into larger organized meanings termed *thematic representations.* Thematic representations reflect the essence of communication and are at the core of attempts to assess the meaning of communications.

6. The necessity for studying both asserted and implied thematic representations is then described. For example, there are times when the implied meaning is the only meaning that makes any sense. Consider the sentence: "Jon was sitting on pins and needles." The explicitly asserted meaning would have Jon a bloody mess, while the implied meaning would likely be the one intended, namely, that Jon was nervous or anxious.

7. In the final stage of the comprehension process, the receiver arrives at one or more *communication beliefs,* which represent what the recipient of the communication believes the communication said, either explicitly or implicitly.

8. Communication beliefs must be distinguished from *referent beliefs.* The latter represent the receiver's beliefs regarding the focus of the communication. Stated somewhat differently, while communication beliefs pose the question "Does the receiver believe *that the communication expresses* proposition X?", referent beliefs ask "Does the receiver believe proposition X?" These are entirely independent issues. The receiver could respond "yes" to the first question and "no" to the second. An example would be, "Yes, the ad did say that the product would remove freckles," and "No, I don't believe that the product is capable of doing what it claims."

9. Having described the process of comprehension, Chapter 2 then goes on to discuss the outcomes of this process. Three *principal outcomes* are identified:

> *non-comprehension:* failing to extract meaning.
> *comprehension:* extracting meanings that were either explicitly or implicitly contained in the communication.
> *miscomprehension:* extracting meanings that were neither contained in nor logically derivable from the communication and/or rejecting meanings that were contained in or logically derivable from the communication.

10. This section concludes by noting that the research plan would focus on studying the sub-process of thematic representation, specifically, whether the communication beliefs that resulted reflected non-comprehension, comprehension, or miscomprehension.

11. The final section of Chapter 2 provides a technical discussion of how miscomprehension may be related to the concepts of deceptive and misleading advertising and to the somewhat different notions of deceptiveness and misleadingness. This section may warrant closer reading by those interested in public policy considerations.

OVERVIEW OF CHAPTER 3: METHODOLOGY

Chapter 3 contains three principal sections. The first addresses how magazines, magazine communications, and magazine readers were selected for the study. The second section describes how comprehension and miscomprehension were measured. The third outlines how the study was actually administered.

Sampling Plans

Clearly, the assessment could not include all magazines, all communications and all individuals who satisfied the study requirements. Some systematic and fair procedure was needed to select representative magazines, communications, and individuals for study. The first portion of Chapter 3 details the sampling plans and procedures that were employed. The application of these plans resulted in the following.

1. A total of 18 different magazines was selected to represent the universe of general circulation magazines across the United States.
2. Six different communications were selected as being representative of those appearing in each of these magazines. Half were advertisements, the other half were editorial passages. Consistent with standard industry practice and nomenclature, these communications were selected so as to represent the basic categories of such communications.
3. A total of 1347 individuals participated in the tests. These individuals were selected on the basis of a national probability sampling design that enables us to project the results to the nation as a whole.

Measuring Comprehension/Miscomprehension

The second stage of the methodology involved developing procedures for assessing comprehension/miscomprehension of the test communications.

True-false quizzes were developed for each communication. All 108 quizzes had the following characteristics:

1. Each quiz contained six true-false items.
2. Each item was a paraphrase of some material meaning contained in the communication. For each quiz, half the items were accurate paraphrases, while the other half were inaccurate.
3. Each quiz included some items measuring asserted meanings, and some measuring implied meanings.
4. For each quiz item, the respondent could answer either true, false, or don't know.

A lengthy test development process, which included scrutiny and evaluation by an outside independent agency (the Document Design Center), insured that the tests were fair and would be readily understood.

Implementation

Once the various samples had been identified and assessment instruments developed, the study was ready for implementation. The third section of Chapter 3 describes the implementation procedures.

In-home interviews were conducted with 1347 eligible respondents screened to insure that they satisfied the study requirements. All eligible respondents claimed to be at least occasional readers of one of the eighteen test magazines.

After a brief introduction, each respondent was given the first of four test communications and asked to "read what it says and tell me when you're finished." Comprehension of this first communication was measured immediately upon completion. This was followed by a brief battery of questions on the respondent's feelings toward, and prior experience with, the product (or topic) that was the focus of that communication.

The same sequence was repeated for the second, third, and fourth communications. Each respondent was thus tested on two advertisements and two editorial communications.

In order to gauge the effects of prior experience and guessing, each respondent then answered two additional quizzes without being shown the test communications upon which the quiz items were based. Thus, each respondent answered six quizzes in all, four for communications that he or she had read and two for communications that had not been provided. During data analysis, these responses were divided so that the first four were sorted into a "communication plus quiz" experimental condition and the latter two into a "quiz only" control condition.

The interview concluded with a final set of questions designed to assess basic sociodemographic information, including the respondent's sex, age, marital status, amount of formal education, income, etc. These data enabled us to determine that the obtained sample was reasonably representative of the universe of magazine readers.

A coda appended to the end of Chapter 3 makes the following points.

1. Though some contrived aspects (such as "forced exposure") were unavoidable, most of the study procedures emphasized the natural over the contrived. As examples: The study used authentic magazine communications, not specially constructed laboratory stimuli; the respondents were representative of the magazine reading public at large; etc.

2. The present investigation embodies precisely the kind of research on basic cognitive processes (including comprehension) recently called for by the National Research Council.[56] Specifically, it represents a relatively rare integration of two different research traditions: large-scale survey research and controlled experimentation.

Having read the Overviews of Chapters 2 and 3, readers are now free either to pursue this material in detail by reading the chapters themselves, or to proceed directly to a discussion of the findings and their implications (Chapters 4 and 5).

---

[56]See Jabine et al., 1984.

II CONCEPTUAL AND METHODOLOGICAL UNDERPINNINGS

2 Conceptual Foundations

The major purpose of this chapter is to detail what *source, message, medium, receiver,* and *comprehension* are taken to mean in the present investigation. Chapter 3 then details how these concepts were "operationalized" (that is, translated into empirical form) so that they could be studied. Because it represents our central focus, the greatest attention in Chapter 2 is devoted to considering the concept of comprehension/ miscomprehension.

A secondary purpose of Chapter 2 is to consider how miscomprehension may be related to the concepts of misleading and deceptive advertising and the related, though not equivalent notions of deceptiveness and misleadingness.

SOURCES

Considerable prior research makes it undeniable that knowing the identity of the source of a message affects the receiver's attention to and perception, comprehension, and evaluation of that message. However, the many factors having higher priority in this investigation dictated that source identity not be a major focus. As detailed in Chapter 3, participants in the study were told only that the communications they would be receiving had appeared in a general circulation magazine. They were given no further information, and left to draw their own conclusions regarding source identity. In the case of advertising, this meant that the identity of most corporate sponsors could be deduced.

MESSAGES

By definition, the notion of comprehension implies "comprehension of what?" Answering this question necessarily presumes that one can identify certain *meanings* contained in the communication and then use these as criteria for gauging correct and incorrect comprehension. That is, assessing comprehension involves providing a test message to the receiver, insuring that the receiver gives it attention, and then determining whether the meanings that he or she extracts from that communication are correct or incorrect.

The chief concern is thus with comprehension of the underlying meanings and not with the surface features of the messages per se. Accordingly, some issues touched on only briefly in this section are left for more extensive consideration in the later section on comprehension.

Content vs. Structure

The message component of the communication process admits to a wide variety of properties and classification schemes.[1] One distinction that can be made is that between message *content* and message *structure*. The latter term refers to such factors as print size, number of colors used, and the spatial and temporal organization of message elements. The manner in which message structure features were handled is described in Chapter 3. Attention is focused here on message content characteristics.

Editorial and Advertising Content

According to standard advertising and magazine industry practice, a magazine's total contents can be apportioned into two mutually exclusive and exhaustive categories—advertising and editorial content. As dictated by Research Objective 4 (see Chapter 1), our interest was in both types of content.

As required by the "Specification for Proposal" initially furnished to the authors, classified advertisements were excluded from consideration. Attention was limited to the broad array of display advertisements that constitute the overwhelming share of magazine advertising content.

In like fashion, editorial content was confined to the features and articles that constitute the core content of magazines. Items such as statements of editorial purpose, place of business, publication policies, letters to the editor, etc. were excluded from consideration. Again, this meant that the vast majority of magazine editorial content qualified for inclusion.

---

[1] See de Sola Pool, Schramm et al., 1973.

Factual and Inferential Content

It is now widely accepted that communication is an active rather than a passive process for both source and receiver. Each receiver enters any communication situation primed with a base of prior knowledge and current expectations which are brought to bear in interpreting and understanding the source's meaning. One aspect of this active process is the generation of inferences from explicit content.[2] Thus, accurate understanding of the meanings explicitly contained in the message represents only *part* of the understanding developed by the receiver.[3] As Woodall, Davis, and Sahin note in regard to television news comprehension:

> Viewers may make inferences concerning a news story in understanding it, . . . some characterized as going beyond immediate story content . . . Until researchers begin to assess a receiver's understanding in terms of inferences made concerning the information, the extent of [comprehension and mis-comprehension] will be difficult to determine.[4]

Accordingly, as was also true of the prior TV study, interest was not confined to the meanings that might objectively be shown to be contained in the message, but also extended to meanings that could be deduced from what had been explicitly stated. The study thus focused on both facts and inferences. These are sometimes referred to below as asserted and implied meanings, respectively.

Material vs. Immaterial Content

Each and every communication can be conceptualized as being comprised of a universe of factual and inferential meanings. As a rule, briefer communications will have correspondingly smaller universes. To illustrate, compare the universe of meanings that might be associated with a single sentence with the universe of meanings likely to be associated with an entire text. When illustrations are involved, as is often the case with a print ad, the universe of meanings can be considerably expanded.

As the universe of associated meanings becomes broader, it becomes clear that no test could possibly focus on all of them. Thus, one needs to ask: Just which meanings associated with a communication should qualify for use in assessing miscomprehension?

One way to address this question is to think of each communication, particularly an advertisement, as consisting of two basic components: one

---

[2]See Ortony, 1978.
[3]See Harris and Monaco, 1977; Olson, 1978; Mitchell, 1983.
[4]Woodall, Davis, and Sahin, 1983, pp. 19–20.

comprised of those elements that focus on presenting and describing the product (e.g., a soft drink), and another consisting of everything else (e.g., the color of the spokesperson's suit). To borrow a legal phrase, there are elements of the communication that are *material* and others that are not.

Both from a public policy[5] and an advertiser's perspective, it is inaccurate beliefs likely to affect the consumer's choice or conduct regarding the advertised product that are of concern; inaccurate beliefs regarding any other aspect of the communication are immaterial.

For example, if readers of a magazine ad tend to believe that the color of the spokesperson's suit was green when it was actually blue, and that spokesperson was promoting a soft drink (not clothing), then the consequences of this erroneous belief would be irrelevant. On the other hand, should consumers miscomprehend the spokesperson's message so that they believe he said that the soft drink contains 100% of the Recommended Daily Allowance (RDA) of Vitamin C when it does not and, further, should they purchase and consume the product on the basis of this faulty miscomprehension, then the adverse consequences across the aggregate of consumers could be substantial. Accordingly, and as was also the case in the prior TV study,[6] attention was limited to material content (both factual and inferential) concerning the object or focus of each communication.

A comment is in order regarding the scope of this material content. It can readily be appreciated that material meanings exist at various levels, from the molar to the molecular. For example, what something is named or called represents a relatively molar material meaning. This is captured by the question, "What is the brand name of the beer being advertised?" The features or general characteristics of the object represent a more molecular level, as reflected by the question, "Does the advertisement claim that the beer is low in calories?" At an even more molecular level, one may ask about the details of these features. This may be illustrated by the question, "What is the number of calories per serving being claimed for the advertised brand?" These latter two questions might be termed "general" and "specific" claims.

Comprehension and miscomprehension likely vary as a function of the level of material meanings under consideration. Specifically, miscomprehension is likely lowest when molar meanings are involved and highest when molecular meanings are involved. It is easier to comprehend a brief name of a product than details regarding its attributes or performance. For this reason, the present assessment focused on intermediate level material content.

---

[5]See FTC, 1983, p. 693; Bailey and Pertschuk, 1984, p. 394; Ford and Calfee, 1986, p. 89.
[6]See Jacoby, Hoyer, and Sheluga, 1980, p.37.

MEDIA

The term *media* refers to the ways in which a source's message is made available to the receiver.[7] At a general level, two categories of media can be distinguished: interpersonal media and mass media.

Interpersonal Media

Originally, all transfer of meaning from one person to another probably occurred in the context of face-to-face interaction. Although spoken language was likely predominant, the physical presence of both source and receiver enabled the former to employ any and all of the basic senses—sight, sound, smell, taste, and touch—to convey his message.

Over the course of evolution, interpersonal communication was extended by media that enabled messages to be transmitted over space and time. As examples, certain sounds and sights, like drum beats and smoke signals, could be detected over several miles. Other visual messages could be used to stand the test of time, such as arrangements of sticks or stones and scratches made on the earth's surface or on papyrus. As these scratches evolved into formalized alphabets consisting of letters and numerals, handwritten messages flourished.

Note that across all such interpersonal media, the distinguishing characteristic is that the transmission of meaning is generally conveyed to one or only a limited number of receivers at a time. Though subsequent development of the telegraph and telephone enabled rapid communication over great distances, these media still required that the parties to the communication be directly connected by the wire over which the communication was transmitted, thereby effectively limiting the number of receivers.

Mass Media

Gutenberg's introduction of the first practical printing press in the mid-1400's made it possible for one party to simultaneously communicate with great numbers of other parties who themselves were separated in time and/or place. The impact of this innovation on mankind and its institutions has been incalculable. Mass literacy and education, something unimaginable in the absence of printing, constitutes one prime example. The use of printed pamphlets to arouse passions, stimulate discontent, and foment successful geo-political revolution is another. More than 400 years later, other technological developments substantially enhanced the ability of one source to simultaneously communicate with many others across time and place.

---

[7]See Schramm, 1973, p. 116.

These include Marconi's demonstration of the first practical wireless transmission of audio signals (radio) in 1895, Zworykin's demonstration of the first practical televised transmission in 1929, and the development of film, phonograph records, audio and video tape, and laser disks.

These developments led to a new category of media which, collectively, are termed the *mass media*. The distinguishing characteristic of the mass media is their "multiplicative power," a term that refers to their "enormous ability to multiply a message and make it available in many places" at the same or different times.[8]

The mass media have been subdivided in various ways. Most typically, they are apportioned into two broad categories: broadcast and print. The broadcast media are usually further subdivided into two sub-categories, namely radio and television. Print, on the other hand, takes a number of different forms. Examples include pamphlets and circulars, billboards and posters, matchbook covers, product packages and labels, package inserts, retail displays, etc. By and large, the two principal print mass media are newspapers and magazines, with each of these forms encompassing a number of more specific varieties.

The initial intent was for the present investigation to examine comprehension/miscomprehension with respect to both newspapers and magazines. But each of these media is highly heterogeneous and, since it was necessary to include in our assessment a reasonable number of examples of each medium studied, we were compelled to restrict our attention to one or the other. Accordingly, attention was confined to general circulation English language mass media magazines that can be purchased at most newstands.[9] Although magazines and newspapers are more similar to each other than they are to either TV or radio, they do differ in a great number of respects, some obvious, others subtle and not so obvious. For that reason, any attempt to generalize from the present findings obtained with magazines to any other print medium would be unwarranted.

RECEIVERS

Receivers of mass media communications vary in a great number of ways. All enter the communication situation with different backgrounds, degrees of knowledge, and current expectations.

---

[8]Schramm, 1973, p. 119.

[9]It is noteworthy that although the *Handbook of Communication* (de Sola Pool, Schramm, et al., 1973) contains separate chapters on broadcasting (Ch. 18), the press (Ch. 16), and even film (Ch. 17), there is no separate chapter devoted to magazines. Attention to this medium is fragmentary and limited throughout the *Handbook*.

One factor of particular relevance is whether the receiver is literate.[10] According to research conducted by the U.S. Department of Education, at a minimum, about one out of eight adult Americans is illiterate.[11] The rates vary by age as follows:

Age	Percent functionally illiterate
20–29 years old	9%
30–39 years old	8%
40–49 years old	13%
50–59 years old	13%
above 60 years old	30%

The rates also differ geographically: 41% of those who are functionally illiterate live in central cities of metropolitan areas, as compared with just 8% in rural areas.

As compared to the TV study, in which the universe of eligible respondents consisted of virtually everyone, the universe of suitable respondents for studying print comprehension/miscomprehension is appreciably smaller.

The universe was further restricted by the need to focus on that subset of individuals who qualified as magazine readers. The universe may be described as individuals aged 18 and older, living in the contiguous 48 United States, who claim to be at least occasional readers of general circulation mass media magazines. As actually implemented, the universe was further restricted to "target audience" individuals, that is, respondents who claimed to be readers of one or more of the eighteen test magazines.

Note that the definition emphasizes "claimed" rather than "actual" readership. This comports with the reliance upon claimed viewership in the earlier TV investigation. It also accomodates the fact that many magazine readers are not subscribers, but either make purchases on an issue-by-issue basis or have access to magazines purchased by others.

Note, also, that the minimum age cut-off was set at 18 years in the present investigation, as contrasted with 13 years in the television study. This was done to comport with customary magazine industry research practice.

Finally, limiting attention to the 48 contiguous states was done in the interest of making the data collection process less costly. There is no a priori basis for believing that rates of comprehension/miscomprehension

---

[10]Northcutt et al., 1975.

[11]Personal communication from Robert Barnes, U.S. Department of Education, in regard to its 1982 "English Language Proficiency Survey" administered by the U.S. Census Bureau. (See U.S. Department of Education, 1986.)

in Alaska and Hawaii would diverge dramatically from those obtained in the population defined.

EFFECTS

A variety of communication effects have been described in the academic and practitioner literatures. One broad distinction is between communications designed simply to educate or inform versus those designed to persuade the receiver to believe or behave in a certain way. Since descriptions of persuasion usually subsume education, this distinction receives no further attention here.

Comprehension as a Principal Communication Effect

Different academic disciplines have focused on the communication *qua* persuasion process and proposed various conceptualizations of how this process presumably works. Of direct relevance to the present discussion is the fact that, in virtually every instance, comprehension plays a central role.

Social Psychological Models

According to one recent review,[12] McGuire's early work[13] represents the first explicit information-processing view of persuasion. This work follows directly from Hovland, Janis, and Kelley's[14] suggestion that the impact of a persuasive communication may be understood in terms of three phases: (1) attention to the message, (2) *comprehension* of its contents, and (3) acceptance of its conclusions. As Eagly and Chaiken point out, the successive formulations offered by McGuire[15] represent the intellectual wellspring from which most behavioral science theorizing and research regarding persuasive communication has emanated.

Invariably, McGuire's formulations include comprehension as a major communication effect. As examples, the 1973 formulation identifies the steps resulting from exposure to persuasive communications as: presentation, attention, *comprehension,* yielding (i.e., agreement), retention, and overt behavior. The 1976 revision refers to: exposure, perception, *comprehension,* agreement, retention, retrieval, decision making, and action. The 1978 version goes from exposure to attention, *comprehension,* agreement,

---

[12]Eagly and Chaiken, 1984, p. 271.
[13]McGuire, 1968a, 1968b, 1969, 1972.
[14]Hovland, Janis, and Kelley, 1953.
[15]More recently these include 1973, 1976, 1978, and 1985.

retention, and behavior. In his 1985 revision, McGuire suggests the follow-ing stages: exposure, attention, interest, *comprehension,* activating rele-vant mental content, acquiring relevant skills, agreement with the message, storing this in memory, later retrieving this from memory, making decisions on the basis of the retrieved information, overt behavior that implements these decisions, and post-behavior reconception and consolidation. Although the specific stages of the process have changed over time, comprehension is a key step in all these formulations.

One important characteristic of McGuire's model is that each of the stages is conceptualized as being a complex process in its own right. Another important characteristic is that inadequacies in any earlier stage presumably exert a negative and limiting impact on subsequent stages.[16] Using the first four stages in the 1985 formulation as an example, if the individual is *exposed* to only 80% of the message and then only pays 70% *attention* to the portion to which he has been exposed, then even if he is 100% *interested* in that portion to which he has attended and accurately *comprehends* 100% of all this information, he will not comprehend all of the source's meanings, but at best only 56% ($.8 \times .7 \times 1.0 \times 1.0$) of those meanings. As evidence of this fact, Stewart (1986) found that the persuasive impact of a message decreased significantly if both comprehension and recall were below average.

Eagly and Chaiken[17] note that while most persuasion researchers either explicitly or implicitly assume message "reception" (defined as attention plus comprehension), relatively few have taken the trouble to empirically verify this assumption. In those instances where reception has been exam-ined empirically, the typical approach involves using recognition and/or recall measures of retention of message content. As noted earlier, such measures are more accurately measures of memory, not comprehension.[18]

It is also worth noting that the expectancy-value approach espoused by Fishbein and Ajzen,[19] which probably represents the second most influen-tial stream of literature on the persuasion process to emanate from a social psychological perspective, essentially posits a five-stage process: exposure to information; belief formation/change; attitude formation/change; inten-tion formation/change; and behavior. The second stage (viz. belief formation/change) is permeated by implicit and explicit considerations related to comprehension.

---

[16]See especially McGuire, 1972.
[17]Eagly and Chaiken, 1984, p. 273.
[18]See Anderson, 1972; Ortony, 1978.
[19]Fishbein and Ajzen, 1975; Ajzen and Fishbein, 1980.

Advertising Models

Modern advertising practice is very much influenced by two classic "hierarchy of effects" formulations. The Lavidge and Steiner version[20] holds that the impact of an advertisement upon the receiver goes through a series of stages. Given exposure to the ad, these stages proceed from awareness of the message, to knowledge, liking, preference, and conviction and, in the ultimate case, culminate in purchase. The second stage, knowledge, encompasses the notion of comprehension. The second classic model, Colley's DAGMAR[21], contains four stages: awareness, *comprehension,* conviction, and action.

Contemporary advertising theory is also much influenced by Krugman's contention that a person's level of involvement will mediate his response to an advertising message.[22] According to this perspective, people attending to an ad under low involvement conditions do not reflect all the effects postulated to be present under high involvement conditions. Specifically, receivers under low involvement do not attend to and "process" the message (that is, evaluate it and purposefully link its content to their pre-existing mental contents) as they are presumed to do under conditions of high involvement.

Of particular relevance to the present investigation, Krugman theorized that television was more likely a low involvement medium while the print media were more likely to generate high involvement. Two reasons were given for this contention. First, with print, both exposure to the ad as a whole and the pace of exposure to its components are under the active volitional control of the receiver. In contrast, as long as he doesn't turn off the TV or switch the station, the TV viewer has no control over either exposure or pace. Second, given exposure, in TV it is the ad that is animated and the receiver that is passive. In contrast, with print it is the ad that is inanimate while the receiver is active.

Recent conceptualizing regarding advertising effects has tended to propose different models, depending upon whether the receiver was or was not involved with the ad. Under conditions of involvement, the classic Lavidge and Steiner formulation is generally elaborated to include what cognitive psychologists have theorized and learned about human information processing. For example, Mitchell[23] suggests that the cognitive effects that intervene between exposure to an ad and a related overt behavioral response (e.g., purchase of the advertised product) may be broken into two broad

---

[20]Lavidge and Steiner, 1961. Also see more recent discussions in Moriarity, 1983 and Preston and Thorson, 1984.

[21]Colley, 1961.

[22]Krugman, 1965, 1966.

[23]Mitchell, 1983.

categories: sensory processing and semantic processing. Consider an advertisement that said: "Prevent colds; Buy Fuzz Cold Medicine." Essentially, sensory processing involves attention to the visual and/or acoustic features of the ad. This would involve identifying letters and words, recognizing sounds (such as "pre" and "vent"), etc.

The second major stage, semantic processing, is concerned with how the person extracts meaning from the communication and then evaluates, modifies, and behaves in relation to this meaning. Semantic processing begins with the individual comprehending components of the message, such as, in our example, "One phrase contained in the ad was 'prevents colds'; another was 'Buy Fuzz Cold Medicine' ". These understandings then become integrated and represented in the individual's mind in terms of specific *message beliefs,* for example, "The ad claims that Fuzz Cold Medicine prevents colds." Message beliefs relate to what the ad said ("The ad claims . . . ") and need to be distinguished from "brand beliefs," discussed below, which refer to the individual's understanding of what the product actually does. The two types of beliefs need not necessarily be consistent.

According to Mitchell, the comprehension process also includes inference making. For example, if one understands that the ad claimed "Fuzz Cold Medicine" prevents colds, one may also believe that, by inference, the ad claimed that Fuzz Cold Medicine also prevents sniffles, runny noses, sore throats, coughing, etc. Hence, one can distinguish between message beliefs based directly on something actually stated in the ad and which may therefore be termed "factual," and those that are derived from something stated in the ad and which may be termed "inferred."

Message belief formation is usually followed by evaluative processing. This involves attaching good-bad, like-dislike evaluations to the factual and inferred message beliefs. For example, if one believes that the ad said that Fuzz Cold Medicine prevented colds, one's reactions might include: "That's good."

The next semantic stage involves the formulation or modification of specific *brand beliefs.* These are distinct from the message beliefs described above. For example, though the individual may believe that the ad claimed that Fuzz Cold Medicine prevents colds (a message belief), based on personal experience with that product, that same individual may also believe that the claim is untrue. The individual may instead choose to believe that, though the ad did make the claim (a message belief), Fuzz Cold Medicine does not prevent colds (a brand belief).

The individual's total set of brand beliefs regarding the referent brand are then integrated into some overall brand attitude. For example: "I don't like Fuzz Cold Medicine." Intentions and overt behavior are presumed to follow such attitudes.

The role of the comprehension process in low involvement situations is less clear and has not been formally addressed in the published literature. While the messages in these instances are generally simpler, it might be hypothesized that miscomprehension is still a serious threat because individuals do not devote as much attention to the message and do not expend as much time and effort in processing as they would in higher involvement contexts.

Consumer Behavior Models

Contemporary models of consumer behavior also explicitly recognize the key role of comprehension. Consider the recent edition of the most widely used text in the field.[24] The authors' general model contains a five-stage information processing component through which all incoming information is filtered prior to being stored in memory. Patterned after McGuire's early work, these stages are: exposure, attention, *comprehension,* yielding/ acceptance, and retention. While these authors contend that the yielding/ acceptance stage is likely absent under conditions of low involvement, they are equally clear in maintaining that comprehension is present under conditions of both high and low involvement.[25] Like the Engel et al. treatment, most other introductory consumer behavior texts also note the importance of comprehension as a reaction to advertising and promotional fare, and as an antecedent to behavior. The most sophisticated treatment appears in Peter and Olson.[26]

In a second influential consumer behavior model,[27] the term comprehension is not explicitly discussed, but the process serves as the key element in perceptual encoding. According to Bettman, " . . . the meaning of a stimulus resides in the assessment of that stimulus by the individual, in how the individual interprets that stimulus, rather than the stimulus itself" (p. 79). Thus comprehension would be a critical element in the processing of consumer-related stimuli.

Summary

As the above review suggests, comprehension is widely believed to be an important communication effect—one that necessarily precedes the formation, implementation, and modification of relevant attitudes, intentions, and behavior. Yet despite the purportedly pivotal role of comprehension, research on communication effects has generally ignored it. At least two reasons may be suggested for this neglect.

First, investigators operating in the realms of social psychology, advertising,

---

[24]Engel, Blackwell, and Miniard, 1986.
[25]See Engel and Blackwell, 1982.
[26]Peter and Olson, 1987.
[27]Bettman, 1979.

and consumer behavior are typically more interested in the stages that are presumed to follow comprehension (namely, attitudes and intentions), and the weight of their conceptual and empirical efforts reflect this orientation.

Second, as previously noted, where effort has been directed toward assessing comprehension, it has in most instances been predicated on the erroneous assumption that retention represents an adequate surrogate for comprehension. For example, if the receiver exposed to a cereal ad can correctly recall the brand name or some other copy point, then many researchers appear ready to assume that the receiver has understood the communication. However, it is both entirely possible and too often the case that the consumers read some information about a product, remember that information and even be 100% accurate in repeating that information days later, yet have zero understanding of what that information means. To illustrate, though it may be 100% accurately recalled, what does the phrase "35 mg. of sodium per serving" appearing in an ad or on a package label actually *mean?* Is that good or bad, high or low, healthful or unhealthful, etc.? The mere retention of information should not be equated with the comprehension of that information. Assessment of comprehension requires a focus on the *meanings* that underlie and are meant to be conveyed by language, not on the language itself.

A Model of Comprehension

Relying upon recent developments in psycholinguistics and cognitive psychology, this section outlines a model of the comprehension sub-process and places it in the context of other communications effects.

The Background of "Givens"

Communication effects may be viewed as arising out of a communication situation consisting of three principal components: the communication, the receiver, and the context or environment in which the receiver experiences the communication (Figure 2.1).

Each of the three components may be partitioned into sub-components. For example, the communication can be described in terms of source, message, and medium. As indicated in the earlier section of this chapter, each of these components is capable of being described in terms of a number of their own sub-components.

Similarly, the receiver may be viewed as consisting of components and sub-components. For present purposes, three primary components can be identified: the individual's current motivational states, prior history, and current expectations. As an illustration of sub-components, past history would include such things as the receiver's cultural milieu and family life, educational experiences, attitudes, values, experiences with the product in question, etc.

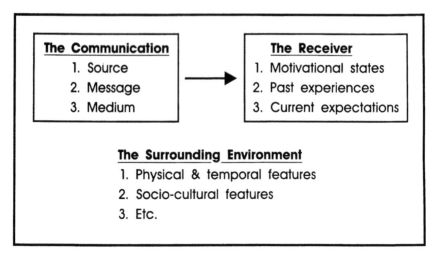

FIG. 2.1.   The Communication Situation

Finally, the environmental context can also be apportioned into its physical, temporal, cultural, subcultural, social, and other characteristics. The context in which a communication is embedded is expected to affect how the receiver interprets and reacts to that communication.

Though entire volumes have been written about each of these components, our purpose here is simply to note that every instance of mass media communication involves the communication itself, a receiver, and a context in which the communication and receiver are brought into contact. These elements constitute the background of "givens" against which the process of comprehension is to be understood.

Communicating Meaning

We begin by presuming that the source of a mass media communication has some thought or feeling which he would like to have the receiver come to understand. Though there may be more than one thought or feeling, and one or more of these might be somewhat unclear to the source himself, let us ignore these possibilities and assume that the source has but one clear thought that he wishes to convey. We call this thought—this internal mental state of the source—his "meaning."

It is an unfortunate fact of human existence that the meanings that exist in the mind of a source cannot be directly transposed into the mind of a receiver. For the source to evoke the intended meaning in the mind of the receiver, he must first convert it into some externally denotable form. Typically, this involves some spoken or written language, visible gestures, etc. This denotable expression, essentially the message and medium, is then conveyed to the receiver who, in turn, decodes this overt expression and extracts meaning from it—hopefully the same meaning intended by the source.

Figure 2.2 depicts the broad outline of this sequence of events. In terms of the vocabulary that has evolved,[28] *meaning structure* is the term used to designate the meanings (thoughts and feelings) as they exist in the minds of both sources and receivers. *Surface structure* is the term used to designate the external, detectable expression of these thoughts—the spoken or written word, visible gestures, etc. In communicating a specific thought (which we shall label Meaning Structure 1), the source uses some surface structure in an attempt to evoke the same thought (Meaning Structure 1) in the mind of the receiver. Conceivably, the source may do a poor job of selecting an appropriate surface structure. For example, he may use an inappropriate choice of words— words that may either inaccurately or ambiguously describe his thoughts.

Assuming that this is not the case and that the source has done a good job of selecting appropriate surface structures, comprehension refers to the process whereby the receiver assigns meaning to these surface structures. This may be the meaning intended by the source, some other meaning, or a combination of the two (see Figure 2.2). Frederiksen has described the situation as follows:

> Understanding, then, may be regarded as a process whereby a listener or reader attempts to infer the knowledge structure of a speaker or writer by using the available linguistic message, contextual information, and his own knowledge store as "data structures" from which the inference is to be made.[29]

Clearly, many factors are involved between the point at which the source decides to convey his meaning to the receiver and the point at which the receiver strives to comprehend. These include the source's assumptions regarding whether the receiver is likely to understand his meaning. They also include the kinds of surface structures that the source believes would be appropriate for conveying this meaning. Additionally, they include the construction of the actual message, its delivery through a particular medium, etc. Our discussion picks up at the point where these tasks have been accomplished and the communication, receiver, and context converge. What are the resultant effects?

Pre-comprehension Effects

We view comprehension as the fifth in a longer series of communication effects, albeit the first effect directly concerned with extracting meaning. Although comprehension is generally considered to be followed by a number

---

[28]See Lindsay and Norman, 1972, 1977.
[29]Frederiksen, 1975, p. 371.

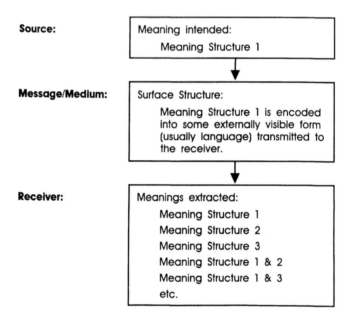

FIG. 2.2.   The Communication of Meaning through Surface Structures

of other mental and behavioral stages, for present purposes it is sufficient to note these in aggregated form, as stages 6 and 7 in Figure 2.3. Readers interested in further elaboration are referred to the social psychological[30] and consumer behavior[31] literatures.

The four stages prior to comprehension may be labeled exposure, peripheral sensory reception, central cortical representation, and attention. Each of these stages represents a complex process in its own right. These stages may be briefly described as follows.

Exposure.   Although the communication, receiver, and context may all converge at the same time and place, there is no guarantee that the receiver will actually be exposed to the message. If the receiver sits down and reads a particular issue of *Time* magazine but does not turn to pages 97-98, then the communications on those pages cannot exert any direct impact upon the receiver (unless, of course, he happens to see them elsewhere or learn of their contents from someone else). Exposure is thus a prerequisite for comprehension.

Note that exposure may come in various forms. At one end of a continuum, exposure may be both passive and unplanned, as is the case with the

[30]For example, McGuire, 1985.
[31]For example, Engel et al., 1986; Peter and Olson, 1987.

1. Exposure

2. Peripheral sensory reception

3. Central cortical representation

4. Attention

*5. Comprehension

6. Post comprehension mental phenomena (i.e., cognitive and affective states and processes such as attitudes, decision making, intentions, etc.)

7. Post comprehension behavioral phenomena (including communicative behaviors, purchase behaviors, etc.)

FIG. 2.3.   Effects That May Result from Communication

television viewer who happens to be exposed to a particular commercial while sitting watching his favorite TV show. At the other extreme, exposure may be the result of a deliberate act taken by the receiver to search out and locate desired information. An example would be the receiver going to the library to locate a recent *Consumer Reports* article on dishwashers. Somewhere in-between would be incidental exposure, that is, happening to be exposed to one type of information while looking for another. The entire issue of exposure warrants more thorough consideration and taxonomic description than it has heretofore been given.

Peripheral Sensory Reception.   Given exposure, the communication may or may not be detected by the receiver's primary sensory receptors of sight, sound, taste, touch, or smell. For example, the print may be too faint to be detected or may be in ultraviolet or infra-red, colors that lie beyond the range of normal human detection. Reception by the peripheral nervous system is thus a second prerequisite.

Central Cortical Representation.   Even given activation of the peripheral sensory system, research concerning that part of the brain called the reticular activating system has shown that not all neuronal transmissions reach the receiver's cortex. For example, studies in which electrodes have been implanted into a cat's cortex have shown that loud noises that would normally be readily detected and produce cortical representations will fail to produce such representations if the cat's attention is diverted by the more engrossing presence of a live mouse. Central cortical representation thus becomes a third prerequisite.

Attention.   While awake, most human beings are immersed in a sea of incoming sensory information. There is no way that anyone could pay attention to all the sensory input that registers cortically. Depending upon such factors as the intensity of the stimulus, the individual's current motivational state, etc., the individual is selective and attends to only a portion of this input. As a result, the vast proportion of cortical stimulation does not register upon consciousness and it is likely that much of this may fail to be translated into psychological form. Hence, attention would appear to be a fourth antecedent of comprehension.

It should be noted that attention to a given communication does not necessarily imply equal attention to all its components. The receiver may pay a disproportionate share of attention to the source, or some feature of the spokesperson (e.g., her clothing), and virtually no attention to the medium (e.g., magazines), the specific vehicle (e.g., *Playgirl*), or the explicitly stated message.

The Comprehension Process

The four prior stages deal with how the external surface structures come to be represented in consciousness. All of this may take but a fraction of a second. To the extent that deficiencies occur at any of these prior stages, they will lead to decrements in comprehension.

At this point, the receiver is aware that something out there has attracted his attention. However, he does not yet know what it means. Comprehension refers to the process whereby the receiver interprets (assigns meaning to) these incoming stimuli.

It is generally agreed that comprehension clearly comes into play under conditions of high involvement. It also seems reasonable to suggest that some form of comprehension occurs under conditions of low involvement. Especially in the case of complex messages, low involvement may result in comprehension which is partial, inaccurate, and/or does not occur at consciously perceived levels.

Once the receiver has given some attention to the communication, the cognitive psychology literature[32] suggests that he begins to process this information at various levels simultaneously in order to extract meaning from what he has just experienced. Two broad approaches have evolved for conceptualizing this process. The first, termed "top-down" processing, emphasizes the pre-existing mental contents that the receiver brings to the situation. The second, termed "bottom-up" processing, places greater empha-

---

[32]See, for example, Estes, 1977; McClelland, 1979; McClelland and Rumelhart, 1981; Rumelhart, 1977; Spiro et al., 1980.

sis upon the physical characteristics of the text itself. As summarized by Tourangeau:

> the two approaches share several important notions—the profound impact of context, the use of prior general knowledge by the reader or listener, and the influence of inferential processes during comprehension. The difference in the approaches lies mainly in their views on the nature of the information we use in interpreting a text. The top-down approach emphasizes large pre-existing structures that can organize an entire text; the bottom-up approach emphasizes lower-level structures that can be used piecemeal.[33]

The large pre-existing mental structures to which Tourangeau refers are usually called "schema" or "schemata"—a concept discussed in some detail below. Interacting with his current expectations and the surrounding environmental context, these schemata supply the individual with hypotheses that he uses as guides to interpreting the text.

The top-down and bottom-up perspectives are complementary rather than contradictory or even competing. Both may be viewed as anchor points, or as roads coming from different directions and leading to that common destination called comprehension. However, since they cannot be described simultaneously, our discussion begins with bottom-up processing. An outline of the model and discussion that follows is provided in Figure 2.4.

While different theorists postulate different numbers and types of stages, for present purposes, it is sufficient to discuss "bottom-up" processing in terms of two broad stages—sensory analysis and semantic analysis.

Sensory analysis involves the identification of selected sensory features of the incoming information and the integration of these features into larger structures. The details differ somewhat, depending upon the sensory characteristics of the incoming information.

Acoustic information is first considered in terms of basic phonetic sounds (e.g., "p"), which are then fused into larger units (namely syllables, e.g., "pre"), and eventually into words (e.g., "prevent").

Visual information in alphanumeric form (i.e., letters or numerals) is first considered in terms of its discrete features. Just as the more than 600,000 words in the English language are made up using only 26 letters, the letters themselves are made up of a smaller number of characteristics termed "critical features." These include lines, segments, curves, juxtapositions, and angles. The features provide the basis for distinguishing one letter or number from another. For example, compare the separate rectilinear features that make up the number "4" with the curvilinear features that make up the letter "c." The features are integrated to form separate letters (or numbers) which are then combined to form letter clusters (e.g., "un")

---

[33]Tourangeau, 1984, p. 74–75.

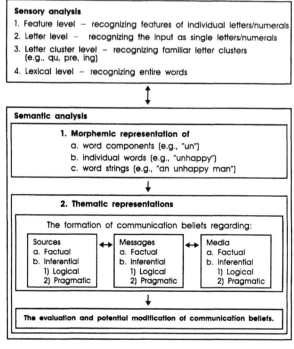

Sensory analysis
1. Feature level – recognizing features of individual letters/numerals
2. Letter level – recognizing the input as single letters/numerals
3. Letter cluster level – recognizing familiar letter clusters
   (e.g., qu, pre, ing)
4. Lexical level – recognizing entire words

Semantic analysis

1. Morphemic representation of
   a. word components (e.g., "un")
   b. individual words (e.g., "unhappy")
   c. word strings (e.g., "an unhappy man")

2. Thematic representations

The formation of communication beliefs regarding:

Sources	Messages	Media
a. Factual	a. Factual	a. Factual
b. Inferential	b. Inferential	b. Inferential
1) Logical	1) Logical	1) Logical
2) Pragmatic	2) Pragmatic	2) Pragmatic

The evaluation and potential modification of communication beliefs.

FIG. 2.4. Outlining a model of the comprehension process

and eventually entire words (e.g., "unhappy") and word strings ("an unhappy man"). A number of different descriptions of this process exist and the multi-stage models outlined by Estes[34] and Rumelhart[35] should be consulted for greater detail on the sensory processing of alphanumeric input.

Visual information in non-alphanumeric form is assumed to go through a similar construction process. For example, the receiver may first identify a smile, then see it as a part of a woman's face, note that this woman has long brown hair, appears to be facing and looking at a man who is wearing an unusual green hat, etc.

Earlier we noted that the context in which communication takes place can influence how the incoming information is interpreted. This can occur even at the level of sensory processing. For example, confronted with a blurred third letter in what appears to be a three letter word beginning ca__, a receiver standing in an automobile showroom is more likely to perceive this word as *car,* while another standing in a pet store is more likely to perceive it as *cat.* By the same token, the receiver's past experiences may combine with (and, at least upon initial reading, entirely

[34]Estes, 1977.
[35]Rumelhart, 1977.

overwhelm) the environmental context so as to lead him to perceive the letters as either *cad, cap, can,* etc.

Semantic analysis refers to the process whereby the sensory input is assigned meaning. We view semantic processing as consisting of two overlapping stages: morphemic and thematic representation.

Just as a phoneme is considered to be the smallest unit of human speech and is the basis for distinguishing one linguistic sound from another, a morpheme is the most basic unit of meaning. According to the dictionary,[36] a morpheme is "a meaningful linguistic unit . . . that contains no smaller meaningful parts."

Morphemes may be represented either by single letters (such as: *a, I*) or by clusters of letters. Such letter clusters may be separate words (e.g., *pin* or *happy*), or be part of some larger clusters of letters that together form a word. As examples of the latter, the single word "unhappy" contains two separate morphemes (or meanings), namely, *not* and *happy*. Similarly, the word "pins" also contains two morphemes, namely *pin* and *two or more*. The latter meaning is conveyed by the single letter *s* which, in English, is used to convey a plural meaning.

The first stage of semantic analysis, *morphemic representation,* involves the receiver assigning molecular and relatively isolated meanings to the incoming sensory data. Each word is given one or more meanings. Since most words contain more than one meaning, morphemic analysis may produce a set of possible meanings for each word. By relying on his past experience (which includes his knowledge of syntax) and his understanding of the context in which the word appears, the receiver reduces this set of meanings to the one meaning considered most likely. For example, consider the word "ball." In isolation, this might mean: (1) a type of plaything (e.g., a football); (2) a spherical object; (3) a level of enjoyment; (4) a formal party; etc. When considered in the context of selected other words ("I had a ball"), the receiver might be more inclined to interpret the meaning one way (e.g., as signifying a level of enjoyment) rather than another. However, as he reads on and recognizes even more words ("I had a ball, but I lost it"), the receiver may come to change his interpretation.

Especially with print communication, note that the assignment of meanings may not occur in the same sequential order as they appear in the external surface structure or are conveyed via the incoming sensory data. The receiver may look at, or come to understand some later word(s) before seeing or interpreting others which come earlier.

By characterizing morphemic representation as molecular and unconnected, we mean to indicate that meanings may initially surface in relative isolation. Though the receiver may understand that "unhappy" represents the combination of two meanings, or that the word "book" represents several

---

[36]Webster's, 1977, p. 749.

meanings, without relating these understandings to any other meanings, he is left with a very limited level of understanding. The receiver does not yet understand how this information "fits in" or can be used. For example, who is unhappy? When or where has this occurred? How long has it lasted or will it last? What caused the unhappiness and what will cause it to dissipate?, etc.

The isolated meanings generated through morphemic representation provide only a superficial, fragmentary, and preliminary level of semantic understanding. It is only when a number of the relatively isolated morphemic representations become integrated to form larger semantic units (e.g., "The old man is unhappy," "The book is on the top shelf.") that we can say that the receiver has arrived at some useful level of understanding of (some or all of) the incoming information. We term these larger units *thematic representations* in order to indicate that the receiver has now integrated a number of molecular morphemic representations into a larger, holistic, meaningful structure.

Thematic representations are not to be confused with the concept of schemata central to the "top-down" conceptualizations. The latter term refers to pre-existing knowledge structures that have been built up over time and that the receiver brings to the situation (see Figure 2.1). These provide coherent generic frameworks used in the interpretation of new incoming stimuli.[37] Schemata often have extensive meaning. For example, the schema "doing laundry" can evoke a whole set of sequentially related thoughts regarding gathering the dirty clothes from the hamper, taking them to the washing machine, adding detergent and fabric softener at the appropriate times, removing the clothes at the end of the spin dry cycle, placing them into a dryer, etc.

In contrast, thematic representations are constructed during the process of comprehending and pertain directly to the situation or communication at hand. They refer to more limited clusters of situation-specific meanings. Understanding that a communication claimed that "the old man was unhappy" does not require that this understanding be enmeshed in any more extensive pre-existing framework.

Each individual possesses a vast repertoire of schema developed from past experience. According to the "top-down" perspective, comprehension typically involves identifying the appropriate schema to match the incoming sensory information. If a schema cannot be found or there are too many discrepancies, a new schema is formed[38] or an existing one is reorganized.[39] Thus, prior knowledge, organized in schemas, influences the manner in which new knowledge is thematically comprehended, organized, and stored.[40]

---

[37]Norman and Bobrow, 1975; Schank and Abelson, 1975.

[38]Via the inference formation process; see Harris, 1981.

[39]Norman & Bobrow, 1975.

[40]Richgels, 1982.

Even the simplest of thematic representations can actually be quite complex. At a basic level, all thematic representations consist of both asserted and implied meanings. *Asserted meanings* are those explicitly expressed in the communication itself. Consider the utterance: "Take Eradicold. It relieves cold symptoms." The asserted meaning is that, according to the communication, something named Eradicold exists which either reduces or eliminates cold symptoms. Asserted meanings are thus based directly on the assertions that can be objectively demonstrated to be present in the communication. Though some assertions can be made via illustration (e.g., a picture of a man swinging a golf club is essentially an assertion that that man is holding a golf club), attention is usually directed to those expressed verbally. In technical terms, an assertion is "a linguistic construction in which a referent is associated with or dissociated from a complement via a verbal connector."[41] In advertising, the referent is usually the advertised brand.

Implied meanings are not explicitly "contained in" the communication but are inferences that the receiver "draws from" the communication.[42] Implied meanings may be of two types—either logical or pragmatic.[43] *Logical implications* are *necessarily* implied. For example, the sentence "Robin is older than Jonathan" necessarily implies that "Jonathan is younger than Robin." Similarly, the sentence "Brand X golf balls have a unique new construction" logically implies that, at least up to that point in time, no other golf ball had been constructed in quite the same way.

Pragmatic implications are inferences the receiver makes that, though they may be correct, either were not explicitly stated nor can be necessarily (logically) inferred from the communication itself. As examples, the receiver may think that: Eradicold is a pharmaceutical product; Eradicold requires no physician's prescription; etc. Or the reader may think that the new golf ball is somehow better than others because of its unique new construction. Harris[44] provides a nice illustration of implied meanings using the following hypothetical audio commercial: "Aren't you tired of the sniffles and runny noses all winter? Tired of always feeling less than your best? Get through a whole winter without colds. Take Eradicold pills as directed." Though not directly asserted nor a necessary logical deduction, the claim that Eradicold pills will prevent winter colds may be easily inferred. Indeed, it would seem pragmatic to do so.

---

[41]Osgood, 1959, p. 45.

[42]Debate exists over whether meanings are actually contained in surface structures. From a philosophical perspective, meanings exist only in the minds of individuals, be they communication sources or receivers. Our use of the phrase "contained in" is meant to suggest that the surface structures are, from the source's perspective, in one-to-one correspondence with the meaning structures that the source had in mind. Clearly, sometimes this may not be the case.

[43]See Harris and Monaco, 1977, pp. 2–3.

[44]Harris, 1977.

According to Ortony, spreading activation (i.e., inference making) is *"the* essential ingredient of the comprehension process."[45] Many other scholars[46] would concur that failure to engage in inference-making generally reflects superficial levels of comprehension. This may be illustrated by the following examples. Consider the phrases "35 mg. of sodium per serving" or "uncured frankfurter; keep refrigerated at 40° F. or below." Though the reader may have a thematic understanding of the asserted meaning inherent in the phrase "35 mg. of sodium per serving," the phrase may not be particularly meaningful. Assuming that the individual has no prior knowledge, is that amount high or low, good or bad, etc.? Similarly, though the reader may understand that the term "uncured meat" means that said product contains no nitrite nor nitrate preservatives, and may also understand that such products are supposed to be refrigerated, the reader may not infer that when such products are not kept refrigerated: they can develop botulism spore, this can happen in as little as 8 hours, the ingestion of said spore is likely to prove fatal, etc.[47]

In some instances, it is actually the inferred meaning, not the asserted meaning, which is the only meaning that makes sense. Consider: "Jon was sitting on pins and needles." Although it is possible to envision Jon sitting on boxes that contained pins and needles, or even that he was actually sitting on a number of flattened needles and closed pins, the thematic representation that most people take away is that Jon was nervous or anxious.[48]

To summarize the notion of thematic representation to this point: "the process of comprehension involves activating concepts related to those of the input and the context, and engaging in inferences based primarily on those concepts."[49] "Both asserted and implied meanings make up what is the semantic content (message) of the communication."[50] Further, the implied meanings are of two basic varieties—either logical or pragmatic. That is, either they are directly and necessarily derivable from the communication itself (logical implications) or they are neither stated in nor logically derivable from the communication, but make sense to the receiver (pragmatic implications).

Regardless of whether they are asserted or implied, it is important to recognize that the receiver generally makes no such distinction. Once the

---

[45]Ortony, 1978; p. 53; italics added.

[46]See, for example, Dascal, 1981; Deighton, 1986; Keenan, 1978; Kintsch, 1978; Langer, 1985, 1986; Schank, 1976; Tierney, Vaughan, and Bridge, 1979; Wittrock, 1981.

[47]See Jacoby, 1981.

[48]Note, also, that a considerable amount of Federal Trade Commission activity in regard to deceptive advertising focuses on implied rather than asserted meanings (see Ford and Calfee, 1986; Preston and Richards, 1986b).

[49]Ortony, 1978, p. 57.

[50]Harris and Monaco, 1977, p. 2.

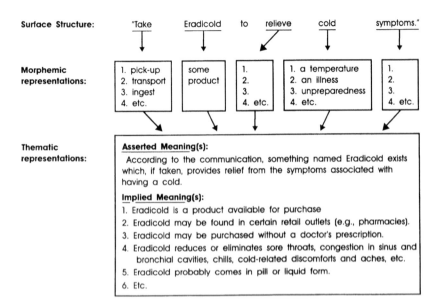

FIG. 2.5.   Illustrating "Bottom-Up" Comprehension

receiver extracts an implied meaning, it may be thought of and retained as having been an asserted fact.[51]

In order to make this abstract discussion more concrete, Figure 2.5 illustrates how a linguistic surface structure may come to be represented morphemically and thematically.

Although the process of thematic representation may already appear complex, at least four additional layers of complexity can be identified. First, one needs to distinguish between fleeting and retained meanings. *Fleeting meanings* are those that are evoked during the instant that the receiver is exposed to the communication and are present only in his short-term memory. If such understandings receive no further cognitive attention (that is, are not thought about, elaborated upon, rehearsed, related to other meanings stored in memory, etc.), they fail to be stored in long-term memory and cannot be expected to exert any impact upon the individual's subsequent mental processing or behavior. In contrast, *retained meanings* are those given further cognitive attention and which, as a result, become stored somewhere in the individual's mental apparatus in the form of *beliefs* such as, "I believe that I read that Eradicold reduces fever and runny noses." It is retained meanings that are of principal concern to writers, advertisers, and regulators. Unfortunately, this means that their conceptualization and assessment may become confounded with the concept of memory.[52]

[51]Harris, Dubitsky, and Bruno, 1983, p. 246.
[52]See Ortony, 1978.

Second, it is important to distinguish between communication beliefs and referent beliefs. These terms correspond to Mitchell's[53] notions of message and brand beliefs, but are given broader meaning here. *Communication beliefs* are retained thematic representations that relate directly to aspects of the communication (*qua* source, message, medium) itself. As examples, the receiver might believe:

1. The ad that he just read said "If you use Crest toothpaste, you'll have fewer cavities" (a communication message belief);
2. the spokesperson pictured in the ad was Robert Young, the actor that played the Dr. Marcus Welby on TV (a communication source/*qua* spokesperson belief);
3. The company paying for the ad was Procter & Gamble (another communication source/*qua* manufacturer belief);
4. by virtue of its seal being used in the ad, the American Dental Association's Council on Dental Therapeutics endorses the use of this product (another source);
5. a professional advertising agency, including copywriters, production people, and so on played a role in developing the ad (more communication source beliefs);
6. by implication, the ad also says using the toothpaste would lead to cleaner, whiter teeth (an inferred communication message belief);
7. the magazine in which he saw the ad was *Time* (a communication medium belief);
8. Etc.

The above beliefs relate to what was explicitly contained in or could be inferred about *the communication itself.* Though these beliefs might be asserted or implied, correct or incorrect, the important thing is that they all focus on what the receiver believes the communication contained and said either explicitly or implicitly.

In contrast, *referent beliefs* pertain to the focus of the communication, that is, to the object or issue of reference. They are essentially post-comprehension mental phenomena. In the above example, they refer to Crest toothpaste itself. While the receiver may have the unshakable communication belief that the ad that he read contained the meaning "If you use Crest toothpaste, you'll have fewer cavities," he may nonetheless also believe that Crest toothpaste does nothing that will materially affect whether one gets cavities or not (a referent belief). In essence, communication beliefs involve the question "Does the receiver *believe that the communication expresses* proposition X?" while referent beliefs pose the question "Does the receiver *believe proposition X?*"

---

[53]Mitchell, 1983.

It is important to point out that, whereas communication beliefs are tied to a specific communication, referent beliefs may have many sources. For example, we may come to believe something about Brand X (e.g., that it soothes sore throats) either because we extracted this meaning from having read an ad, heard this information from a trusted friend, heard it from our physician or pharmacist, had previously used the product and experienced these effects for ourselves, etc. Thus, the individual may form referent beliefs as a consequence of evaluating and then accepting a communication belief.[54] By the same token, a relevant referent belief may have been formed as a result of some prior experience and thus be available to affect the formation of communication beliefs (specifically, how the individual comprehends or miscomprehends the incoming information). As with communication beliefs, referent beliefs may be based on either asserted or implied meanings.

Given that our focus is on comprehension, this investigation limits attention to communication beliefs, and excludes referent beliefs.

A third layer of complexity stems from the fact that virtually as soon as they are formed, asserted and implied communication beliefs may become involved in a process of evaluation (see Figure 2.4). Consider the following as representing several communication beliefs formed by the reader of a toothpaste ad.

Asserted content:

1. The ad that I read said: "If you use Crest toothpaste, you'll have fewer cavities." That's a benefit.
2. The ad that I read was sponsored by Procter & Gamble. They're a good company.
3. The ad that I read contained a photo of a smiling woman. I like people who seem happy.
4. The ad that I read used a cursive script style superimposed on a pale pink background. That's too feminine for me.

Implied meanings:

5. The ad implies that if you use Crest toothpaste, you will be able to get by with fewer visits to the dentist. That's terrific.
6. The ad implies that regular brushing with Crest will lead to cleaner teeth. I'd like that.
7. Etc.

---

[54]See Ortony, 1978, p. 59.

Once having formed a communication belief, the receiver begins to consider each belief in terms of evaluative and affective terms. Receivers implicitly ask and answer such questions as: Is that good or bad?; Do I like it or dislike it?; etc. If the individual is incapable of answering these questions, then the meaning associated with that belief may be limited.

The fourth layer of complexity relates to the fact that communication beliefs may apply to any aspect of the communication (see Figure 2.4). Thus, the receiver may form communication beliefs not only regarding the message content ("It said if you use Crest toothpaste, you'll have fewer cavities") but also regarding:

a. all other message features ("It used an ascending cursive script against a pale pink background, and this suggested femininity to me.")
b. the source (or, in this instance, various asserted and implied sources— the Procter & Gamble Co., the advertising agency, the spokesperson, the smiling model, the American Dental Association), and
c. the medium ("I believe that the ad that I just read appeared in *Time* magazine.").

Moreover, there are opportunities for beliefs formed regarding one aspect of the communication to affect beliefs regarding any other aspect. For example, one might believe that the particular vehicle in which the message appears is the *National Enquirer,* and this may affect how the message is understood, especially the kinds of inferences that are made.

As another example, upon reading a news article, the receiver may believe:

a. the article claimed that the source to which the words in quotation marks were being attributed was President Reagan
b. the message clearly stated that the source believed the Star Wars Strategic Defense Initiative should be scrapped.

Yet he may find these two (source and message) communication beliefs to be incongruous and therefore decide either to disbelieve or modify one or both of these.[55] Thus, as a result of interaction with some other part of the communication and one's prior experience, 100% correct comprehension of one part of a communication could be converted to some form of miscomprehension. For example: "I thought that I heard the source say X, but I must have been mistaken since I don't really believe he would say such a thing."

Despite the fact that the subsequent communication effects (which include such things as attitudes, decision making, intentions, and overt behavior) have received more attention, it should be clear that the comprehension process is quite complex and merits considerable attention in its

---

[55]See Osgood et al., 1957.

TABLE 2.1
Comprehension Process Outcomes

I. Non-comprehension. (No meanings extracted)

II. Comprehension of:

- a given asserted meaning, or
- a given logically implied meaning, or
- several asserted meanings, or
- several logically implied meanings, or
- all asserted meanings, or
- all logically implied meanings

in:

- one, or
- some, or
- all components of the communication.

III. Miscomprehension

- Complete miscomprehension. (Extracting thematic meanings which are entirely incorrect)

- Partial miscomprehension. (Combining logically independent meanings, some accurate and others inaccurate)

- Confused miscomprehension. (Extracting logically incompatible meanings and not being able to identify which of the two is correct

- Derived miscomprehension. (Extracting only a portion of the thematic meaning, leading to faulty inference-making)

own right. This investigation focuses on one segment of the process, namely, thematic representations. It does not consider either prior comprehension phases (namely, sensory analysis or morphemic representation) nor does it address any post-comprehension phenomena (e.g., referent beliefs).

Comprehension Process Outcomes

The model outlined in the previous section focused on the *process* of comprehension. Except in passing, it did not address the *outcomes* of this process. The question of outcomes is particularly important when one deals with a dynamic mental process, since it is generally only the outcomes of the process that may be directly assessed. Expanding on a framework proposed elsewhere,[56] Table 2.1 outlines a number of possible immediate outcomes that may result from the receiver's attempt to extract meaning from incoming stimuli. These may be organized into three categories: (1) non-comprehension, (2) complete and accurate comprehension, and (3) miscomprehension. Each of these categories is discussed in turn.

Non-Comprehension

In giving attention to a communication, the receiver either will extract some meaning from the experience or will extract no meaning. We use the

---

[56]Jacoby, Nelson, and Hoyer, 1982, p. 64.

term non-comprehension to refer to the receiver's inability or lack of desire to extract any thematic meaning whatsoever from the communication. This would entail the failure to form any (source, message, or media) communication beliefs. Accordingly, we suspect that total non-comprehension is a relatively rare occurrence.

Partial non-comprehension, however, is likely the most typical experience, particularly for communications containing many meanings. The receiver generally will extract some thematic meanings and fail to extract others. Extracted meanings may be further sorted into those which reflect complete and accurate comprehension and those which reflect various forms of inaccuracy and are therefore instances of miscomprehension.

Comprehension

Although the notion of "complete and accurate comprehension" may seem simple enough, the phrase actually encompasses a myriad of complex issues. One such issue is whether it refers only to the source's asserted meaning, or also includes the implications that are or might be derived.

On the one hand, several lines of thought suggest that implications warrant inclusion in the notion of "complete and accurate comprehension." First, as noted during our discussion of the comprehension process, the receiver who extracts only the asserted meaning is often left with a superficial level of understanding. The receiver who makes inferences is able to arrive at a fuller and more useful level of understanding. Second, logically implied meanings *necessarily* follow from asserted meanings. Hence, they would warrant inclusion on these grounds alone. Third, if a sufficient proportion of readers take away a common pragmatic meaning that is incorrect, then the communication may be characterized as being misleading.[57] Hence, pragmatic implications also warrant consideration.

On the other hand, arguments can be offered against subsuming implied meanings within the notion of "complete and accurate." Since they are not logical derivations, pragmatically implied meanings may be more a function of the receiver's unique mental state than of the communication itself.

Even if one limits attention to logical implications, arguments can also be offered against their inclusion. Most importantly, just because one or more meanings may be logically derived from a given assertion, it does not follow that any or all of these meanings were necessarily in the source's mind when he initiated the communication,[58] nor that he would choose to

---

[57]This possibility is discussed at greater length in the final section of this chapter.

[58]Clark (1977) distinguishes between *authorized* and *unauthorized* inferences. The former are those which the source intended the receiver to draw, while the latter are ones the source did not intend to be drawn. The line between the two is not always easily recognizable, and unauthorized inferences may be drawn either because the receiver misinterprets or because the source uses language that, by normal agreement, should be taken as meaning something other than was intended. Also see Wittrock, 1981, p. 251.

adopt and/or communicate them even after their logical relationship to his asserted meaning were brought to his attention.

The issue of whether "complete and accurate comprehension" should apply to implied meanings is obviously a complex one. Our solution for the present study has been to adopt an intermediate position. The case for including logical implications seems sound, while the case for including pragmatic implications is less so. Accordingly, our assessment focuses primarily on asserted and logically implied meanings and contains only a small proportion of pragmatic implications.

The notion of "complete and accurate comprehension" possesses additional complexity. This is because the communication may contain two or more asserted meanings. What if one of these is "completely and correctly comprehended" and the other is not? Even if it contains only a single asserted meaning, the number of logically implied meanings may be many (see Figures 2.2 and 2.5). Moreover, both asserted and implied meanings may be extracted from attending to any component of the communication (i.e., sources, messages, media). Accordingly, the notion of "complete and accurate" comprehension could refer either to: one specific asserted meaning, one specific logically implied meaning, several asserted meanings, several logically implied meanings, all asserted meanings, and/or all logically implied meanings contained in one, some, or all components of the communication.

As this analysis suggests, assessing comprehension is necessarily tied to the identification of a universe of content. Earlier in this chapter we identified the universe of interest as material meanings of both the factual and inferential variety.

Miscomprehension

As used here, the term miscomprehension refers to a variety of problems. The common underlying theme is that the receiver either: (1) extracts an asserted meaning that was not asserted, or a logically implied meaning that could not be logically inferred from the communication, or (2) rejects either asserted and/or logically implied meanings that were in fact asserted in, or could logically be derived from the communication. As suggested by our previous discussion, the opportunity for some form of miscomprehension increases as both the domain of asserted and logically implied meanings increases and as this domain extends to all components of the communication.

Several forms of miscomprehension can be identified. One extreme is *complete miscomprehension,* a situation in which the meaning(s) extracted is (are) entirely incorrect. This occurs when the receiver either entirely rejects a correct meaning (believing that the communication did not assert nor logically imply X when, in fact, it did) or accepts an entirely incorrect meaning as having been asserted or logically implied. An example would be a situation in which an ad asserted that an advertised car cost $15,749 and the receiver believed the communication to have said that the car costs $18,749.

Two observations must be made regarding the notion of complete miscomprehension. First, the significance of such miscomprehension can vary along a continuum from trivial to substantial (or mild to severe). As an example, believing that the aforementioned communication claimed that the car cost $15,750 would represent a trivial instance of miscomprehension, whereas believing that it had said the car cost $25,750 would represent a more severe instance.

Second, virtually any communication can be considered to contain a number of asserted and logically implied meanings. The notion of "complete miscomprehension" could refer to a single such meaning or to some greater number of meanings. When two or more meanings are involved, we can identify the potential for a second form of miscomprehension, namely, partial miscomprehension.

Partial miscomprehension refers to those situations in which the receiver extracts two or more logically independent meanings, a portion of which is correct and another portion of which is incorrect. For example, suppose an ad asserted: "This car averages 25 MPG on the highway and costs $15,749." The receiver might believe that the communication claimed the car obtained 35 MPG on the highway (an inaccurate belief) and cost $15,749 (an accurate belief).

Confused (or ambiguous) miscomprehension represents a third type of miscomprehension. It involves the receiver extracting two or more logically incompatible meanings, recognizing this incompatibility, and not knowing which of the meanings is correct. As a result, when asked to indicate the meanings contained in the communication, the receiver may select one or the other, thereby incorrectly suggesting comprehension, or may be even more inclined to respond "I'm not sure" or "I don't know."

A fourth form of miscomprehension may be labeled *derived miscomprehension*. This stems from combining full and accurate comprehension of some meanings with the non-comprehension of others. Such partial comprehension can often lead to "don't know" responses as well as to significant miscomprehension.

To illustrate, suppose that a 61-year-old survey respondent came upon the following question: "How many times have you voted in statewide elections held in the state in which you now reside? In answering, please think only in terms of the last 8 years." Assume, further, that he came to a complete and accurate understanding of the thematic meaning contained in the first sentence. If he failed to attend to or understand the thematic meaning contained in the second sentence, he might base his answer on the entire period during which he resided in that state. If this were since he was 21 years old and of voting age, his answer might be something like: "Twenty times; every other year since I've been 21." Thus, by not obtaining the full thematic meaning asserted across the entire communication, it becomes possible to draw logical inferences that cause us to extract an incorrect meaning.

Though the taxonomic distinctions noted above are probably neither exhaustive nor entirely mutually exclusive, the discussion does serve to illustrate several basic points.

1. Miscomprehension is not necessarily the obverse of comprehension.
2. When it does occur, miscomprehension displays various forms and degrees. It may even appear together with comprehension.
3. Miscomprehension refers directly to both asserted and logically implied meanings, and indirectly to pragmatically implied meanings.
4. Miscomprehension is a complex phenomenon and, as such, warrants serious attention in its own right.

Post-Comprehension Effects

As suggested by Figure 2.3 and noted in our discussion of the comprehension process, one can anticipate that both comprehension and miscomprehension will usually lead to various effects. These include the development and/or modification of other cognitive and affective states and processes. As one specific example, communication beliefs may serve to influence the formation or modification of associated referent beliefs. These, in turn, may affect attitudes, intentions, and a variety of other mental phenomena. They may also eventually influence various behavioral phenomena, such as the receiver's subsequent communicative behaviors (e.g., "Did you see that funny Wendy's commercial in which an elderly woman shouts, 'Where's the beef?!'?'") and acquisition behaviors (e.g., the purchase of a Wendy's hamburger).

Except for a discussion of how miscomprehension relates to the notion of deceptive/misleading advertising (which follows immediately below), the treatment of these subsequent mental and behavioral phenomena are beyond the scope of this monograph. Again, the interested reader is referred to the seminal work in social psychology[59] and consumer behavior[60] for a discussion of these issues.

Summary

No single investigation could possibly study all aspects of comprehension/ miscomprehension as outlined above. Accordingly, this study focuses on

---

[59]For example, McGuire, 1985.
[60]For example, Engel et al., 1986; Peter and Olson, 1987.

semantic processing, leaving the more fundamental problem of sensory processing for others better suited to the task.

Within the domain of semantic processing, the study focuses on thematic representation, not morphemic representation. Though the latter topic is of great concern and definitely deserves considerable attention, it is beyond the scope of the present project.

Within thematic representation, attention is directed to both asserted and implied meanings. In regard to the latter, our attention is principally directed to logical rather than pragmatic inferences.

Inasmuch as understanding that is fleeting is, by definition, inconsequential, our efforts are directed toward retained meanings—at least those that qualify as having been retained for several seconds. We do not, however, focus either on: (1) the evaluations or affect associated with any retained meaning; (2) the potential or actual interactions between and among various communication beliefs, nor (3) the various potential or actual interactions between communication and referent beliefs.

In regard to outcomes, this study examines both comprehension and miscomprehension.

RELATING MISCOMPREHENSION TO DECEPTIVE/MISLEADING COMMUNICATIONS

Noting that a basic consumer right is the right to be informed, Chapter 1 indicated that the regulatory agencies have taken an active interest in insuring that the information that is provided is neither deceptive nor misleading. Considered in the context of these concerns, an important question is: How does miscomprehension relate to the notions of deceptive and misleading communications?[61]

As discussed in work commissioned by the Food and Drug Administration,[62] reference to the dictionary suggests that *deceptive* and *misleading* are distinguished in terms of the source's intent and actions. *Deceptive* implies a deliberate act on the part of the source to lead the receiver astray, whereas *misleading* implies that the receiver has been led astray for any of a number of reasons, which may or may not be attributed to the source. Although the regulatory agencies use the terms interchangeably, *misleading*

---

[61]The notion of deceptive and misleading communications refers to communications (such as advertisements, package labeling, etc.) that cause some meaningful number of "reasonable consumers" to be led astray regarding some material aspect of the product in question. The question of what constitutes information that is deceptive/misleading (or is likely to deceive/mislead) is also relevant to the trademark and trade dress arena, where the analogous terms are "consumer confusion" and "likelihood of confusion."

[62]Jacoby and Small, 1975.

may be viewed as incorporating and being broader than *deceptive,* while at the same time being less pejorative. The earlier miscomprehension monograph[63] contended that, while miscomprehension and deception were conceptually independent, miscomprehension was a necessary, albeit insufficient, condition for determining whether a communication was misleading.

Our current views reflect evolution and change. We no longer believe that miscomprehension is a necessary prerequisite for establishing that a communication is misleading. As will be illustrated below, whether or not a communication is *actually* misleading or deceptive may be independent of whether that communication has been miscomprehended. On the other hand, miscomprehension may be an essential component of the notions of deceptive*ness* and misleading*ness.* This merits explanation.

A Policy-Oriented Framework

The reader is asked to consider Figure 2.6, which has been adapted from an exhibit provided in the earlier TV report[64] in order to more clearly illustrate the relationship between the concept of miscomprehension and the concepts of misleading/deceptive and misleadingness/deceptiveness. The box at the left depicts Product X (or Service X), an independent entity that may be described in terms of its objectively verifiable features and characteristics. For example, one may verify that Brand X breakfast cereal contains raisins but does not contain blueberries. On the other hand, the box on the right is meant to portray the consumer's relevant referent beliefs regarding Product X. These may be veridical (e.g., Brand X contains raisins but no blueberries), completely non-veridical (e.g., Brand X contains blueberries, but no raisins), or some combination of the two (e.g., Brand X contains both raisins and blueberries).

Note that there are several routes by which the consumer may arrive at these product-oriented referent beliefs. Generally they may result from personal experiences (Route 1) or from attending to some communication regarding Brand X. The latter may be mass media communications (e.g., advertisements, package labeling, news stories, etc; Route 2), or interpersonal communications (e.g., word-of-mouth communications from friends and neighbors, conversations with sales clerks, etc.; Route 3). Our focus is on the mass media advertising communications, one variety of the 2A→2B→2C sequence. For the moment, it is important to recognize that the consumer's relevant referent beliefs may come from any one of a number of different sources. Further, even the receiver's own personal experiences (e.g., eating Brand X breakfast cereal at a friend's home and not realizing that the friend added blueberries on her own) may lead to non-veridical referent beliefs.

---

[63]Jacoby, Hoyer, and Sheluga, 1980, pp. 40–42.

[64]See Jacoby, Hoyer, and Sheluga, 1980, p. 36.

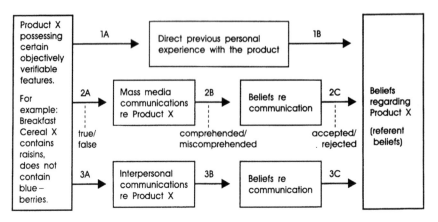

FIG. 2.6.   A Policy-Oriented Model of the Belief Formation Process

The difference between communication beliefs and referent beliefs outlined earlier also bears repeating. Succinctly described, communication beliefs pose the question "Does the receiver believe *that the communication expresses* proposition X?" whereas referent beliefs ask "Does the receiver believe proposition X?" Note that these are entirely independent issues. The receiver could respond "yes" to the first question and "no" to the second: "Yes, the ad did say that the product would remove freckles," and "No, I don't believe that the product is capable of doing what it claims."

Now consider an advertisement for Brand X which, via either direct assertion or logical implication, makes Representation A—a representation that can be objectively demonstrated to be either true (for example: "Brand X does contain raisins") or false (such as "Brand X does not contain raisins" or "Brand X contains blueberries"). The truth or falsity issue focuses on the question of whether the communication represents objective reality (link 2A) and is reflected in the notion of "advertising substantiation." This issue and its assessment are made independently of whether the receivers to whom the communication is directed actually comprehend or miscomprehend that communication.

The receiver who devotes attention to this communication will form various communication beliefs (link 2B). As examples, he may come away with any of the following meanings:

1. The ad said A ("The cereal contains raisins").
2. The ad did not say A.
3. The ad said "not A" ("The cereal does not contain raisins").
4. The ad said B ("The cereal contains blueberries").
5. Etc.

Meaning 1 represents accurate comprehension of the meaning actually asserted or logically implied; all other extracted meanings represent some form of miscomprehension.[65] Note that miscomprehension refers to link 2B and is conceptually independent of whether the communication actually does or does not misrepresent (that is, can or cannot be substantiated; link 2A). For instance, the ad may make a valid claim ("Brand X contains raisins") which the receiver may miscomprehend, believing that *the ad said* something else ("Brand X contains no raisins"). Or the ad may make a false claim ("Brand X contains no raisins") which the receiver may either comprehend (i.e., believe that *the ad said* that Brand X did not contain raisins) or miscomprehend (e.g., believe that *the ad said* that Brand X did contain raisins). Again, the focus is on what the receiver believes the ad said, not what the ad did in fact say or imply. In other words, the subject of comprehension/miscomprehension refers to describing the relationship depicted by link 2B.

Finally, there are the receiver's referent beliefs regarding the product itself. Recall that such beliefs have many potential sources, including understandings derived from mass media communications (link 2C), word-of-mouth communications from friends and family (link 3C), one's own past experiences (link 1B), etc. Thus, irrespective of whether he has comprehended or miscomprehended the communication (link 2B), the receiver may accept or reject what he believes it to say about the product in question (link 2C). That is, one can arrive at a deceptive/misleading belief for any one of a number of reasons, some of which may be entirely independent of any manufacturer-controlled communication.

Consideration of how the elements comprising Route 2 of Figure 2.6 may operate suggests a number of interesting possibilities (see Table 2.2). In some cases, a person could be misled because he *correctly* comprehended the communication while in other cases he could be misled because he *mis*comprehended the communication. As examples, a person could be misled due to:

1. a communication that expresses a misrepresentation (Tier 2 in Table 2.2) that he accurately comprehends (Tier 3) and accepts as being true (Tier 4); see case 6 of Table 2.2;
2. a communication that expresses no misrepresentation (Tier 2), but is somehow miscomprehended (Tier 3) with the miscomprehension then being accepted as fact (Tier 4); see case 4; or
3. a communication that contains no misrepresentations (Tier 2) and is correctly understood (Tier 3), but is dismissed as being untrue; see case 2.

Regardless of the reason why he is misled, the result is the same in all

---

[65]For purposes of simplification, we ignore the possibility that the receiver may extract multiple meanings involving a combination of Meaning 1 with some other meaning.

TABLE 2.2
Relating Miscomprehension to Deceptive/Misleading and Deceptiveness/Misleadingness

Examples

Tier	Case 1	Case 2	Case 3	Case 4	Case 5	Case 6	Case 7	Case 8
1: *Products* or services having objectively verifiable features	Brand X breakfast cereal — Presence of raisins; absence of blueberries							
2: *Communications* re Products/Services containing asserted or logically implied meanings which can be demonstrated to be true or false. The communication represents:	"Brand X contains Raisins"				"Brand X contains no raisins" (a misrepresentation)			
3: The receiver's resultant *communication beliefs*. These may reflect either non-comprehension, comprehension or miscomprehension. Person believes communication represents:	"Brand X contains raisins" (Comprehension)		"Brand X contains no raisins" (Miscomprehension)		"Brand X contains no raisins" (Comprehension)		"Brand X contains raisins" (Miscomprehension)	
4: The receiver's associated *referent beliefs* (which may or may not be influenced by his comprehension or miscomprehension of the communication). Person believes:	"Brand X contains raisins"	"Brand X contains no raisins"	"Brand X contains raisins"	"Brand X contains no raisins"	"Brand X contains raisins"	"Brand X contains no raisins"	"Brand X contains raisins"	"Brand X contains no raisins"

three cases: the person has been led astray so that he believes something regarding a material aspect of the product that is not true. The receiver may come away from the communication with an erroneous referent belief either because he correctly comprehends the ad but doesn't believe what it says, or because he incorrectly interprets the ad and believes this interpretation.

Communications That Are Actually Misleading/Deceptive

What does this imply regarding the relationship between miscomprehension and misleading/deceptive communications?

First, let us emphasize the importance of distinguishing between actually being misled and the potential or likelihood of being misled. Consistent with our earlier writings, we believe that whether a communication is *actually* deceptive or misleading requires demonstrating: (1) that the receiver has fallacious *referent* beliefs and (2) that these have been *caused* by the communication in question. Accordingly, we continue to subscribe to the definition that the senior author developed for use by the Food and Drug Administration.[66] In generalized form, it states that a misleading or deceptive communication is one that:

1. causes,
2. either through its verbal content, design, structure, and/or visual artwork, or the context in which it appears,
3. at least N%
4. of a representative group of relevant consumers
5. to have a common
6. impression or *belief regarding the* advertised *product, brand, or service* (i.e., a referent belief)
7. that is incorrect or not justified.

Unfortunately, the demonstration of such a cause-effect relationship requires elaborate testing procedures in order to rule out the possibility that the fallacious referent belief is caused by something other than the communication in question, such as word-of-mouth communications or firsthand experience with the product. Such testing is exceedingly difficult to conduct, especially for established products where the consumer is likely to have a network of relevant pre-existing beliefs.

---

[66]See Jacoby and Small, 1975.

Communications That Are Likely to Mislead/Deceive

The regulatory agencies have adopted a less stringent approach. Instead of relying on carefully controlled experimental tests to convincingly demonstrate that an erroneous belief was actually due to the communication in question and to nothing else, they focus on the communication's *potential* to mislead. The regulatory standard "is whether the act or practice is likely to mislead"[67] or has a "tendency or capacity to mislead."[68]

The regulatory agencies thus focus on deceptive*ness* rather than actual deception. "The law doesn't want to know what the consumer thinks is true; it wants to know what the consumer thinks the ad claimed".[69] Under these circumstances, "it would follow that the appropriate research question would be 'Does the ad convey this statement?' rather than 'Do you believe this statement?' "[70]

In other words, while demonstrating that something is *actually* deceptive or misleading (at tier 4 in Table 2.2) would require a carefully controlled assessment of the causes of referent beliefs, demonstrating that a communication has the *potential* or *is likely* to deceive (that is, possesses the quality of "deceptive*ness*" or "misleading*ness*") simply involves an assessment of communication beliefs (at tier 3 in Table 2.2). Because the link (2B in Figure 2.6) is direct and no other communication sources are involved, it is much easier to demonstrate that an ad caused a fallacious communication belief than it is to demonstrate that the ad caused a fallacious referent belief.[71] Although miscomprehension and deceptiveness/misleadingness are conceptually quite different and independent as operationalized under these circumstances, miscomprehension appears to be a necessary ingredient for the notion of deceptiveness/misleadingness. This statement warrants further explanation.

According to the Federal Trade Commission majority statement, communications will be subject to regulatory action if they make a claim or representation that reflects three essential ingredients:

1. the representation is "likely to mislead consumers";
2. the people in question are "reasonable consumers";
3. the representation is "material" so that accepting the representation as true "is likely to affect the consumer's conduct or decision with regard to a product or service."[72]

---

[67]FTC, 1983, p. 689.

[68]Bailey and Pertschuk, 1984, p. 379.

[69]Preston, 1983, p. 301.

[70]Preston, 1983, p. 300.

[71]A further discussion of the rationale underlying the regulatory focus on potential rather than actual deception can be found in Preston, 1983, pages 294–301, and in Ford and Calfee, 1986.

[72]Federal Trade Commission, 1983, pp. 689–690.

Thus, in those situations where attention is confined to "reasonable consumers" and "material representations," the issue of "likely to mislead" is effectively reduced to a question of miscomprehension.

Acting on "False and/or Misleading" Communications

Reconsider the eight cases outlined in Table 2.2. Cases 1 through 4 describe situations where the assertion in the communication is truthful, while cases 5 through 8 describe situations where the representation is demonstrably false. In these latter circumstances, ad substantiation research (focusing on link 2A of Figure 2.6) would reveal the claims to be false, and regulatory action would be warranted on these grounds alone. There would appear to be no need for consumer-based data. Indeed, one might find that the ad is correctly comprehended and not deceptive (case 6), or incorrectly comprehended and not deceptive (case 8). Despite the fact that the ad was not deceptive, action would be warranted on the grounds that the ad was false. Of course, demonstrating likelihood of deception (cases 5 and 6) would provide additional grounds for action. Note, however, that in certain instances, regulators might choose to take no action whatsoever. "Puffery" provides an excellent example.

Given that false advertising can be detected and eliminated via ad substantiation research, the principal value of the deceptiveness doctrine would seem to apply when the representations made in the communication (link 2A) are not false, but some substantial number of reasonable consumers are shown to extract erroneous communication beliefs (link 2B). Let us consider the possibilities on a case-by-case basis, bearing in mind that the representations actually being made in the communication (link 2A) can be shown to be true.

Case 1 presents no problem. The communication itself, and the consumer's communication and referent beliefs, are all veridical.

Case 2 does pose a problem. Though the communication contains a truthful representation and the consumer correctly comprehends this representation (i.e., forms an accurate communication belief), the consumer nonetheless maintains an inaccurate referent belief regarding some material aspect of the product. The communication is thus not likely to mislead, but the consumer is misled (perhaps due to prior personal experience or other communications). It is debatable whether such a communication can or should be the focus of regulatory action.

Case 3 describes a situation where there is miscomprehension (an erroneous communication belief) and the communication possesses a high degree of that quality termed "likely to deceive." However, as reflected by the relevant referent belief, there appears to be no actual deception. In many such instances, the regulatory agency may choose to take no action at all, since there would appear to be no probable injury (financial or otherwise) that would result from such miscomprehension.

Case 4 appears to best reflect the kind of situation that regulatory focus on the subject of deception was intended to address. In this situation, though the communication contains a representation which is true, there is something about that communication which leads reasonable consumers to extract an erroneous communication belief (at tier 3) which, in turn, leads to or reinforces an erroneous referent belief (at tier 4) and may then "affect the consumer's conduct or decision with regard to (the) product or service." For example, an ad for an in-home pregnancy test may truthfully claim to provide results "in as soon as 10 minutes," thus not misrepresenting the fact that it may take up to 30 minutes to learn the results. But if, as a result of reading this ad, a substantial number of reasonable target consumers believe the ad said it provides results in "10 minutes or less," and also believe this to be true of the product, we have a situation where the ad is "likely to mislead" in some material respect. Such advertising needs to be revised so as to thwart the formation of such erroneous communication (and referent) beliefs.

Several concluding observations are in order. First, note that, in terms of the framework outlined here, the notion of "likely to deceive" requires the formation of erroneous communication beliefs (on material matters by some number of reasonable consumers). It seems to us that, to be actionable, said miscomprehension should be accompanied by corresponding erroneous referent beliefs. Otherwise, the situation is trivial. Though it demonstrates that the communication has a high likelihood to mislead, no one will actually be misled as a consequence.

For example, even though a communication may be shown to possess a high degree of deceptiveness/misleadingness, it does not necessarily follow that even a single consumer will actually be misled/deceived. Believing that an ad for Brand X claimed it would "give you the whitest teeth in the whole wide world" (a communication belief) doesn't necessarily lead to accepting this claim as being true of Brand X (a referent belief).

Second, good judgment, and possibly regulatory restraint, may best be exercised in situations where, although the communication gives rise to both erroneous communication and erroneous referent beliefs (i.e., is both likely to mislead and does in fact mislead), no behavior based on such deception ever occurs. That is, consumers may be deceived, but never injured, because they never act on the basis of this deception. Should finite and precious regulatory resources be expended on such situations?

Finally, note that the above analysis suggests that regulatory actions taken on the basis of likely deception are perhaps only appropriate in those instances where the representations in a communication can be substantiated (i.e., are true). If an ad claim cannot be substantiated, then the question of whether or not it is also deceptive may be irrelevant. A demonstration of misrepresentation should, by itself, provide a sufficient basis for requiring remediation.

3 Methodology

Remaining at a conceptual level, the previous chapter specified the kinds of messages, media, receivers, and effects of interest in this study. The present chapter indicates how these specifications were implemented to select the specific messages, media, and receivers used in the investigation and to assess the effects of interest, namely comprehension/miscomprehension.

Clearly, assessment was feasible for only samples of all nationally circulated magazines, all the content within these magazines, and all magazine readers. Since our interest was in generalizing from the respective sample findings to each of these domains as a whole, the sampling plans had to generate reasonably comprehensive and representative coverage of each domain. The various sampling plans are described below. They are followed by a discussion of the assessment instrument and testing procedures. It should be noted that in order to avoid re-inventing the wheel and to maximize the utility of our findings for communication practitioners, standard industry nomenclature and practice was relied on in most instances.

SAMPLING PLANS

Sampling Plan for Magazines

There are hundreds of nationally circulated magazines. Beyond the top 100 or so, however, circulation and audience[1] drop dramatically. To insure that the study would not be faulted for focusing on relatively obscure and

---

[1] Audience is defined as circulation times number of readers per copy.

unrepresentative magazines, and also to insure that standard industry data would be available for the magazines selected, we concentrated on "newstand" magazines available to the public and having widespread national audiences. The study thus excluded from considerations periodicals published by labor unions, automobile associations, veterans associations, fraternal organizations, and so on. Also excluded were professional and scholarly periodicals such as the *American Psychologist, Journal of Marketing Research;* etc.

The selection of target magazines was made with an eye toward magazine content. According to standard industry practice, a magazine's total content is apportioned into two mutually exclusive categories. Any given item is classified as being either advertising or editorial content.[2] Each of these categories is quite broad and encompasses many subvarieties. Rather than constructing de novo classification schemes, we relied on those used by the following syndicated services which regularly issue reports on the advertising and editorial content of major magazines.

1. *Hall's Magazine Reports*[3] contain analyses of the *editorial* content of 60 major consumer magazines (see Appendix A). The December issue for monthly magazines and the January 1st issue for weekly magazines provide summaries of the linage devoted to each type of editorial content for the calendar year just concluded.
2. *Publishers Information Bureau (PIB): Magazine Total and Class Totals Index*[4] provides summaries of the linage devoted to each type of advertising content for the 121 major magazines indicated in Appendix B of this study.

Since the intent of this project was to use advertising and editorial messages from each test magazine, it was further decided to limit attention to magazines for which data were provided in *both* the Hall's and PIB reports. Of the 60 magazines listed in Hall's, 52 were also listed in PIB. Three of these (*Family Weekly,* the *New York Times Magazine,* and *Parade*) were eliminated because they were newspaper supplements rather than general circulation "newstand" magazines. Two (*Sunset, Southern Living*) were eliminated on the grounds that they possessed primarily regional, as opposed to national, appeal. This left a set of 47 potential test magazines.

It was considered important to have access to the audience data for each

---

[2]As used in this context, the term "editorial content" encompasses all non-advertising material, including articles, features, etc.

[3]Published by the R. Russell Hall Company, 544 Old Post Road, Greenwich, CT.

[4]Published by the Magazines Publishers Association, 575 Lexington Avenue, New York, NY.

magazine, since these data are acknowledged to represent the single best estimate of total readership. The two major syndicated services that provide audience measurements[5] are the Simmons Market Research Bureau (SMRB)[6] and Mediamark Research Inc. (MRI)[7] Both services produce essentially the same rank orders in terms of readership, though MRI provides higher estimates. It was decided to rely on the SMRB approach, as it appeared to be more widely used throughout the industry.

The SMRB data are provided in Appendix C. The 122 separate entries include data for the three newspaper supplements deleted above, several daily newspapers (*The New York Times,* the *Wall Street Journal*), major magazine networks (e.g., Ziff-Davis Magazine Network, CBS Magazine Network), and duplicate listings for 11 magazines, one for "net" and the other for "gross."

Of the 47 magazines that passed the Hall's-PIB screening process, only 36 are listed in the SMRB Media and Markets report. Listed in order of size of total adult (over the age of 18) audience, these 36 magazines are identified in Appendix D. The sampling plan called for using every other magazine on this list, leaving 18 test magazines. This set is considered reasonably representative of the universe of generally circulated and widely read national "newstand" magazines. (For example, note that the set of 18 test magazines contains virtually the same ratio of monthly-to-weekly magazines as in the PIB set of 121 magazines.)

To select a specific issue of each magazine for use as the test issue, a date in April 1984 was randomly selected and the first issue of each magazine appearing on or after that date was included. None of the issues selected was an atypical, "special" issue.

Sampling Plan for Magazine Content

Having selected the specific test magazines, the next task was to identify and sample the content of these magazines.

Types of Content

As noted, standard industry practice is to partition magazines into advertising and editorial content. These categories can be subdivided in a number of ways. To comport with industry practice, reliance was placed upon the "Industry class" divisions provided by the PIB reports and the "Major level" divisions provided in the Hall's reports. As illustrated in

---

[5]See *Magazine Age,* April and May 1983 issues.
[6]Specifically, the SMRB Study of Media and Markets.
[7]Which issues the MRI Reports.

Appendices E and F, there are 29 major Industry class ("100 level") categories in the PIB reports and 18 "100 level" categories in the Hall's reports.

Using one ad from each of the 29 PIB categories for all 18 test magazines would have yielded (29 PIB categories × 18 magazines =) 522 test ads. Using one editorial communication for each of the 18 categories in the Hall's system would have yielded an additional (18 categories × 18 magazines =) 324 non-advertising stimuli. The combined total of 846 stimuli would have resulted in a study of gargantuan proportions. Relying upon the advice of our statistical consultant,[8] it was considered adequate to employ 3 advertising and 3 editorial communications from each of the 18 magazines, thus yielding a total of 108 test stimuli.

Two separate matrices were developed as a basis for answering the question "Just which *types* of advertising and editorial content should be tested?" The first matrix provided, for each of the 18 test magazines, the proportion of each magazine's linage that was devoted to each of the 29 PIB advertising categories during all of 1982 (Table 3.1). The second matrix provided the proportion of each magazine's linage that was devoted to each of Hall's 18 categories during all of 1982 (Table 3.2).

The initial inclination was to select, for each magazine, the three advertising and three editorial content categories having the highest linage proportions in that magazine. It soon became obvious this method would result in most test advertisements being drawn from only five of the 29 PIB categories: toiletries and cosmetics (D 100); food (F 100); beer, wine, and liquor (F 100); cigarettes (G 100); and automotive (T 100). This would have produced too narrow a universe of content. On the other hand, it did not seem reasonable to include test communications from categories that accounted for such miniscule proportions as .01 and .02 percent of the content of that magazine.

Accordingly, the following procedure was followed to insure that the types of advertising and non-advertising content selected for study would be sufficiently representative:

1. The categories labeled "Miscellaneous" in both the PIB and Hall's systems were eliminated from consideration. This left 28 PIB and 17 Hall's categories.

2. Next, inspection of the data suggested that a minimum cut-off of 2% be established. That is, at least 2% of a magazine's content had to be devoted to a particular "major level" or "industry class" category before that category would be eligible for inclusion in the study. The number of eligible categories for each magazine is listed at the bottom of Tables 3.1 and 3.2. For example, five of the 29 PIB categories met this criterion for

---

[8]Professor Jacob Cohen, New York University.

TABLE 3.1
Test Magazine Advertising Content Broken Down According to PBI "Industry Class" Categories

		Reader's Digest	Time	Ladies Home Journal	Good House-Keeping	Woman's Day	Sports Illust.
A100	Apparel	.2	.3	2.8	3.9	3.8	1.9
B100	Business	2.0	3.5	3.6	2.2	.2	2.2
B200	Insurance	1.3	1.2	—	—	—	1.4
B300	Office Equipment	.3	3.8	.2	.2	.1	2.0
B400	Publishing	1.7	2.4	.7	3.5	1.6	1.0
B500	Industrial Material	.9	.8	.1	.1	.3	.1
B600	Freight, Industrial	—	.4	—	—	—	—
D100	Toiletries, Cosmet.	1.9	.3	8.7	10.0	8.0	.6
D200	Drugs	3.8	.4	2.3	3.2	3.1	.7
F100	Food	5.7	.1	11.9	15.4	15.1	.2
F200	Confectionery	.5	.1	.5	1.0	.8	.3
F300	Beer, Wine, Liquor	1.5	3.7	.3	.5	.1	6.6
G100	Cigarettes	.1	5.8	9.1	—	8.0	8.7
G200	Jewelry	1.6	1.2	.1	.5	.3	1.9
G300	Entertainment	.4	.5	.1	.2	.1	.2
G400	Sporting Goods	.1	.1	.4	1.7	2.2	1.5
G500	Miscellaneous	1.4	1.5	1.2	1.7	1.6	1.2
G600	Retail	2.9	.3	1.6	2.5	4.1	1.5
H100	Household Furnish.	.6	—	1.6	2.8	2.5	.2
H200	Household Equipmt.	1.6	.4	1.0	2.6	1.8	.2
H300	Home Ent. Equipmt.	1.4	1.1	.5	.2	.3	2.7
H400	Soaps	.3	—	1.6	2.0	1.9	—
H500	Building Materials	.5	.4	.2	.8	.3	.5
T100	Automotive	3.4	9.1	—	.3	.1	10.2
T200	Gasoline	.9	1.1	—	.1	—	.4
T300	Aviation	—	.2	—	—	—	—
T400	Travel	.7	2.4	.1	.2	.1	1.0
T500	Agriculture	—	—	—	—	—	—
T600	Horticulture	.2	—	.1	.2	.2	.2
No. of eligible categories		5	7	6	10	8	6

67

Life	Redbook	Pop. Mech.	Outdoor Life	Mech. Illust.	House Beaut.	Madem.	Family Handyman	Bon Appetit	GQ	Cuisine	Met. Home
.9	3.3	.4	1.0	.2	.2	10.9	.3	.3	20.1	.3	.2
2.5	1.4	5.4	1.3	6.9	.5	2.1	3.2	.9	.8	.5	.6
1.2	.1	.1	—	.1	.1	—	.2	—	—	—	.8
1.1	.1	.2	.3	.2	.1	.1	.2	.1	—	—	.3
.4	2.1	1.8	1.8	2.3	1.3	.8	4.2	3.2	.5	2.2	2.0
.2	—	.1	—	—	.2	—	—	.2	—	.6	.1
.1	—	—	—	—	.2	—	—	—	—	—	—
.9	9.3	.1	—	.1	.7	20.1	—	—	7.0	—	1.8
.6	2.4	.3	.5	.2	—	2.2	.2	—	.8	—	.1
1.9	12.4	—	.1	—	1.3	.8	—	11.0	.1	7.0	4.6
.1	1.4	—	—	—	.2	.3	—	.7	.1	.4	.4
6.7	.2	1.1	2.3	1.0	1.5	2.2	.3	11.2	4.4	5.5	6.9
5.7	7.6	4.1	6.4	7.0	5.6	3.2	4.0	4.3	.9	7.2	6.5
3.2	.3	.5	.8	.4	—	1.2	—	.1	2.4	—	.3
1.6	.1	.1	.1	.1	—	—	.1	.4	.1	—	.2
1.2	.8	1.9	12.3	2.7	.1	—	.3	.2	—	—	—
.6	.8	6.9	5.4	5.0	1.8	1.1	3.9	1.1	1.2	1.3	1.7
.7	1.4	6.5	3.9	5.2	14.5	5.4	6.6	7.1	7.7	1.5	6.4
.8	1.8	.3	.1	.1	12.9	.6	.2	3.6	.1	2.4	7.8
.6	1.1	1.4	.4	.8	2.9	—	2.0	7.6	—	5.4	3.1
2.4	.3	.3	.3	.5	.4	.1	.2	.3	2.7	.1	2.1
—	1.0	.2	.1	.3	.3	.1	.4	.6	—	.4	.1
.1	—	6.5	1.2	6.5	3.6	—	16.1	.2	—	.2	1.5
3.3	—	9.4	7.2	7.6	.6	.2	4.0	1.4	.3	.2	2.1
.3	—	1.0	.8	1.1	—	—	.5	—	—	—	—
—	—	.1	—	.1	—	—	—	—	—	—	—
1.5	.1	—	4.2	—	.9	—	—	2.4	1.0	.5	.6
—	—	.2	.1	.2	—	—	.1	—	—	—	—
.1	—	1.9	1.3	1.7	.5	—	3.3	—	—	—	.1
6	6	6	7	8	5	7	9	8	6	6	9

TABLE 3.2
Test Magazine Editorial Content Broken Down According to
Hall's "Major Level" Categories

		Reader's Digest	Time	Ladies Home Journal	Good House-Keeping	Woman's Day	Sports Illust.
100	National Affairs	7.3	10.7	.8	.3	.2	.5
200	Foreign	6.4	10.9	.7	.7	—	.1
300	Amusement	.3	2.6	2.9	1.5	.2	.6
400	Beauty & Grooming	—	.1	3.1	3.2	3.4	.1
500	Building	.8	.2	.2	.3	1.4	—
600	Business & Industry	1.3	4.1	.8	.5	1.1	.2
700	Children	1.4	—	1.5	.8	1.7	—
800	Gardening–Farming	.3	—	.9	.2	.6	—
900	Food & Nutrition	.7	.2	10.4	10.7	9.9	—
1000	Health	6.9	.7	4.5	3.5	2.3	.1
1100	Home Furnishings	.1	.1	4.6	6.5	7.8	—
1200	Sports/Recr/Hobby	2.5	1.2	.1	.1	.2	39.1
1300	Travel–Transport.	1.9	.1	.3	.7	.7	.4
1400	Wearing Apparel	—	.2	2.4	2.7	6.3	.3
1500	Culture–Humanities	18.6	6.6	9.7	1.9	2.5	1.5
1600	General Interest	11.6	2.6	3.1	3.8	3.1	2.0
1700	Miscellaneous	1.9	1.5	2.5	1.8	2.3	1.8
1800	Fiction–Stories	1.5	—	4.5	7.6	.6	—
	No. of eligible categories	6	6	10	7	8	2

Reader's Digest (B 100, D 200, F 100, G 600, and T 100); seven met this criterion for *Time* magazine (B 100, B 300, B 400, F 300, G 100, T 100, and T 400).

3. Three advertising and three editorial categories for each magazine were then randomly selected from among the eligible categories (i.e., those meeting the 2% cut-off criterion) for each magazine. When considered across all 18 magazines, this approach meant that only eight of the remaining 28 PIB advertising content categories had no chance of being represented in the study.[9] None of the 17 Hall's editorial content categories were eliminated as a result of employing the 2% criterion. After deleting the two "Miscellaneous" categories and then eliminating those content categories that had less than a 2% representation in that magazine, the study could be considered representative of 17 (out of 18) Hall's editorial content categories and 20 (out of 29) PIB advertising content categories.

4. Applying the 2% criterion as a basis for category eligibility produced

_____
[9]These categories are: insurance; industrial materials; freight and industrial; confectionary; entertainment; gasoline; aviation; and agriculture.

| | | Pop. | Outdoor | Mech. | House | | Family Handy- | Bon | | | Met. |
Life	Redbook	Mech.	Life	Illust.	Beaut.	Madem.	man	Appetit	GQ	Cuisine	Home
9.6	.4	.6	2.2	.9	—	.3	—	—	.1	—	.1
8.7	—	.2	—	—	.2	—	—	—	—	—	—
8.1	1.0	—	.1	—	—	1.9	—	—	3.0	—	.4
.7	2.6	.2	—	—	.3	8.8	—	—	3.3	—	.1
—	.3	8.5	.3	15.8	7.0	.3	20.0	—	.4	.1	7.1
2.1	1.2	.6	.2	.6	—	1.0	.2	—	.6	—	.8
.7	3.2	.1	—	.3	.1	—	1.5	—	—	—	—
—	.2	2.1	—	2.7	3.3	—	7.6	—	—	.1	1.5
2.4	7.8	—	.4	—	6.3	2.8	.1	38.0	1.5	41.7	7.1
3.1	1.5	.2	1.1	—	—	2.6	.4	—	.7	—	—
—	2.4	5.8	.2	6.9	24.3	1.1	9.7	1.5	2.2	4.9	23.5
3.7	.1	6.5	35.0	1.4	.2	.4	1.3	—	2.1	.1	.2
.6	.3	15.6	1.3	14.5	1.7	.3	2.0	2.6	4.1	10.0	1.5
1.4	3.6	.1	—	—	.4	13.0	.1	—	23.8	—	.2
15.3	4.8	4.3	1.3	2.4	.6	10.7	—	—	4.1	1.3	1.2
3.1	1.6	1.1	3.2	1.8	1.8	2.0	1.4	—	1.3	1.8	1.6
1.7	1.8	1.9	2.3	2.4	2.6	1.9	2.8	1.4	1.8	2.7	3.2
—	14.2	—	—	—	—	1.1	—	—	—	—	—
9	7	6	4	6	5	6	5	2	7	4	4

two magazines which had fewer than three eligible editorial content categories. *Sports Illustrated* had two eligible categories (Sports, Recreation, and Hobby, 39.1%; and General Interest, 2.0%). *Bon Appetit* also had only two eligible content categories (Food and Nutrition, 37.9%; and Travel, 2.6%). No other magazine had fewer than four eligible advertising content categories from which to select three for use in the study.

Given that *Sports Illustrated* and *Bon Appetit* concentrate such a substantial amount of their editorial content on only one of the 17 content categories, it was decided to proceed as follows. For *Bon Appetit*, two items of editorial content were selected from the Foods and Nutrition category and the remaining item was taken from the Travel category. For *Sports Illustrated*, two editorial content items were selected from the Sports, Recreation, and Hobby category—one for sports and the other for recreation—and one item from General Interest.

The above procedure was designed to generate a total of 108 test stimuli—six stimuli (three advertising and three editorial) for each of the 18 magazines. The specific ad and ed categories selected for testing via this procedure are provided in Table 3.3. Across the set of 18 magazines, communications were selected from all 17 eligible editorial content categories and 19 of the 20 eligible advertising content categories.

Size of Content

The above discussion focused on the *types* of content to be included. Another fundamental issue concerns the *size* of each content item. To address this consideration, for each magazine, a tally was made of the number of ads appearing in each of nine sizes. These data are provided in Table 3.4, from which it can be seen that one size—the full-page ad—accounted for 53.9% of all advertising content in the sample selected. Further, it was the only size that was present in all 18 magazines, and the most frequent size in 16 of these. Because there seemed to be no a priori reason for the full-page ads in a given magazine to be any better or more poorly comprehended than would larger or smaller ads placed in that magazine, it was decided to use only full-page ads.

Having decided on the size of the advertising stimuli, the next step was to decide on the size of the editorial stimuli. Clearly, it would be unreasonable to compare comprehension of a full page ad with comprehension of a full page of editorial content. On the one hand, ads typically have a great amount of white space and relatively few words. On the other hand, an ad may actually convey much more information if one considers that "one picture is worth a thousand words." Hence, there appears to be no way to generate truly comparable stimuli.

Since one accepted way for comparing ad and ed content is in terms of total linage, it appeared reasonable to rely on an analogous index, the total number of words, as a basis for generating sets of advertising and editorial stimuli containing roughly comparable amounts of reading matter.

For each of the 18 magazines, the number of words appearing in each full-page ad for each of the test categories was tallied. These data are summarized in Table 3.5. Next, the median number of words was calculated for each category. To insure that each test ad was representative of the ads in that category, the following rule was applied: to be eligible for selection, an ad had to contain between ± 30% of the median number of words for ads in that category in that magazine. For example, if the category median was 120 words, to be eligible, an ad had to contain between 84 and 156 words. Taking the middle 60% effectively eliminates outliers.

The actual ad selection procedure involved cataloging all the full-page ads found for the three categories in each magazine. The number of words in each ad was counted and a median derived for each category. The ± 30% of the median decision rule was then administered. In cases where two or more ads fit this criterion, the test ad was randomly selected from among that set.

TABLE 3.3
Specific Ad and Ed Content Categories Selected for Each Magazine

Magazine	Ad Categories			Ed Categories		
	1	2	3	1	2	3
Reader's Digest	Drugs	Business	Retail	National affairs	Health and med. svcs.	Culture & humanities
Time	Office equip.	Business	Travel	Foreign affairs	Business & Industry	Amusement
Ladies Home J.	Cigarettes	Drugs	Food	Amusement	Food & nutrit.	Culture & humanities
Good Housekeep.	Toiletries	Apparel	Drugs	Wearing apparel	Health & med. svcs.	Fiction
Woman's Day	Entertainment	Toiletries	Apparel	Beauty & grooming	Home furn.	Wearing apparel
Sports Illust.	Beer, Wine, Liq.	Home enter.	Cigarettes	Sports/recr./hobby	Sports/recr./hobby	General interest
Life	Automotive	Jewelry	Business	Foreign affairs	Amusement	Business & industry
Redbook	Apparel	Food	Drugs	Children	Fiction	Foods & nutrit.
Pop. Mechanics	Building mater.	Automotive	Retail	Gardening	Travel & transp.	Home furn.
Outdoor Life	Entertainment	Automotive	Travel	Sports	National affairs	General interest
Mech. Illustrated	Publishing	Building mater.	Sporting goods	Travel & transp.	Gardening	Building
House Beautiful	Retail	Household furn.	Household equip.	Home furnish.	Building	Gardening
Madamoiselle	Apparel	Drugs	Cigarettes	Beauty & grooming	Health & med. svcs.	Culture & humanities
Family Handyman	Publishing	Business	Automotive	Building	Gardening	Gardening
Bon Appetit	Cigarettes	Retail	Household furn.	Food & nutrit.	Food & nutrit.	Travel & transp.
G.Q.	Apparel	Beer, Wine, Liq.	Jewelry	Travel & transp.	Wearing apparel	Beauty & grooming
Cuisine	Food	Publishing	Household equip.	Travel & transp.	Home furnish.	Food & nutrit.
Metropolitan Home	Home Enter.	Household equip.	Beer, Wine, Liq.	Home furnish.	Food & nutrit.	Building

TABLE 3.4
Proportion of Each Size Ad Appearing in the 18 Test Magazines*

Magazine	> Two	Two	Full	3/4	2/3	1/2	1/3	1/4	< 1/4
Bon Apetit		.09	.48		.04	.13	.11		.15
Cuisine	.04		.43			.09		.09	.36
Family Handyman	.05		.29			.15		.24	.27
Good Housekeeping	.01	.07	.53		.09	.14	.16		
GQ		.07	.56	.01		.19	.10	.04	.03
House Beautiful		.09	.47		.05	.05	.25		.07
Ladies Home Journal		.06	.45	.10		.18	.04	.17	
Life	.02	.03	.80			.08		.07	
Mademoiselle		.13	.63		.03	.03	.09		.09
Mechanics Illustrated		.07	.47			.12	.12	.14	.09
Metropolitan Home		.06	.31		.01	.01	.11		.50
Outdoor Life	.02	.07	.26		.07	.02	.08		.49
Popular Mechanics		.07	.54	.12		.04	.06	.03	.14
Reader's Digest	.07	.11	.63			.20			
Redbook		.22	.54	.12		.10	.02		
Sports Illustrated	.04	.11	.67					.11	.07
Time		.10	.71		.03		.06	.03	.06
Woman's Day		.07	.67	.08		.14		.04	
Totals	1.2%	7.8%	53.9%	3.1%	2.8%	9.7%	6.4%	5.2%	9.9%

*This tally excludes classified advertising.

In a few instances, the test issue of the magazine contained no advertisements for a particular category that had been targeted for use. Based on the rationale that the type of communication was more important than the specific magazine from which it came, in these cases, full-page ads representing that product category and meeting the number-of-words criterion were selected from one of the other test magazines. Thus, in a few instances, more than three ads were selected from some magazines while fewer than three were selected from others.

A matching procedure was applied as the basis for selecting the editorial

TABLE 3.5
Number of Words per Full-Page Advertisement

Magazine	$\bar{x}$	n	range	total
Bon Apetit	71.50	6	18–137	429
Cuisine	157.80	5	53–357	789
Family Handyman	443.60	5	292–748	2218
Good Housekeeping	100.35	17	8–271	1706
G.Q.	105.62	8	8–270	845
House Beautiful	202.60	5	`24–336	1013
Ladies Home Journal	87.10	10	14–268	871
Life	114.20	10	11–304	1142
Mademoiselle	99.62	8	13–165	797
Mechanics Illustrated	271.75	4	12–392	1087
Metropolitan Home	83.83	6	9–138	503
Outdoor Life	130.67	3	43–226	392
Popular Mechanics	319.12	8	69–587	2553
Reader's Digest	200.00	6	121–291	1200
Redbook	111.33	6	18–116	204
Sports Illustrated	115.00	4	19–184	460
Time	143.50	4	13–420	574
Woman's Day	99.18	11	15–260	1091
TOTAL Mean:	145.54	126	71.50–443.6	18338
Median:	114.60			

stimuli. Specifically, for each magazine, the median word ranges for the three ad categories were used as the basis for selecting the three editorial stimuli. For each of the three editorial content categories used for that magazine, the first editorial passage in the magazine that fell into one of the three median ad ranges was selected. Note that most of these editorial passages were segments taken from larger pieces. In these instances, the segment was used only if it could be completely understood without reference to the remainder of the article. No segment was selected where comprehension required that it be read in the context of earlier or later material. Where available, accompanying illustrations were included so as to increase comparability to the advertisements. As for the ads, there were instances where article categories could not be found in the April issue of a particular magazine. In those cases, a procedure identical to the ad selection substitute procedure was employed.

To avoid problems that might have resulted from using reproductions of the stimuli (particularly in those instances where color was involved), 120 copies of each test magazine were secured, so that actual tear sheets were used. Each test communication was cut from the magazine and mounted on a separate acetate-covered looseleaf page, with no other material appearing in the surrounding context. Each respondent was given only the four test pages, one at a time, for the communications on which he or she was to be tested.

Sampling Plan for Respondents

A nationally projectible in-home probability study was conducted, with the sampling plan calling for 1350 respondents living within the contiguous United States. As detailed below, the sample was stratified according to the primary gender orientation of the magazine (i.e., whether to males, females, or both). For purposes of assessing miscomprehension, each respondent was tested on four of the 108 test communications—two advertisements and two editorial passages—producing 50 replicates per communication. As described below, each respondent also participated in a "control condition." This yielded an additional 25 replicates per communication.

A set of screening questions was used to insure that all respondents were 18 years of age or older and were magazine readers.[10] A relatively broad criterion of readership was employed so that individuals were included if they claimed that they usually read at least some portion of a nationally circulated magazine at least once a month.[11] While it might be argued that since 25% to 35% of the adult population is considered to be functionally illiterate and such a screening procedure likely eliminates such individuals from consideration, the counterargument is that such marginal readers generally don't read magazines. Thus, whether they miscomprehend the contents of said magazines is immaterial. In this regard, note that the screening procedure also eliminates good readers if they claim that they usually do not read magazines. An example would be a person who reads one or two newspapers a day and/or several books a month. Though they

---

[10]See Appendix G, Screener Questionnaire, Questions a, b.
[11]See Appendix G, Screener Questionnaire, Question c.

may be good readers, such indivi !uals are not relevant for determining the extent to which the universe of *magazine* readers comprehend/ miscomprehend what they read in magazines.

Up to this point, these sampling procedures refer to the universe of magazine readers as a whole and appear not to accomodate for the fact that different magazines have different target audiences. Given 18 test magazines with varying incidences of readership and 108 test communi- cations, attempting to test each magazine using only people who claim to be readers of that particular magazine (or test each advertisement only with people who claim to be users of the advertised product and each editorial passage only with people who claim to be interested in that content) would have increased the project costs manyfold. Accordingly, three separate tactics were employed to better accomodate the notion of target audience.

First, the 18 test magazines were sorted into three categories, based on their primary gender orientation and audience.[12] Specifically, six of the magazines were classified as appealing principally to men, nine were classi- fied as appealing principally to women, and the remaining three as appealing equally to both sexes. These distributions are as follows:

Principally Women	*Principally Men*	*Both men and women*
1. Ladies' Home Journal	1. Sports Illustrated	1. Reader's Digest
2. Good Housekeeping	2. Popular Mechanics	2. Time
3. Woman's Day	3. Outdoor Life	3. Life
4. Redbook	4. Mechanics Illustrated	
5. House Beautiful	5. Family Handyman	
6. Mademoiselle	6. G.Q.	
7. Bon Appetit		
8. Cuisine		
9. Metropolitan Home		

The sample was stratified so that no males were tested on stimuli taken from female-oriented magazines and no females were tested on stimuli taken from male-oriented magazines. Both males and females were tested on stimuli taken from the three magazines considered to appeal equally to members of both sexes.

Second, the data were separately analyzed first for the entire sample of magazine readers and then for the following subgroups: (1) people who claimed to be subscribers to the magazines on which they were tested; (2) people who, while not subscribers, claimed to be at least occasional

---

[12]See Simmons's 1983 Study of Media and Markets.

readers of the magazines on which they were tested; (3) people who claimed to be at least occasional users of the products described in the test ads on which they were tested; and (4) people who indicated that they would, at least occasionally, read material such as the editorial passages on which they were tested.

Third, based on their responses to a series of screener questions (described below), only individuals who claimed to be regular readers of one or more of the test magazines were interviewed. Since each respondent saw communications from four different magazines, the chances were at least 4 out of 12 for females and 4 out of 9 for males that they would be "target audience" respondents.

The sample utilized in this investigation was the subcontractor's[13] National Probability Sample designed by Dr. Richard Maisel in June, 1982. The sample was selected on the basis of the 1980 household counts as reported by the United States Census Bureau in the Master Area Reference File (MARF). The sample was selected using the principles of area probability sampling. The specific design used in the sample is similar to that developed by W. Edwards Deming[14] and uses a single stage of selection with equal-sized primary sampling units (PSU's), each having an equal probability of selection.

All households in the United States, excluding Alaska and Hawaii, were divided into nine regional strata, each of which was then further divided into a metropolitan stratum and a non-metropolitan stratum. The eighteen strata were then further subdivided into a total of 100 substrata. The number of substrata within each of the eighteen strata was proportional to the number of households within the region. Each substratum within a region contained the same number of households.

Two equal-sized Primary Sampling Units were then randomly selected within each substratum, giving the sample 200 PSU's. The PSU consisted of a set of contiguous Census-defined Block Groups and/or Enumeration Districts which contained approximately 4,000 households. The set of households used in any specific survey are then randomly selected within the PSU using one of the standard procedures for selecting samples of households within larger Primary Sampling Units.

A total of 90 sampling points was required to complete the 1,350 in-home personal interviews. The selection of the individual sampling points was made from the basic Guideline Research Corporation National Probability Sample. This involved a three-step process, as follows:

---

[13]The subcontractor, Guideline Research Corporation, is a large full-service market research organization headquartered in New York City. (See Honomichl, 1986.)

[14]See Deming, 1960.

1. The 200 Primary Sampling Units, as described above, were intermingled by cross-numbering each replicate's sampling points.
2. Since the study was to involve only those households with "A," "B," and "C" counties (as per A.C. Nielsen Company designations), all PSU's in "D" counties were eliminated. While "D" counties represent 64.6% of all U.S. counties, they contain only 13.7% of the total U.S. population (see Table 3.6). Note that reliance upon the Nielsen system for clustering counties represents an accepted advertising and marketing practice.
3. Utilizing a formula provided by Dr. Maisel, every "nth" sampling point was eliminated from the list of remaining PSU's until 90 sampling points remained.

A two-tiered respondent selection process was employed. Every household was designated as either a male or female household. Within that household, only a member of the gender indicated could serve as a respondent.

Households were designated as either male or female by means of a "Household Listing Booklet." Once a household address was listed, a

TABLE 3.6
The A.C. Nielsen System for Clustering Counties

Category	Operational Definition	No. of U.S. Counties	% of Total U.S. Population
A Counties	All counties belonging as of June 19, 1981 to the 25 largest SCSAs or SMSAs according to the 1980 Census of Population.	183	40.9%
B Counties	All counties not included under A that are either over 150,000 population or in SCSAs or SMSAs over 150,000 population according to the 1980 Census of Population.	414	30.0%
C Counties	All counties not included under A or B that are either over 40,000 population or in SCSAs or SMSAs over 40,000 population according to the 1980 Census of Population.	515	15.4%
D Counties	All remaining counties.	2,023	13.7%
	Totals:	3,135	100.0%

Note: SCSA (Standard Consolidated Statistical Area) and SMSA (Standard Metropolitan Statistical Area) are defined by the Federal Government Office of Management and Budget.

pre-printed "F" or "M" next to the listing line indicated whether that household was "Female" or "Male." This designation never changed for that particular household. A "Female" household was always screened on a pink questionnaire form and a "Male" household was always screened on a blue form.

When screening a particular "male" or "female" household, all members of the designated gender, 18 years of age or older, were listed on a grid, from oldest down to youngest.[15] The designated respondent within each household was then selected by means of a different computer generated random number strip that had been affixed to the top of each screening form. The "designated respondent" was the individual whose name appeared on the line with a number that corresponded to the first random number on the strip. This individual was the only person within that household eligible for that interview.

ASSESSMENT INSTRUMENTS AND INDEPENDENT VARIABLES

Both open-ended and closed-ended assessment procedures were employed.

Open-ended Assessment

Immediately after reading each test communication, the respondent was asked standard open-ended questions designed to elicit his or her playback of the "main point(s)" of that communication.[16] The rationale for collecting these data was multi-faceted. Most importantly, this procedure insured that we would be assessing retained rather than fleeting meanings. Second, to the extent possible, it was considered desirable for our current procedures to be comparable to those used in the earlier TV investigation. Since open-ended questions preceded closed-ended questions in that study, they were also included here. Third, it was felt that an informal examination of these open-ended responses might provide some insight into the nature and underlying reasons for miscomprehension. Fourth, once gathered, these data would be available for future analysis. As compared to beginning an open-ended assessment study from scratch, a relatively small incremental cost was attached to collecting such data here.

---

[15]See Appendix G.
[16]See Questions 3a and 3b of the Main Questionnaire; Appendix G.

Closed-ended Assessment

The open-ended assessment was immediately followed by a closed-ended assessment. Of the variety of closed-ended formats that might have been employed, each has compensating advantages and disadvantages. In instances where the communication consists of a single phrase or sentence and the universe of meanings is relatively small, one can develop detailed multiple choice formats that require considerable respondent time to assess each of the target meanings.[17] However, in the present instance, the communications generally consisted of a number of sentences (some totaling a few hundred words) representing a broad universe of associated meanings. It was not considered feasible to develop time-demanding, detailed multiple-choice tests for assessing these meanings. In contrast, a true-false format permits more rapid testing of a greater number of meanings. Other advantages of the t-f format are that: (1) it is easy to administer; (2) it can be used across broad educational segments of the populace; and (3) it provides a straightforward means of objective scoring.

A separate "modified true-false" quiz was developed for each of the 108 test communications. Each quiz contained six items and each item could be answered using one of three explicitly provided response options: true, false, and don't know. This procedure is essentially the same as that proposed by Harris for studying inferences made from textual material.[18] The inclusion of a "don't know" option also reduces pressures for guessing and permits more accurate estimates of miscomprehension.[19]

To compensate for yea-saying response tendencies, each quiz contained an equal number of true and false items.

Approximately half the items on each quiz assessed asserted meanings while the other items assessed implied meanings. Across all 108 communications (as well as for the subsets of 54 advertisements and 54 editorial communications) there were an equal number of facts and inferences. Asserted meanings (or "facts") were tested via statements that were paraphrases of objectively ascertainable information explicitly stated in the communication. In half the cases, these statements were true; in the other half, they were false. Implied meanings (or "inferences") were tested via statements that contained meanings one might derive from that communication. Across the aggregate, half these inferences were true and half were false.

The quiz development and refinement process went through several stages designed to insure that the quiz items focused on comprehension, not recall, and were not biased so as to produce inaccurate estimates of

---

[17]See Jacoby, Nelson, and Hoyer, 1982.
[18]Harris and Monaco, 1977, pp. 10–11.
[19]See Schmittlein & Morrison, 1983.

miscomprehension. First, under the direction of the junior author, a team of graduate students knowledgeable with respect to the comprehension literature in general and the work of Anderson[20] (regarding paraphrase questions) and Harris and Monaco[21] (regarding distinguishing between logical and pragmatic inference) in particular, developed pools of quiz items for each of the 108 test communications.

When developing items to assess factual content, the principal focus was on developing "paraphrase questions." As Anderson notes:

> The argument that paraphrase questions assess comprehension is very simple . . . [In] order to answer a question based on a paraphrase, a person has to have comprehended the original sentence, since a paraphrase is related to the original sentence with respect to meaning but unrelated with respect to the shape or the sound of the words.[22]

In contrast, items that are simple re-statements may be answered correctly on the basis of recognition memory, not comprehension, a possible consequence of which would be inflated levels of comprehension.

The inferential items were developed with the distinction between logical and pragmatic implications in mind. All inference items in the test pool were then independently evaluated and categorized as being either logical or pragmatic. Across the two graduate students, the level of agreement was 91%. Discrepancies were resolved via discussions with the junior author. Next, the junior author scrutinized and, as necessary, revised the various items and generated six-item quizzes for each communication. In keeping with the arguments outlined in discussing the conceptual foundations (see Chapter 2), 92% of these items focused on logical implications; only 8% addressed pragmatic implications.

The six-item quizzes were then sent to the senior author and reviewed in two phases. During the first phase, the quiz items were considered independently of the communication upon which they were based. This was done to insure that the items could be understood on their own. Modifications were considered, and some of these implemented after consultation between the authors. During the second phase, each question was considered in the context of the communication on which it was based. Again, various modifications were considered, some of which were implemented after discussion between the authors.

All 108 communications and their corresponding quizzes were then sent

---

[20]Anderson, 1972.
[21]Harris and Monaco, 1977.
[22]Anderson, 1972, p. 150.

to a subcontractor, the Document Design Center[23], for independent review and, as necessary, revision. After satisfying themselves that each of the 108 communications could be meaningfully comprehended in its own right, the DDC staff evaluated the corresponding quizzes. The objective was to insure that these quizzes could be easily understood and would provide a reasonable and fair basis for assessing comprehension. This review resulted in editorial changes in a number of the quizzes.

The DDC also conducted an analysis of the graphic and linguistic features of the 108 communications and, for each, provided the following indices for use in the later analyses:

Graphic Features

Average line length (no. of words)
Average line length (no. of characters)
Mean characters per sq. in.
Percent of page covered by text
Number of headings or boldface
Percent of total words in headings
Number of consecutive words in all caps
Right margin—ragged or justified
Left margins—ragged or justified
Margins—mixed
Presence of photo or drawing
Color photo
Number of type sizes
Number of different type styles
Predominant type size

Linguistic Features

Number of sentences
Mean sentence length (in words)
Sentence fragments (% of sentences)
Passive verbs (% of all verbs)
Noun strings (% of all words)
Personal pronouns (% of all words)

---

[23]The DDC, a subsidiary of the American Institutes for Research (AIR), includes communication specialists and researchers with backgrounds in psychology, linguistics, psycholinguistics, writing, law, and design whose principal focus is on easy text comprehension. Among other projects, the DDC regularly conducts seminars on the subject of writing manuals, forms, and other documents so that the people who use these documents can understand them.

Nominalizations (% of all words)
Number of lists
Items per list
Parallel lists
Percentage of one syllable words
Adjectives (% of all words)

The entire set of quizzes was then reviewed by the staff at Guideline Research Corporation to insure that, based upon their experience in the realm of consumer and market surveys, the quiz items would pose no difficulties for respondents.

Finally, using an average of 8 respondents per quiz, a subsample (24) of the quizzes was pre-tested in January 1985 at central location testing sites in Indianapolis, Indiana and Austin, Texas. The 24 quizzes were not selected at random. Rather, they were those which the authors thought might be the most difficult or unclear. The respondents were told that they were participating in a pre-test, the objective of which was to insure that the materials that would be used in the test proper were easily understood.[24] After reading one of the 24 pre-test ad communications, they were given the corresponding quiz and told that the page:

> contains six statements that we're thinking of using next month. As I mentioned, we'd like to make certain that they are easily understood. We don't need your answers. All you have to do is simply indicate if the statement is clear to you. Please read the first statement. If the entire statement is clear to you, simply write "OK" next to it. If certain portions of the statement are not clear to you, or if you don't understand it, simply circle those words or phrases which are not clear.

Each respondent evaluated four different quizzes. The quizzes were provided in counterbalanced order both across and within respondents in order to minimize order effects.

Analysis of these data revealed no consistent problems with any of the (24 stimuli × 6 quiz items/ea. =) 144 pre-tested items. On fewer than 10% of the items (13 out of 144) did two of the respondents circle the same word or phrase as being troublesome. Upon examination, most of these "problems" turned out not to be problems at all.

In a number of instances, the respondents wrote in an explanation for their underlining which revealed that they comprehended the quiz item, but were unwilling to accept its proposition as being true. Such comments

---

[24]See Appendix H.

pertain to referent beliefs, not to the communication beliefs that are formed as part of the comprehension process (cf. Chapter 2).

In a number of other instances, the difficulty arose from the need to have 50% of the items be incorrect representations (i.e., convey a meaning that was contrary to what had been conveyed by the communication itself)—a requirement not explained to the respondent. It was clear in these instances that the respondent had correctly comprehended both the communication and the "false" quiz item, and the problem stemmed from the respondents rejecting the "false" quiz item because they made the erroneous assumption that the item was supposed to be an accurate representation of the communication.

In yet another instance, respondents indicated that while they understood the item, they felt its wording could be improved and went on to suggest such improvements.

Collectively, the pre-test findings generated strong confidence that the entire set of quiz items would be readily comprehended by the universe of interest. Although it is always possible that any level of obtained miscomprehension could be due to miscomprehension of the quiz items and not of the communication itself, as the steps described above indicate, great care was taken to minimize this possibility.

It should be pointed out that this series of steps bears on the question of whether meanings are "contained in" surface structures or only in the minds of sources and receivers. Though no effort was made to have the original communication sources themselves evaluate the quizzes in terms of their fidelity to the source's intended meaning, the elaborate sequence of stages in the quiz construction process serves to insure a degree of triangulation on the meanings that might be "contained in" the communication. The convergence of all those involved in the process suggests that we can be reasonably comfortable that the quizzes do assess the meanings being conveyed.

Once all the survey instruments had reached their final version, the materials and procedures were evaluated via a pilot investigation conducted in a New York suburban community (Massapequa, Long Island). As this investigation revealed, interviewers could easily understand and follow the procedures and the interview itself was smooth-flowing and did not result in respondent fatigue.

An attempt was made to include all 54 non-advertising test communications and their corresponding quizzes in Appendix I. As a number of authors and/or publications denied our request for permission to reproduce, only about half of these communications have been included. As was done with the previous TV study, the advertisements and their corresponding quizzes are not provided in order to preserve confidentiality.

ADMINISTRATION PROCEDURES

Implementation of the in-home interviews was handled by Guideline Research Corporation. Preparation of field materials was customized for each sampling (cluster) point as well as for each respondent within the cluster point.

Each interview consisted of two basic questionnaires, a Screener Questionnaire and a Main Questionnaire.[25] Both came in two basic versions, one for each sex. The contents of each questionnaire were customized for each individual respondent to insure that the sequence of communications both within and across respondents was randomized and counterbalanced over sex and PSU. Thus, each communication appeared an equal number of times in each of the four test positions. This meant that respondents were not only randomly selected, but also randomly assigned to test stimuli, thereby enhancing both external and internal validity.

The collation process entailed handwriting each stimulus code number onto each questionnaire and then matching each stimulus to the appropriate questionnaire. Questionnaire and stimuli were then clipped together and placed into an envelope marked with a cluster point number. Each envelope contained 15 customized questionnaires/stimuli. These were then double-checked against the master listing by an individual not involved in the collation process.

The finished packets were shipped to each cluster point, accompanied by a letter containing one set of Supervisor Instructions and a set of detailed Interviewer Instructions for each interviewer.[26] Each interviewer received a thorough personal briefing on the study procedures and conducted a practice interview before proceding on the project. All interviews were conducted during May, 1985.

Screener Questionnaire

The purpose of the Screener Questionnaire was to eliminate households and individuals who did not fit either the universe definition or the requirements of the sampling plan.

Question 1 eliminated those households that did not qualify for the study by virtue of having no individuals over 18 years of age of the gender called for by the Screener Questionnaire.

The purpose of Q.2 and Q.3 was to identify the entire pool of potentially eligible respondents in that particular household and then, by means of the previously described random number tape strip, to identify the one person from that pool who was the designated respondent. This person was the only individual in the household who could qualify for participation in the

---

[25]See Appendix G.
[26]See Appendix J.

study. (Up to three attempts were made to contact and interview this individual.)

Questions 4a and 4b inquired regarding the potential respondents' television viewing habits. These questions were similar to the screening questions in the TV investigation and served three purposes. First, they were to identify that subset of respondents who would have qualified for both TV and print investigations. (Since approximately 98% of the sample replied affirmatively to these questions, the separate analysis originally intended for this subgroup was not warranted.) Second, they provide a framework and a smooth-flowing procedure for asking the corresponding magazine questions. Third, since the respondent was likely to have already replied affirmatively to these questions, they reduced the pressure for yea-saying and overclaiming on the critical magazine questions that followed.

Based on the suggestions of others,[27] Question 5a ("Now thinking about magazines, do you usually read or look through some portion of a magazine at least once a month?") was worded to comport with common industry practice. Questions 5b and 5c were designed to assess the number and specific identities, respectively, of the magazines that were read.

The twelve-component Question 6 series was introduced by handing the respondent a card that, for males, listed the 9 magazines relevant for males and, for females, the 12 magazines for females. These cards also contained the names of two fictitious magazines: *American Unicorn* and *News of the Globe.* This series of questions served several important functions.

First, it was designed to determine whether the designated respondent had previously heard of or was a "regular reader" (defined as having read or looked through at least one out of two issues) of any of the relevant test magazines. To maximize the likelihood of including "target audience" respondents, those individuals who reported not being regular readers of at least one of the relevant test magazines were eliminated from further consideration. Questions 6e through 6l asked whether the Designated Respondent, or any other individual in the household, either currently or previously subscribed to any of the magazines.

Another purpose of the Question 6 series was to eliminate from further consideration individuals who replied affirmatively in regard to either of the two fictitious magazines, since these individuals might be prone to lying on other items as well.

Only after successful completion of the Screener Questionnaire was the Main Questionnaire administered to the designated respondent.

---

[27]Particularly Marvin M. Gropp, Vice President, Research at the Magazine Publishers Association.

Main Questionnaire

The Main Questionnaire for each respondent[28] contained four components: (1) a general introduction, (2) four test communications, along with corresponding open- and closed-ended comprehension assessment questions and a battery of several communication-specific interest and evaluation items, (3) two "control" quizzes, and (4) a concluding sociodemographic battery.

Introduction

The introduction to the Main Questionnaire informed the respondent that he or she would be given four different items (two advertising and two editorial communications) taken from the magazines appearing on the screener list, and would then be asked a few questions regarding each of these.

Test Communications and Assessment

The respondent was then handed the first communication and told (Q.2): "Please read what it says and tell me when you're finished." Respondents were given as much time as they desired and record was made of the amount of time taken. Across all respondents and test stimuli, this averaged 48.8 seconds (median = 29.7 seconds). Given the objective of striving for 100% attention, when compared with Batra and Ray's[29] observation that "approximately 4 seconds are spent on the average magazine advertisement page," it can be seen that our respondents did indeed devote substantial attention to each communication. They knew that they were in a test situation and were clearly devoting greater attention to these communications than would typically be the case. As with the TV investigation, immediately upon completion, the respondent was asked the two open-ended assessment questions: "What was the *main* message of the ad/passage you just read?" (Q3a), and "What *other* points were in the ad/passage you just read?" (Q3b).

These items were directly followed by the six-item quiz designed to assess comprehension/miscomprehension of that communication. The quiz was introduced as follows:

> I'm going to give you page listing six statements about the ad you just read. The purpose of these statements is to find out how well this ad did in getting its message across. Please answer these questions based *only* on what you just read *and not* on anything else you might have known about the subject

---

[28]See Appendix G.
[29]Batra and Ray, 1983, pp. 128–129.

before now. Just read each statement and circle whether you think it is true or false.

Several additional points are worth noting. First, the procedure involves "forced exposure"—a direct request for the respondent to read the material. This contrasts sharply with the selective self-exposure that characterizes normal magazine reading. Respondents were given a pre-specified communication to read—one they might not have read had they been browsing through a magazine on their own. The basic justification for this procedure stems from our interest in comprehension per se, not in comprehension under varying levels of exposure, attention, etc. As the reader may recall from Chapter 2, there are theoretical reasons for believing that decrements in any information processing stage prior to comprehension will place corresponding limits on comprehension itself.[30] Had we not insured 100% exposure, 100% attention, etc., it could have been argued that low comprehension rates might not truly reflect miscomprehension as much as failures at some earlier stage.

Relevant evidence on this point comes from the magazine comprehension study conducted by Morris, Brinberg et al.[31] That study employed two different sets of instructions. Those respondents told to pay attention "primarily" or "solely" to the ads embedded in a test magazine recalled 25% to 50% more information and exhibited lower rates of miscomprehension on a subsequent modified t-f quiz than did those respondents given the magazine and simply asked to read it, paying attention to both the articles and the advertisements.

Second, by removing the communication from view and then testing for comprehension, the procedure has the potential to introduce a mild confound between memory and comprehension. We emphasize "mild," because the assessment occurred virtually immediately after exposure, not days, hours, or even five minutes afterward. More importantly, great care was taken (e.g., via the development and use of paraphrase questions; the assessment of inferences which necessarily stem from asserted meanings; etc.) to insure that the assessment focused on the comprehension of underlying meanings rather than on memory for surface structures.

Third, the introduction to each quiz used language that focused the respondent's attention on communication beliefs rather than on referent beliefs (see Chapter 2). When introducing each quiz, the interviewer said: "Please answer these questions based on what you just read *and not* on anything else you might have known about the subject before now." Next, the top of each quiz began: "Based upon the passage (ad) you just read,

---

[30] See McGuire, 1972.
[31] Morris, Brinberg et al., 1986.

which of the following statements is True and which is False? Remember: Base your answers only upon what you think the passage (ad) said or implied." In this respect, note that our language is comparable to that used by the Educational Testing Service in introducing the reading comprehension section of their Scholastic Aptitude Test (SAT), a test given annually to millions of high school juniors nation-wide: "Answer all questions following the passage on the basis of what is *stated* or *implied* in the passage."

Fourth, the measurement approach may be more likely to underestimate miscomprehension than to overestimate it. Consider the principal outcomes that may result from the transfer of meaning from source to receiver. The receiver may extract: (1) one or more beliefs, all of which accurately reflect content, (2) one or more beliefs, all of which inaccurately reflect content, (3) two or more beliefs that are at variance with each other (i.e., produce ambiguity), neither of which accurately reflects content, or (4) two or more beliefs that are at variance with each other, only one of which accurately reflects content. In the last instance (i.e., where the receiver comes away with meaning structures 1 and 2, one of which is an accurate reflection), if the quiz item asks "Is MS1 correct?", the individual is likely to respond affirmatively and leave it at that. It will therefore never be known that he or she also extracted a second meaning structure which was essentially incorrect.

Immediately after completing the comprehension quiz for the first item, the respondent was asked a series of questions pertaining to that communication. The specific wording varied slightly, depending upon whether the test communication was an advertisement or an editorial passage.

Question 5 probed the respondents' affect, or feelings, regarding the communication itself, specifically, whether they liked or disliked it. This question was included because recent research has indicated that affect can have an influence on other related cognitive processes such as memory storage[32] and information processing.[33]

Question 6a then asked whether the respondent recalled having previously seen that communication (and, if so, how often, cf. Q.6b), or some other communication directly bearing on the same topic.

For the advertisements, Q7a asked if the individual had ever previously bought or used that particular product category (e.g., breakfast cereals). If so, Q7b probed how frequently. Given an affirmative response to Q7a, Q7c asked if the individual had ever purchased or used the specific brand (e.g., Post's Raisin Bran) that was featured in the ad and, if so, how frequently (Q7d). The Q7 series for editorial content consisted of a single question that inquired how often the individual read material on the same topic.

---

[32]Srull, 1984; Moore & Hutchinson, 1983.
[33]Petty, Caccioppo, and Goldman, 1981.

Series Q6 and Q7 were asked because, as mentioned previously, readers comprehend incoming stimuli on the basis of schema stored in memory, and one of the major determinants of these schema is past experience (Norman & Bobrow, 1975). As a result, it was felt that these variables might prove to be important predictors of miscomprehension.

For both ad and editorial communications, a final question (Q8) asked the respondent to indicate how important he or she thought the referent of the communication was in terms of his or her everyday life. This question served as an indicator of referent involvement. As mentioned previously, miscomprehension should be higher in instances where involvement is low.

Upon completion of these items for the first test communication, the respondent was handed the second test communication, and the same sequence of events ensued. The two open-ended questions were followed by a six-item comprehension quiz. In turn, this was followed by a brief battery on affect toward, knowledge of, and previous experience with the product/topic in question.

For the third and fourth test communications, the same sequence of events followed each presentation.

Assessment-Only Control Condition

Even without reading the test communication, an individual might be able to answer the quiz items correctly by relying on prior experiences. To achieve some idea of the magnitude of this possibility for each item, the next portion of the Main Questionnaire required that respondents answer two additional quizzes without being provided the test communications on which the quiz items were based. These quizzes were introduced with the simple request, "Which of these following statements is True and which is False?" The order and sequence of administration of these control quizzes were also randomly counterbalanced. In all, there were 25 "control" (or "quiz only") respondents for each of the 108 test communications.

Sociodemographics

The main questionnaire concluded with a battery of sociodemographic items designed to assess marital status (Q9), level of education (Q10), employment status (Questions 11a and 11b), and annual family income (Q.12).

Response Rates and Sample Composition

Response Rates

Table 3.7 provides a breakdown of what transpired with each household and person contacted. In all, there were 5488 attempts to contact households and, within households, the designated respondent. For approximately 30% of households, either no one was found at home after three attempts or the designated respondent could not be reached after three attempts.

Of the 3801 contacts actually made, in 31.2% of households the individual approached at that household refused to respond to the screener questionnaire and in 5.6% of households the person subsequently identified as the designated respondent refused to continue with the screening process. There is no way of knowing whether these households would have contained an eligible respondent, or whether those persons identified as the designated respondent would have been found to be eligible after responding to all the screener questions.

Of the households that did consent to be screened, 15.5% were eliminated because they did not contain a person 18 years of age or older of the gender called for by the randomization procedures. Another 10.5% were

TABLE 3.7
Response Rates

	Total Attempts		Total Contacts		Total Eligible	
Total households	5,488	100.0%	3,801	100.0%	1,421	100.0%
No one at home (3 attempts)	1,416	25.8	—		—	
Refused screening	1,186	21.6		31.2	—	
No female 18 or older in female-designated households (Q. 1)	211	3.8		5.6	—	
No male 18 or older in male-designated households (Q. 1)	375	6.8		9.9	—	
Designated respondent not at home (after 3 attempts)	271	4.9	—		—	
Designated respondent refused screening	211	3.9		5.6	—	
No magazines read (Q. 5a)	218	4.0		5.7	—	
Do not read any listed magazines (Q. 6c)	173	3.2		4.6	—	
Read/subscribe to bogus magazines (Q. 6d, f, g)	6	0.1		0.2	—	
Eligible designated respondent refused main questionnaire	50	0.9		1.3		3.5
Mid-interview terminations	21	0.4		0.6		1.5
Completed interviews	1,350	24.6		35.5		95.0

eliminated because they claimed either not to read magazines regularly in general, not to read regularly at least one of the test magazines, or to read regularly one of the two bogus magazines.

Of the 1421 households containing an eligible designated respondent after the screening process, 3.5% refused to participate and another 1.5% terminated at some point during the administration of the Main Questionnaire. Thus, 95% of those known to be eligible actually participated in the study.

The obtained refusal rates compare quite favorably with those reported in the recent "Refusal Rate" benchmark study that identified national norms.[34] Based on almost 1.4 million interviews conducted in September 1985 by 46 member companies of the Council of American Survey Research Organizations (CASRO), this investigation found that 38% of the people asked to participate in surveys declined to do so. Importantly, in those interviews where the screening instructions required that a potential respondent be ruled ineligible to participate, the person was counted as a legitimate respondent since, technically speaking, he or she had cooperated.

Applying the same criterion to the 3801 contacts made in the present investigation, it can be seen that the four refusal categories produce a combined refusal rate (31.2 + 5.6 + 1.3 + .6) of 38.7%. This rate is actually better than national average because the above-cited investigation reported refusal rates to be considerably higher (47%) for interviews that lasted more than 12 minutes, and for those conducted in person (54%) as compared to those conducted over-the-phone (30%). Given that the present study involved in-person interviews lasting considerably longer than 12 minutes, the obtained 38.7% refusal rate can be seen to be much lower than national norms for similar interviews.

Sample Composition

Table 3.8 provides a thumbnail sketch of the sociodemographic composition of the obtained sample. Since our universe definition limited attention to individuals 18 years of age and older who claimed to be readers of general circulation mass media magazines (see Ch. 2), it would be inappropriate to compare these data to the corresponding figures for the total U.S. population. Accordingly, they are compared to the figures provided in the Simmons Market Research Bureau (SMRB) "1983 Study of Media and Markets." Projecting to 165 million Americans, this report provides total audience data for over 100 magazines as well as for several magazine networks and daily and weekend/Sunday newspapers. Hence, it is not an entirely accurate description of our intended universe, although it more faithfully reflects this universe than do Census Bureau figures for the entire population.

---

[34] *Your Opinion Counts*, 1986.

TABLE 3.8
Sociodemographic Composition of the Sample

| | Sample | | SMRB |
	n	%	%
Sex			
Male	557	41.4	47.4
Female	790	58.6	52.6
Age			
18-24	172	12.8	17.4
25-34	385	28.6	23.4
35-44	266	19.7	16.8
45-54	154	11.4	13.7
55-64	166	12.3	13.3
65+	188	14.0	15.5
No Answer	16	1.2	
Income			
Under $10,000	158	11.7	
$10,000-14,999	124	9.2	
$15,000-19,999	122	9.1	
$20,000-24,999	146	10.8	
$25,000-34,999	265	19.7	
$35,000-49,999	178	13.2	
$50,000-74,999	89	6.6	
$75,000+	19	1.4	
Refused	246	18.3	
Education			
8th grade or less	44	3.3	13.7
Attended high school (1-3 yrs.)	132	9.8	14.2
Graduated high school	554	41.1	39.9
Attended college (1-3 yrs.)	213	15.8	16.5
Grad. 2 yr. college	87	6.5	
Grad. 4 yr. college	198	14.7	15.7
Attended grad. school	42	3.1	
Completed advanced degree	70	5.2	
Refused	7	.5	
Marital status			
Single	254	18.9	20.5
Married	891	66.1	62.3
Widowed	97	7.2	7.7
Divorced	77	5.7	9.5[a]
Separated	21	1.6	
Refused	7	.5	
Employment status			
Not employed	578	42.9	41.8
Employed 30+ hrs/wk	619	46.0	50.2
Employed 29- hrs/wk	150	11.1	8.0

[a]Combined percentage for divorced and separated.

As compared to the SMRB data, our sample includes more women, and more people in the 25–44 year age brackets. Especially when taking into account the fact that the SMRB data includes individuals who claim to be newspaper readers but not magazine readers—which would explain why the SMRB sample is less educated—it can be seen that our sample represents the magazine reading public reasonably well.[35]

Post-Administration Quality Controls

Upon completion and return of the interview schedules to the subcontractor, all were checked for completeness and legibility.

Next, callback "validations"[36] were conducted by WATS Interviewing Network, an independent telephone research facility. Twenty-five percent of each interviewer's work was validated to insure that: (1) the designated respondent was, in fact, interviewed; (2) the respondent qualified for the study; (3) the interview was conducted in the respondent's home; and (4) exhibit materials were shown during the course of the interview.

When discrepancies arose, validation was escalated to 100%. This effort revealed problems with three respondents in one cluster. These interviews were eliminated from the study, thereby leaving a total of 1347 usable respondents.

All data were then 100% key-verified prior to being transferred to tape. That is, all data were keypunched onto cards twice, with the duplicate cards being physically compared so as to identify discrepancies. In this manner, virtually all keypunching errors could be detected and eliminated. This process insured the accurate transfer of responses from the "paper" questionnaire to the computer tape.

SUMMARIZING THE VARIOUS
UNIVERSE–SAMPLE CORRESPONDENCIES

Table 3.9 summarizes the various universe-sample correspondencies.

The universe of magazine readers was represented by a sample of 1347 qualified respondents. The universe of magazines was represented by 18 general circulation mass media magazines. The universe of magazine communications was represented by 108 advertising and editorial stimuli selected from these test magazines.

---

[35]The SMRB data for income are not provided since (a) their question asks for individual income while ours inquires as to "total family income," and (b) the two studies used incompatible income level breakdowns.

[36]See Appendix K.

TABLE 3.9
Summarizing the Universe-Sample Correspondences

	Number	Relevant Universe
1. Sample of respondents	1,347	Magazine readers
2. Sample of magazines	18	Magazines
3. Total sample of test stimuli	108	Magazine communications
a. advertisements	54	
b. editorial passages	54	
4. Communications tested per respondent		
a. in full test (communication followed by quiz)	4	
b. in no communication, quiz only control	2	
5. Communication tests (readings) across respondents		
a. full test (1347 × 4 =)	5,388	
b. quiz only control (1347 × 2 =)	2,694	
6. Items per test quiz	6	
7. Unique quiz items (108 × 6 =)	648	Meanings
8. No. of meanings tested per respondent		
a. in full test (communication presented; 4 × 6 =)	24	
b. in quiz only control (2 × 6) =	12	
9. Tests of meanings across all respondents (1347 × 4 × 6 =)	32,328	

A total of 648 different test items, six per communication, was used to assess the universe of material meanings associated with the communications. Since some communications contained fewer than six distinct meanings, the questions for a given communication sometimes overlapped (i.e., two questions tapped into the same meaning). Accordingly, it might be best to view the universe of meanings as being represented by 32,328 separate tests of meanings.

PRINCIPAL DEPENDENT MEASURES

As described, each respondent read four print communications and responded to four quizzes designed to assess comprehension/miscomprehension of these communications. Upon completion, each respondent completed two additional quizzes, this time without benefit of having read the related communication. Given the number of planned respondents, this design produces 25 "no communication, quiz only" control respondents and 50 "communication plus quiz" respondents for each of the 108 test communications. A number of relevant dependent measures can be derived from this design. Figure 3.1 depicts how the data from the 75 respondents to each quiz were summarized.

Condition:

	Quiz Only Control Condition (n = 25)	Communication + Quiz Experimental Condition (n = 50)

ITEM

1: % correct:
    % incorrect:
    % D.K.:

2: % correct:
    % incorrect:
    % D.K.:

3: % correct:
    % incorrect:
    % D.K.

4: % correct:
    % incorrect:
    % D.K.:

5: % correct:
    % incorrect:
    % D.K.:

6: % correct:
    % incorrect:
    % D.K.:

OVERALL

    % correct:
    % incorrect:
    % D.K.:

FIG. 3.1.   Data Summarization Sheet Used for Each Quiz

Note that all quiz items were carefully constructed to be unambiguously true or false. They also underwent a series of independent reviews and test stages, all designed to insure that they were faithful paraphrase translations of the textual material and could be easily comprehended. These precautions served to reduce, insofar as possible, the likelihood that an indication of miscomprehension would be due to miscomprehension of the quiz items rather than miscomprehension of the test communications themselves.

Even assuming that our efforts in these regards were 100% effective, various other sources of error are possible. First, even though the respondent might have no difficulty comprehending the quiz item, he might not have given 100% attention to the communication. Thus, even a highly intelligent, top-notch reader might provide an incorrect response. As described earlier, our procedures were designed to maximize attention, thereby reducing this possibility for error.

Second, due to guessing, a respondent might provide a correct answer when he actually did not comprehend, or vice versa. Provision of the "don't know" options was designed to minimize guessing and thereby eliminate such error.

Third, regardless of whether respondents knew or did not know the correct answer, it was possible for them to make simple recording errors when entering their responses and, in this way, provide answers that did not reflect what they had in mind. We assume that such instances were negligible and, in any case, tended to cancel each other out. Accordingly, we can assume that the data upon which the cell entries in Figure 3.1 are based reflect what the respondents actually had in mind.

Note that if the respondent answered "true" when the answer was indeed true, or answered "false" when the answer was indeed false, the response would be scored as being "correct." Similarly, if the respondent answered "false" when the answer was true, or replied "true" when the answer was false, the response would be scored as "incorrect." Figure 3.2 illustrates these basic outcomes and the principal indices that may be derived.

Under the present circumstances,[37] it may be argued that a don't know (DK) response represents a form of miscomprehension[38] and should therefore be added to the Percent Incorrect to arrive at an overall estimate of miscomprehension. According to this logic, it is possible to consider Percent Incorrect, on the one hand, and the sum of Percent Incorrect + Percent Don't Know, on the other, as representing lower and upper thresholds, respectively, with the true level of miscomprehension residing somewhere between the two. Just how one would locate the precise level of miscomprehension within this range would depend upon the assumptions made in interpreting the Don't Know responses. At least five plausible approaches exist: either 100%, 50%, 33.3%, 25.3%, or 0% of the DK responses could be supposed to represent miscomprehension.

At one extreme, it could be argued that the respondent's inability to extract any meaning so shortly after reading a communication reflects confusion and necessarily implies miscomprehension. According to this rationale, all DK responses would therefore be interpreted as miscomprehension.

A less extreme approach would be to contend that, had simple true-false items without a DK response option been used, the respondent who was inclined to answer DK would be forced to choose either true or false. Assuming an equal number of correct and incorrect true and false items, one could expect the respondent to provide an accurate response half the

---

[37]Where: much attention was lavished on the quiz items to insure that their meanings were easily understood; the respondents knew they were participating in a "test" situation and therefore devoted considerable attention to reading the brief communications; all respondents gave some appropriate response to the open-ended questions, thereby indicating no instances of total non-comprehension.

[38]Perhaps "confused miscomprehension" or the potential for "derived miscomprehension;" see Chapter 2.

The quiz item
was actually:

		True	False
The respondent replied:	True	1 Comprehension	4 Miscomprehension
	False	2 Miscomprehension	5 Comprehension
	Don't Know	3 ?	6 ?

Indices:
    % Correct = cell 1 + cell 5
    % Incorrect = cell 2 + cell 4
    % Don't Know = cell 3 + cell 6

FIG. 3.2.   Deriving Percent Correct, Percent Incorrect, and "Don't Know" Indices

time and an inaccurate response the other half of the time. Hence, 50% of the DK responses would be allocated to miscomprehension.

The rationale underlying the third procedure emphasizes respondent confidence. The availability of a DK option provides an "easy out." In some instances, respondents may check DK when they are leaning in a certain direction, but are not entirely confident of these inclinations. Accordingly, it may be reasonable to view the total DK response as consisting of three roughly equal components: one third representing those who are inclined toward a correct response, one third who are inclined toward an incorrect response, and one third who represent a hard core of actual "don't know." Under these circumstances, it would be entirely appropriate to add 33% of the DK response to the Percent Incorrect rate in order to arrive at a revised estimate of overall miscomprehension.

The fourth approach would be to allocate the DK responses in direct proportion to the observed occurrence of correct and incorrect responses on the grounds that this is what a forced choice procedure would likely have produced. As detailed in Chapter 4, the obtained Percent Correct value is 63.1% and the obtained Percent Incorrect value is 21.4%. This is equivalent to a ratio of 74.7% to 25.3%. Hence, it could be argued that 25.3% of all DK responses should be interpreted as miscomprehension and thus added to Percent Incorrect to arrive at the best estimate of overall miscomprehension.

Finally, the most conservative position of all would be to assume that, had respondents wanted to make some other response, they would have. Hence, all DK responses must represent "don't know" and nothing else. Ergo, nothing should be added to Percent Incorrect to estimate the true level of miscomprehension.

No doubt, additional arguments could be offered for and against each approach, and other adjustment procedures can be identified. We chose not to be advocates for any one of these over the others. Accordingly, the principal dependent measures provided in Chapter 4 are Percent Correct, Percent Incorrect and Percent DK.

CODA

Although the methodology reflects a blend of "real world" and "contrived" aspects, the orientation throughout emphasized the natural over the contrived. As examples, the communication stimuli were not textual materials specially created for the tests. Rather, all were authentic communications that had actually appeared in major magazines. Further, they were provided in authentic—not photo-reproduced nor re-typed—form and were systematically selected to represent standard industry classification categories. Respondents were representative of the population at large and were selected in accord with accepted industry practice for defining magazine readers.

In these regards, the present investigation is far removed from the kinds of research typically conducted on reading comprehension.[39] As Neisser,[40] Tourangeau,[41] and others note, that research tradition consists primarily of studies involving impractical problems performed in unnatural settings by unrepresentative samples. As a consequence, much of the work lacks the "ecological validity" emphasized by Brunswik[42] and his followers.[43]

On the other hand, the procedures did involve several features that departed from the typical natural circumstances under which magazines are read. In all instances, however, these departures were based either on sound theoretical requirements,[44] or empirical necessity.[45]

In many respects, the present investigation exemplifies precisely the kind of fundamental research on cognitive processes called for by the National Research Council.[46] Specifically, it represents a relatively rare

---

[39]See, for example, the research described in the *Journal of Experimental Psychology,* the *Journal of Verbal Learning and Verbal Behavior,* or the volumes by LaBerge and Samuels, 1977, and Spiro et al., 1980.

[40]Neisser, 1976, 1978, 1982.

[41]Tourangeau, 1984, pp. 91-92.

[42]Brunswik, 1956.

[43]For example, Petrinovich, 1979.

[44]Reducing contextual distractions and "forcing" exposure and attention were dictated by our interest in studying comprehension per se, not in studying comprehension under varying levels of exposure, distraction, and attention (cf. McGuire, 1972).

[45]As examples, there is no practical way to assess comprehension other than to use tests; using a "no communication, quiz only" control group represents the only practical way to assess pre-exposure knowledge levels and guessing rates.

[46]See Jabine et al., 1984.

integration of two very different research traditions: survey research (which typically involves random selection and large-scale probability surveys) and experimental research (which typically involves random assignment to experimental and control groups created by, and under the control of, the investigator).

It is also noteworthy that, by virtue of the systematic sampling designs employed across a number of the research facets (including respondents, communication vehicles, and communications within these vehicles), the present investigation moves closer to the notion of a generalizability study as articulated by Cronbach et al.[47]

---

[47]Cronbach et al., 1972.

III THE FINDINGS AND THEIR IMPLICATIONS

4 Findings

This chapter presents the basic findings; the following chapter discusses these findings and their implications. The present chapter is organized in three sections.

The first section discusses the findings as they relate to accurate comprehension—one of the five major questions specified in the "Objectives" section of Chapter 1.

The second section focuses on miscomprehension, specifically, on addressing the remaining four principal questions posed in the "Objectives" section of Chapter 1.

The final section discusses a number of ancillary findings pertaining to miscomprehension.

OVERVIEW

An overview of the extent to which readers understood, misunderstood, or did not understand the magazine communications they read (as reflected in their Correct, Incorrect, and Don't Know answers) is shown in Table 4.1[1]

Readers were questioned about the magazine communications under two test conditions:

---

[1]To enhance clarity of exposition, most of the percentages reported in the body of the text have been rounded off to the nearest whole integer. Those reported in the accompanying tables have been rounded off to the nearest tenth.

TABLE 4.1
An Overview of the Aggregate Findings for the
"Communication + Quiz" and "Quiz Only" Test Conditions

	Communication + Quiz	Quiz Only
% Correct	63.1%	31.7%
% Incorrect	21.4	17.0
% Don't know	15.5	51.5

Note: Due to rounding, the quiz-only values add to more than 100%.

- *Exposed:* After reading each of four magazine communications, they were asked six questions developed to test comprehension of the meanings conveyed by that communication.
- *Non-exposed:* They were then asked six questions about two other communications, without having an opportunity to read them.

The reason for this "exposed/non-exposed" study design was to evaluate the extent to which prior knowledge or personal experience, rather than comprehension, may have led some respondents to answer questions correctly.

Not surprisingly, those people who were asked questions about a communication without having seen it were more than three times as likely to answer "don't know" than readers who had an opportunity to read the communication before responding.

On the other hand, readers who did see the communication before being questioned about it were far more likely to give specific answers. As might be expected, people who had an opportunity to read a communication were twice as likely to answer questions about its content correctly than people who were asked the questions without having seen the communication.

Readers who had an opportunity to see the communication before being questioned about it were slightly more likely to answer questions incorrectly than people who were asked the questions without having seen the communication.

Those people exposed to the communication had a higher rate of incorrect responses than those not exposed to the communication. This is because exposure to the communication results in a marked decrease in "Don't Know." This decrease in Don't Know divides into a marked increase in correct answers and a slight increase in incorrect answers.

COMPREHENSION

What is the Average Level of Comprehension?

Unadjusted Comprehension

A fundamental question is: "To what extent do magazine readers understand what they read?" One approach to answering this question is to focus on the degree to which respondents operating under the "communication + quiz" condition correctly answered the quiz questions. This approach is in keeping with the procedure typically employed by educational institutions, namely, assigning a grade based on the number (or percent) of test questions answered correctly. As indicated in Table 4.1, on average across the entire set of 108 communications, a single reading of a magazine communication results in 63% correct answers to questions on the meanings conveyed by that communication (S.D. = 9%; median = 66%). The variation in level of correct answers ranged from a high of 83% to a low of 37%.

Adjusted Comprehension[2]

The above approach may be flawed, however, at least insofar as it is used to measure comprehension as a product of attention to the communication. Consider the following illustration. A student may begin a new class already knowing the correct answers to some of the questions that will be included on the final exam. Under such circumstances, though the student comprehends the intended meaning and obtains a correct answer on the final, it would be an error to conclude that this was a result of the experiences that occurred in connection with the class.

In similar fashion, the respondents did not enter our assessment situation as blank slates. As a result of either prior exposure to advertising and/or personal experience with the product, some may have already known the correct answer to some quiz questions.

It is also a virtual certainty that some proportion of a "total correct" score represents fortuitous guessing rather than actual comprehension.

It would be desirable to make some adjustment to the average Percent Correct scores for the communications in order to allow for successful guessing, prior knowledge, and the difficulty of the quizzes. One possibility that suggests itself is simply to subtract the scores of the "quiz only" control condition from those of the "communications + quiz" condition. However, such an adjustment would not only require making dubious psychometric assumptions, but would also imply the untenable proposition that a communication might not be comprehended merely because its recipient had

---

[2]Those not interested in technical discussion can easily skip to the next section, "Does comprehension vary by type of content?," without any loss of meaning.

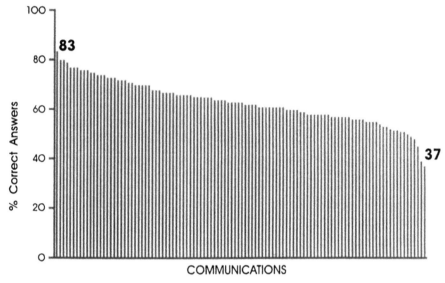

FIG. 4.1. *Comprehension:* Percent of Correct Answers Elicited By 108 Magazine Communications

prior understanding of its content. Efforts to translate the findings into absolute rates of comprehension are doomed to failure.[3]

However, the average Percent Correct, Percent Incorrect, and Percent Don't Know for subsets of the 108 communications can be adjusted to take into account the effects of differences in the performance on the quiz questions as reflected in the scores of the "quiz only" condition. Predicated upon the rationale outlined in Cohen and Cohen,[4] the average percent scores of subsets of communications can be adjusted using the analysis of covariance, with the "quiz only" scores serving as the adjusting covariate. These adjusted means may then be compared with each other.

Accordingly, Table 4.2 provides both the unadjusted and adjusted data for advertising vs. editorial communications and asserted vs. implied meanings. As can be seen from this table, the magnitude of the differences between the corresponding values is negligible.[5] (This is a joint consequence of the generally small differences between the unadjusted means of

---

[3]Jacob Cohen, personal communication.

[4]Cohen and Cohen, 1983, Chapter 10.

[5]It should be noted that the sample sizes for total tests of meanings (n = 32, 328), quiz questions (n = 648) and readers (n = 1,347) are so large that even small differences of 1 or 2 percentage points are statistically significant. Hence, the emphasis in these instances is placed on the magnitude of the differences rather than on statistical significance. By comparison, the samples of magazine communications (108 total; 54 ad, 54 ed) are relatively small. It therefore makes greater sense to assess statistical significance in these instances (Jacob Cohen, personal communication).

the subsets to be compared and the low correlations between the paired quiz means in "communication + quiz" conditions.) In only one instance (the Percent Correct for facts) the two estimates diverge by 1.5%; in another instance (the Percent Correct for inferences) the estimates diverge by 1.2%. In none of the remaining ten instance do they diverge by more than a half percent. Based upon these findings, it was decided to rely upon the unadjusted findings throughout the remainder of this report.

Does Comprehension Vary by Type of Content?

As can be seen in the following, advertising in mass media magazines was associated with a higher level of correct answers than was the editorial content in those same magazines (see Table 4.2).

Factual content elicted higher levels of correct answers than did inferential content, in which the meanings were implied rather than asserted.

MISCOMPREHENSION

The findings pertaining to miscomprehension are presented in two sections. The present section considers miscomprehension in terms of four of the principal objectives of the investigation.[6] The next section addresses the relationship of miscomprehension to a number of ancillary issues.

TABLE 4.2
Comparing Unadjusted and Adjusted Percentages for Different Types of Content

	% Correct		% Incorrect		% Don't Know	
Total	63.1		21.4		15.5	
(108 communications)						
	Unadj.	*Adj.*	*Unadj.*	*Adj.*	*Unadj.*	*Adj.*
Advertising Content	65.4	64.9	19.3	19.4	15.3	15.6
(54 communications)						
Editorial Content	60.8	61.3	23.4	23.4	15.8	15.4
(54 communications)						
Level of Significance	< .01	< .02	< .01	< .01	n.s.	n.s.
($p = \ldots$)						
Facts	63.6	65.1	20.3	20.0	16.0	15.6
Inferences	62.3	61.1	22.4	22.8	15.2	15.4
Level of Significance	n.s.	< .01	n.s.	< .01	n.s.	n.s.
($p = \ldots$)						

Note: The tests of significance refer to advertising vs. editorial content and facts vs. inferences, not to adjusted vs. unadjusted.

---

[6]See the Objectives section of Chapter 1.

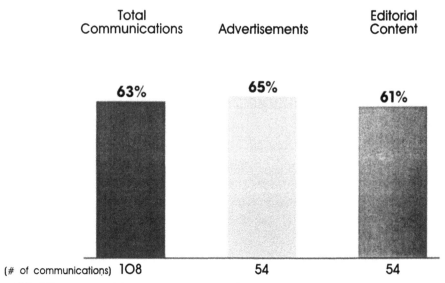

FIG. 4.2.   Percent of Correct Answers Elicited By Magazine Advertisements Vs. Editorial Content

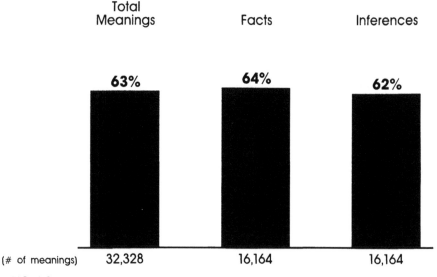

FIG. 4.3.   Percent of Correct Answers Elicited By Facts Vs. Inferences

What is the Average Level of Miscomprehension?

The question "To what extent do magazine readers misunderstand what they read?" may be considered in terms of four principal universes: readers, magazines, magazine communications, and the meanings contained in these communications. Thus, it can be rephrased as four separate questions:

1. What proportion of the material *meanings* contained in the test communications was miscomprehended?
2. What proportion of the 108 test *communications* was miscomprehended?
3. What proportion of 18 test *magazines* had their material content miscomprehended?
4. What proportion of magazine *readers* miscomprehended at least some portion of the magazine communications they read?

Proportion of Meanings Miscomprehended

The first question concerns the overall extent to which the meanings associated with the material information content were miscomprehended. Each of the 1347 respondents read four communications and answered six quiz questions per communication. Thus, there were a total of 32,328 separate tests of meanings.

As the findings reported earlier in Tables 4.1 and 4.2 reveal, an average of 63% of the questions relating to magazine contents was answered correctly. An average of 21% of the meanings was clearly misunderstood. In addition, the percentage of Don't Know answers averaged 16%. Thus, 37% of the 32,328 tests were answered either incorrectly or Don't Know.

Proportion of Communications Miscomprehended

At least some degree of miscomprehension was associated with each and every one of the 108 test communications. Stated somewhat differently, 100% of the 108 test communications evidenced some degree of miscomprehension.

Table 4.3 presents the Percent Incorrect and Percent Don't Know data for each of the 108 communications. The percentage of Incorrect answers ranged from a low of 6% to a high of 32%. The percentage of Don't Know answers ranged from a low of 4% to a high of 32%.

Proportion of Magazines Miscomprehended

Since all of the 108 test communications elicted some degree of miscomprehension, it follows that none of the test magazines was immune. Each of the 18 test magazines (or 100% of this sample) had some of its material content misunderstood by at least some of the respondents who read communications taken from that magazine.

Proportion of Readers Who Miscomprehended

Each of the 1347 respondents was tested on four communications. Multiplying the sample of 1347 readers by four communications results in

TABLE 4.3
Percent Incorrect, Percent Don't Know, and Percent Correct Response with Each Test Communication

Rank	Stimulus Number	Type of Stimulus	% Incorrect	% Don't Know	% Correct
1	16	Ed	32.4	30.5	37.1
2	135	Ed	32.3	15.7	52.0
3	165	Ed	31.7	7.3	61.0
4	91	Ad	31.7	4.2	64.0
5	14	Ed	31.3	13.9	54.8
6	124	Ed	31.0	18.3	50.7
7	104	Ed	30.0	13.3	56.7
8	42	Ad	29.6	7.7	62.7
9	123	Ad	29.3	31.7	39.0
10	15	Ed	29.0	6.0	65.0
11	36	Ed	28.9	26.5	44.6
12	186	Ed	28.9	17.8	53.3
13	155	Ed	28.6	10.9	60.5
14	62	Ad	28.4	13.7	57.8
15	176	Ed	28.1	15.7	56.2
16	184	Ed	28.0	24.0	48.0
17	94	Ed	28.0	10.0	62.0
18	116	Ed	27.7	14.3	58.0
19	174	Ed	27.6	16.7	55.7
20	146	Ed	27.3	7.7	65.0
21	46	Ed	26.6	18.7	54.7
22	154	Ed	26.5	10.9	62.6
23	173	Ad	26.1	19.0	54.9
24	151	Ad	25.4	22.9	51.7
25	126	Ed	25.3	23.3	51.4
26	166	Ed	25.3	17.7	57.0
27	13	Ad	25.0	18.0	57.0
28	51	Ad	25.0	12.0	63.0
29	95	Ed	25.0	5.0	70.0
30	34	Ed	24.7	16.3	59.0
31	74	Ed	24.7	15.3	60.0
32	93	Ad	24.7	13.3	62.0
33	156	Ed	24.6	16.0	59.4
34	83	Ad	24.3	14.2	61.5
35	84	Ed	24.1	19.4	56.5
36	145	Ed	24.0	15.0	61.0
37	115	Ed	23.8	19.1	57.1
38	41	Ad	23.6	15.7	60.7
39	141	Ad	23.4	15.7	60.9
40	142	Ad	23.2	7.1	69.7
41	31	Ad	22.9	28.1	49.0
42	22	Ad	22.9	26.8	50.3
43	12	Ad	22.9	15.0	62.1
44	181	Ad	22.9	10.7	66.3
45	85	Ed	22.6	24.7	52.7

TABLE 4.3 (Continued)

Rank	Stimulus Number	Type of Stimulus	% Incorrect	% Don't Know	% Correct
46	35	Ed	22.6	20.1	57.3
47	56	Ed	22.3	17.0	60.7
48	64	Ed	22.3	13.7	64.0
49	161	Ad	22.1	12.6	65.3
50	163	Ad	22.0	14.7	63.3
51	66	Ed	21.9	9.5	68.6
52	125	Ed	21.7	20.3	58.0
53	25	Ed	21.7	20.1	58.2
54	134	Ed	21.6	18.7	59.7
55	24	Ed	21.4	28.6	50.0
56	52	Ad	21.1	12.6	66.3
57	183	Ad	21.0	9.3	69.7
58	21	Ad	20.9	23.7	55.3
59	32	Ad	20.7	27.3	52.0
60	44	Ed	20.7	18.0	61.3
61	72	Ad	20.6	16.7	62.7
62	133	Ad	20.6	14.7	64.7
63	92	Ad	20.2	15.4	64.4
64	11	Ad	20.2	12.8	67.0
65	26	Ed	20.0	21.8	58.2
66	82	Ad	20.0	14.7	65.3
67	86	Ed	19.9	12.7	67.3
68	175	Ed	19.6	6.9	73.5
69	114	Ed	19.3	24.3	56.3
70	143	Ad	19.3	8.5	72.2
71	185	Ed	19.0	23.8	57.1
72	45	Ed	18.6	13.7	67.7
73	103	Ad	17.7	17.7	64.6
74	144	Ed	17.7	8.3	74.0
75	105	Ed	17.7	7.1	75.2
76	75	Ed	17.3	24.2	58.5
77	61	Ad	17.3	23.0	59.7
78	73	Ad	17.3	15.4	67.3
79	54	Ed	17.3	5.8	76.9
80	136	Ed	17.0	15.6	67.4
81	53	Ad	16.0	26.0	58.0
82	43	Ad	16.0	7.0	77.0
83	33	Ad	15.7	30.0	54.3
84	71	Ad	15.7	16.0	68.3
85	111	Ad	15.6	14.0	70.4
86	102	Ad	15.3	12.5	72.2
87	164	Ed	15.3	9.0	75.7
88	182	Ad	15.1	13.8	71.2
89	55	Ed	14.9	9.0	76.0
90	171	Ad	14.7	12.3	73.0

TABLE 4.3 (Continued)

Rank	Stimulus Number	Type of Stimulus	% Incorrect	% Don't Know	% Correct
91	76	Ed	14.6	21.0	64.4
92	132	Ad	14.6	14.0	71.3
93	113	Ad	14.6	6.7	78.7
94	121	Ad	14.5	24.3	61.1
95	23	Ad	14.3	14.0	71.7
96	112	Ad	14.3	12.4	73.3
97	131	Ad	13.9	19.7	66.3
98	106	Ed	13.4	11.8	74.8
99	152	Ad	13.1	21.2	65.7
100	172	Ad	12.9	4.1	83.0
101	122	Ad	12.7	17.6	69.6
102	162	Ad	12.3	10.3	77.3
103	153	Ad	12.2	13.6	74.2
104	63	Ad	12.0	8.0	80.0
105	81	Ad	9.2	11.9	78.9
106	101	Ad	8.9	11.2	79.9
107	96	Ed	8.6	18.1	73.3
108	65	Ed	6.2	18.0	75.8

5388 "readings." Respondents were able to answer all six questions correctly in only 10% of these readings. Readers misunderstood some portion of what they read in 74% of the readings. Most misunderstood only one or two of the six quiz questions. In the remaining 16% of the readings, the readers answered Don't Know to at least one of the test questions.

When shifting the focus from readings to *individuals,* it becomes clear that being able to understand one communication does not necessarily mean that a person will comprehend the contents of another communication correctly.

When tested across four communications, only three (.2%) of the 1347 respondents were able to answer all 24 quiz questions correctly. Not shown in Table 4.5 is the fact that another 18 respondents (1.4%), though making no incorrect answers, provided at least one Don't Know response.

Thus, more than 98% of the readers misunderstood at least some portion of the four communications on which they were tested. Some degree of miscomprehension characterizes virtually the entire magazine reading public.

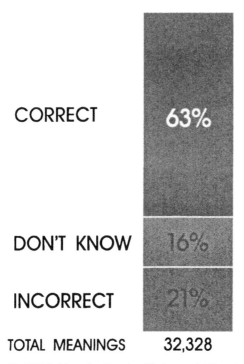

CORRECT   63%

DON'T KNOW   16%

INCORRECT   21%

TOTAL MEANINGS   32,328

FIG. **4.4**.   Extent To Which Magazine Readers Understand/Misunderstand The Meaning Of What They Read

What is the Normative Range of Miscomprehension?

A "normative range" of magazine content miscomprehension can be identified by deriving the interquartile range,[7] which is defined as the span encompassing the middle 50% of all scores. The interquartile range for percentage of Incorrect answers extended from 16–25%. Thus, one quarter of the communications had less than a 16% miscomprehension rate and one quarter had more than 25%.

Do Rates Differ for Advertising vs. Editorial Content?

Another important question is: "Do magazine advertisements and editorial communications elicit different levels of miscomprehension?" There do appear to be differences. Editorial content is associated with a significantly

---

[7]The "interquartile range" is employed in preference to "plus-or-minus one standard deviation from the mean" because it more clearly describes the spread.

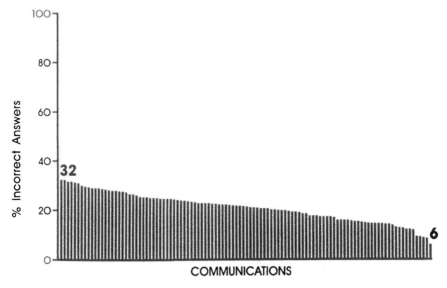

FIG. 4.5. *Miscomprehension:* Percent Of Incorrect Answers Elicited By 108 Magazine Communications

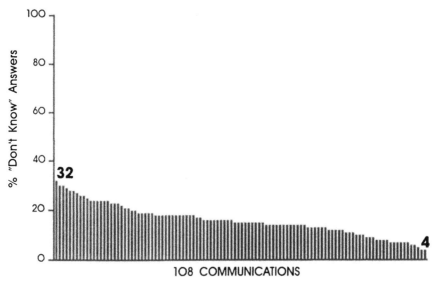

FIG. 4.6. *Noncomprehension:* Percent of "Don't Know" Answers Elicited by 108 Magazine Communications

($p < .01$) higher rate of miscomprehension (23%) than is advertising (19%). On the other hand, there was no material difference between these two types of communication in terms of the incidence of "don't know" response; it was 16% for both (see Table 4.2).

TABLE 4.4
Comprehension/Miscomprehension/Noncomprehension Rates for Readings

Percent of readings in which:	Correctly	Incorrectly	Don't know
All 6 items were answered	9.6	0.7	1.6
5 items were answered	24.3	0.2	1.1
4 items were answered	28.0	1.9	2.2
3 items were answered	21.0	9.9	6.0
2 items were answered	10.2	24.3	13.5
1 item was answered	3.7	37.0	24.6
0 answered	3.2	26.0	51.0

Note: Base = 5388 readings (= the number of respondents × the number of communications tested per respondent).

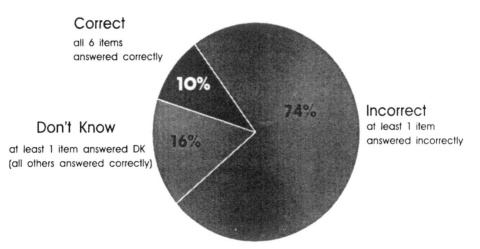

Base: 5388 Readings

FIG. 4.7. Extent To Which Readers Understand, Misunderstand Or Don't Understand One Magazine Communication

The normative range of miscomprehension elicited by magazine advertisements is 15–23%; the normative range of miscomprehension elicited by magazine editorial content is 19–28%.

The apparent superiority of advertising over editorial communications warrants some discussion. As detailed in Chapter 3, the advertising and editorial communications were made comparable in terms of having roughly equivalent amounts of reading matter. However, these two types of communications could not be made equivalent in all respects. As a rule, the advertisements contain accompanying illustrations as well as more varied and larger typefaces. These differences in graphics may help to account for the better performance on the advertising communications.

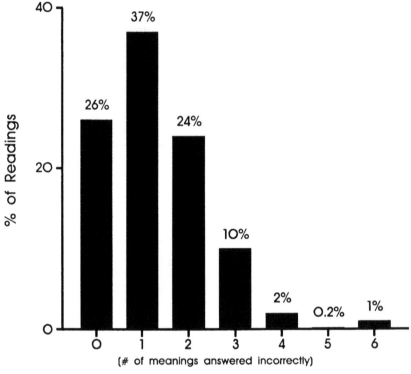

Base: 1,347 Readers X 4 test communications each = 5,388 Readings

FIG. 4.8.   The Extent To Which Readers Misunderstand Any Part Of One Magazine Communication

Are There Basic Sociodemographic Differences?

The final principal question of interest is: "Are demographic characteristics of readers related to their miscomprehension of magazines?"

A number of different sociodemographic characteristics were assessed. These included each respondent's sex, age, marital status, employment status, race, years of formal education, and total household income for the preceding year. Only three of these factors exhibited any noteworthy relationship to overall miscomprehension.

The relationship between *age* and miscomprehension is depicted below. From here it can be seen that readers over the age of 54 tended to miscomprehend slightly more than did those in the other age groups. A Tukey-HSD procedure indicated that the 55-64 and 65+ age groups were significantly different ($p < .05$) from the other groups (i.e. miscomprehension was greater). However, while this relationship is statis-

TABLE 4.5
Comprehension/Miscomprehension/Noncomprehension Rates
for Individuals
Base = 1347 individuals

% of Individuals Answering	Correctly	Incorrectly	Don't Know
All 24 items	0.2	0.0	0.1
23 items	0.4	0.0	0.0
22 items	0.6	0.0	0.0
21 items	3.5	0.0	0.1
20 items	5.3	0.0	0.0
19 items	7.1	0.0	0.2
18 items	10.3	0.0	0.1
17 items	11.2	0.0	0.1
16 items	10.4	0.0	0.4
15 items	11.4	0.0	0.4
14 items	11.7	0.1	0.1
13 items	7.1	0.0	0.7
12 items	5.1	0.7	1.3
11 items	4.7	1.0	1.0
10 items	4.2	2.9	2.3
9 items	1.3	4.6	2.4
8 items	2.2	6.3	3.7
7 items	1.4	8.8	5.4
6 items	0.5	13.0	6.9
5 items	0.7	15.6	7.8
4 items	0.3	17.2	11.1
3 items	0.1	14.4	11.4
2 items	0.1	9.9	11.6
1 item	0.1	3.9	12.8
0	0.1	1.6	20.1

tically significant, the difference is so small so as to have little practical applicability.

A more significant trend was evidenced in the case of *education.* As level of formal education increased, miscomprehension tended to decrease. A Tukey-HSD procedure indicated that readers with less than a 9th grade education miscomprehended significantly more than all other groups. Also, the some high school, high school graduate, and some college groups miscomprehended significantly more ($p < .05$) than did the readers with advanced degrees, some graduate school, and college degrees; the differences within these two clusters were not significant.

A small inverse relationship was found between *income* and miscomprehension. As income increased, miscomprehension tended to decrease. A Tukey-HSD procedure indicated that readers with incomes under $10,000 miscomprehended to a statistically significantly greater extent than readers with over $25,000 in income. Also, readers with incomes of $10,000-$14,999 and $20,000-$24,999 miscomprehended more than those with incomes of over $35,000 ($p < .05$).

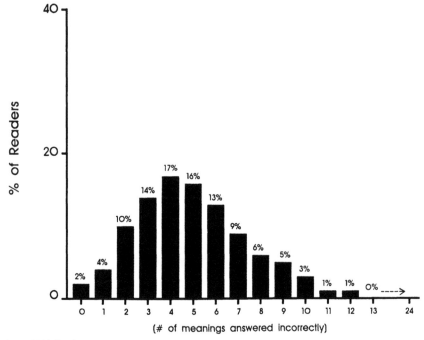

Base: 1,347 Readers

FIG. **4.9.** The Extent To Which Readers Misunderstand Any Part Of Four Magazine Communications

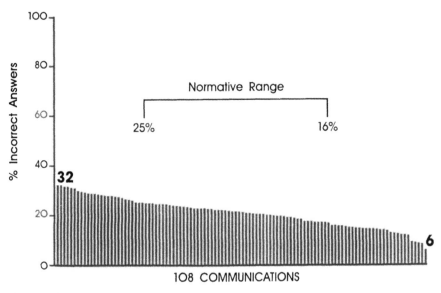

FIG. 4.10. Normative Range of Miscomprehension Elicited By Magazine Communications

116

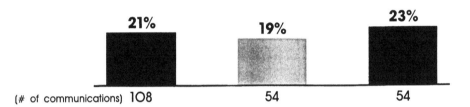

	Total Communications	Advertisements	Editorial Content
	21%	19%	23%

(# of communications) 108   54   54

FIG. 4.11.   Percent Of Incorrect Answers Elicited By Magazine Advertisements Vs. Editorial Content

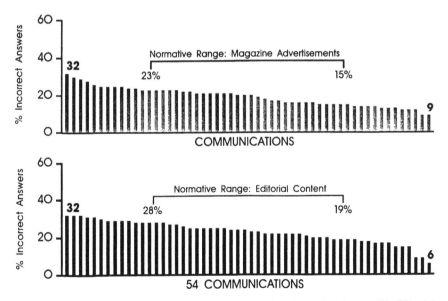

FIG. 4.12.   Normative Range of Miscomprehension Magazine Advertisement Vs. Editorial Content

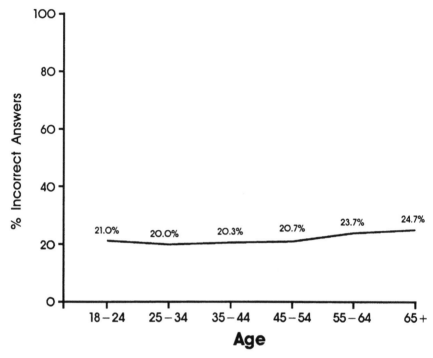

FIG. 4.13. The Relationship Between Age and Miscomprehension

Finally, when considered across all 18 magazines, the miscomprehension rates for males and females were not significantly different from each other. That is, the male respondents misunderstood the contents of the 9 magazines to which they were exposed at the same levels that the females misunderstood the contents of the 12 magazines on which they were tested.

However, an interesting gender-related finding emerges when attention is confined to the three magazines that were tested with both groups (namely, *Reader's Digest, Time,* and *Life*). Though there was no meaningful difference when overall miscomprehension was examined (23.1% for females vs. 24.7% for males), there was a significant difference when facts and inferences were considered separately. Specifically, although there was no significant difference between the sexes when it came to inferential content (24.7% for women vs. 24.6% for men), women evidenced significantly lower levels of miscomprehension with respect to factual content (21.1% vs. 24.7%, respectively; $p < .05$). Lest too much be made out of this finding, note that it is based on a limited number of test magazines and respondents.

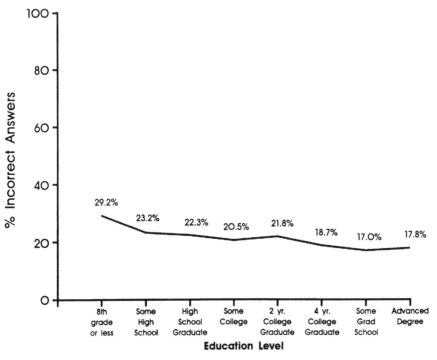

FIG. 4.14.   The Relationship Between Formal Education And Miscomprehension

ANCILLARY ISSUES

This section considers the findings pertaining to a number of relevant issues not subsumed by the basic objectives that prompted this investigation as defined in Chapter 1. These ancillary results are discussed in terms of four subsections:

- message factors;
- medium factors;
- receiver factors; and
- measurement considerations.

Message Factors

Facts vs. Inferences: The Miscomprehension of Asserted vs. Implied Meanings

As discussed in Chapter 2, comprehension necessarily involves the reader in a process of identifying the factual meaning(s) actually asserted in

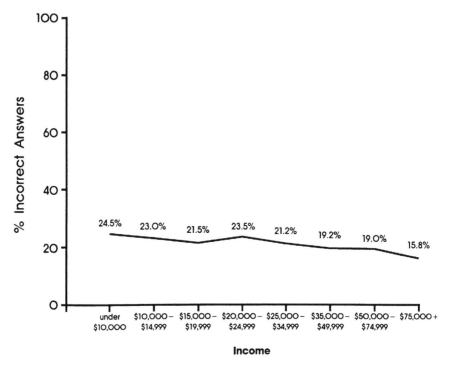

FIG. 4.15.   The Relationship Between Income And Miscomprehension

the communication as well as in a process of generating a set of inferential meanings that are or may reasonably be implied from that communication. Hence, it is meaningful to ask: "Are there any differences in the extent to which people misunderstand facts or inferences?"

The data for the entire set of 108 communications reveal that facts are associated with a lower percentage of Incorrect responses than are inferences. Table 4.6 reveals that this relationship also holds true when averaged across all 108 communications as well as for the subsets of advertising and editorial communications in particular. Interestingly, though facts are better understood than inferences, the inferred meanings derived from the advertisements were actually associated with a lower Percent Incorrect score (22%) than were the factual meanings drawn from the editorial communications (24%). However, this difference is statistically not significant.

Miscomprehension and Message Structure Features

The advertisements and editorial communications were subjected to a detailed analysis of both their linguistic and graphic features. In total, 12 language features and 15 graphics features were carefully assessed.[8] It

---

[8]These indices were described in Chapter 3.

TABLE 4.6
Miscomprehension for Facts vs. Inferences

	% Incorrect	% DK
A. *Overall*	21.4%	15.5%
B. *Facts* (for all communications)	20.3	16.0
C. *Inferences* (for all communications)	22.4	15.2
D. For ads:		
Facts	17.3	16.6
Inferences	21.5	14.2
E. For eds:		
Facts	23.1	15.3
Inferences	23.5	16.2

was expected that these features might account for some of the variation in Percent Incorrect scores.

To test this notion, these variables were entered into a regression analysis as predictor variables, with the dependent variable being Percent Incorrect. The obtained relationships were quite small. When considered in terms of the multiple tests involved, these relationships were nonsignificant. Similarly, correlations for the Don't Know scores were small and nonsignificant (see Table 4.7).

Miscomprehension and the Varieties of Editorial and Advertising Content

An earlier analysis compared the miscomprehension rates for the 54 advertising vs. 54 editorial communications. Comparisons can also be made within each of these categories, although it must be emphasized that the number of test communications representing each subcategory becomes quite small (usually 2 to 4) and tests of significance based on such small numbers would be virtually meaningless.

Editorial Content. Appendix E identifies the major categories that *Hall's Magazine Reports* uses to describe editorial content. Except for the Miscellaneous category, all were represented in this investigation. Table 4.8 compares these categories in terms of both Percent Incorrect and Percent Don't Know. It can be seen from this table that miscomprehension was substantial across all categories. The level of Incorrect answers ranged from 20–23%. The level of Don't Know answers ranged from 6–23%.

Advertising Content. Appendix F identifies the 29 major content categories used in the *Publisher's Information Bureau (PIB) Reports*. As detailed in Chapter 3, the present investigation utilized 19 of these 29 categories. As Table 4.9 reveals, Percent Incorrect ranged from a low of 14% to a high of 27% and Percent Don't Know ranged from a low of 9% to a high of 22%.

TABLE 4.7
Correlations Between Stimulus Factors and
Miscomprehension

Variable	% Incorrect
A. *Linguistic Variables*	
Number of Sentences	− .04
Mean of Sentence Length	.06
Sentence Fragments	− .06
Passive Verbs	.05
Noun Strings	− .03
Personal Pronouns	− .05
Nominalizations	.04
Number of Lists	− .03
Items Per List	− .01
Parallel Lists	− .01
Percentage of One-Syllable Words	.00
Adjectives	.02
B. *Graphic Variables*	
Average Line Length (words)	.04
Average Line Length (characters)	.06
Mean Characters/sq. in.	.05
Percentage of Page Covered by Text	− .09
Number of Headings of Boldface	− .04
Percentage of Total Words in Headings	− .01
Consecutive Words in All Caps	.00
Margins − Ragged Right	− .12
Margins − Ragged Left	− .01
Margins − Mixed	.10
Photo or Drawing	− .10
Color Photo?	− .10
Number of Type Sizes	− .06
Number of Type Styles	− .05
Type Style	.06

Again, given the very small numbers of communications involved for each subcategory, interpretations that extrapolate beyond these data would be quite risky.

Medium Factors

The present investigation was restricted to "major national magazines." As shown in the Publishers Information Bureau categories (Appendix B), such magazines may be sorted into a number of subvarieties based upon the nature of their typical content and intended audience. Tables 4.10–4.12 compare the Percent Incorrect and Percent Don't Know data for these subvarieties in terms of overall, editorial and advertising communications.

These data reveal few differences across the various types of magazines

TABLE 4.8
Miscomprehension Levels for the Varieties of Editorial Content

Rank	Ed Category	% Incorrect	% DK	# of Comm.
1	National Affairs	28.5%	13.8%	2
2	Building	26.8	18.0	4
3	Sports/Hobby	26.8	15.5	3
4	Beauty & Grooming	26.4	13.8	3
5	Food/Nutrition	25.4	12.4	6
6	Business & Industry	25.3	23.3	2
7	Children	24.7	15.3	1
8	Foreign Affairs	23.1	22.3	2
9	Culture/Humanities	23.0	22.6	3
10	Health & Medical Services	22.8	6.9	3
11	Amusement	22.5	18.5	3
12	Home Furnishings	22.4	16.5	5
13	Gardening	21.4	10.9	4
14	Transportation/Travel	20.9	16.9	6
15	General Interest	20.8	15.8	2
16	Fiction	19.9	20.5	2
17	Wearing Apparel	19.5	12.9	3
				54

overall, and slightly greater differences when considered separately by type of content.

It must again be emphasized that, given the very small number of magazines in each subcategory, generalizations beyond these data would be quite risky.

Receiver Factors

Portions of our earlier discussion focused on whether miscomprehension was related to various sociodemographic characteristics of the respondents. The following analyses focus on a number of other respondent characteristics.

Target vs. Non-Target Audience

The earlier TV study was criticized on the grounds that the communications were tested on a broad cross-section of viewers, including some number of individuals for whom they were not intended. It was contended that miscomprehension of a given communication should be assessed only among those for whom that communication was developed and intended, namely, the target audience.

Various efforts were made in the present study to focus attention on target audiences. Women respondents were given only female-oriented or gender-neutral communications, while men were given only male-oriented or gender-neutral communications.

TABLE 4.9
Miscomprehension Levels for the Varieties of Advertising Content

Rank	Ad Category	% Incorrect	% DK	# of Comm.
1	Toiletries	26.7%	12.9%	2
2	Automotive	23.9	19.1	4
3	Jewelry	22.0	18.8	2
4	Sporting Goods	22.0	14.7	1
5	Travel	20.8	21.1	2
6	Drugs	20.8	16.1	5
7	Apparel	20.7	10.3	5
8	Cigarettes	19.5	13.7	4
9	Beer, Wine & Liquor	19.4	21.6	3
10	Retail	18.9	15.8	4
11	Business	18.2	18.2	4
12	Household Furniture	17.7	13.6	2
13	Food	17.4	12.6	3
14	Household Equipment	17.1	12.9	3
15	Publishing	17.0	11.9	3
16	Building Materials	15.8	9.4	2
17	Entertainment	14.8	18.4	2
18	Home Entertainment	14.6	19.1	2
19	Office Equipment	14.3	14.0	1
				54

TABLE 4.10
Miscomprehension by Type of Magazine

Rank	Magazine Type	No.	% Incorrect	% DK
1	Outdoor & Sports	1	23.1%	17.0%
2	Fashion & Service	1	22.7	12.1
3	Mechanics & Science	2	22.4	12.1
4	Weeklies & Biweeklies	2	22.0	20.6
5	Home	2	21.5	15.3
6	Monthlies	6	21.2	16.8
7	Women's	4	20.1	14.1
		18		

In addition, a series of Screener questions assessed magazine readership in a number of ways. Respondents were asked to indicate magazines that they personally read and/or subscribed to, and to identify any magazines to which other members of their household subscribed. Analyses were then conducted to identify differences in miscomprehension between readers and non-readers, personal subscribers vs. non-subscribers, and family subscribers vs. non-subscribers.

TABLE 4.11
Miscomprehension by Type of Magazine: Eds Only

Rank	Magazine Type	No.	% Incorrect	% DK
1	Mechanics & Science	2	26.0%	12.1%
2	Monthlies	6	25.7	17.5
3	Outdoor & Sports	1	25.7	13.5
4	Home	2	23.7	15.9
5	Weeklies & Biweeklies	2	22.2	21.1
6	Fashion & Service	1	20.4	13.0
7	Women's	4	20.0	13.8
		18		

TABLE 4.12
Miscomprehension by Type of Magazine: Ads Only

Rank	Magazine Type	No.	% Incorrect	% DK
1	Fashion & Service	1	25.6%	10.9%
2	Weeklies & Biweeklies	2	21.3	19.6
3	Women's	4	20.2	14.5
4	Home	2	19.8	14.8
5	Outdoor & Sports	1	19.3	22.0
6	Mechanics & Science	2	18.8	12.1
7	Monthlies	6	17.5	16.4
		18		

Results of these analyses indicated virtually no differences in Percent Incorrect responses across the three sets of subgroups. Readers of a magazine[9] were as likely to miscomprehend a communication from that magazine as were nonreaders of that magazine, and personal subscribers[10] were as likely to miscomprehend as non-subscribers.

Other Individual Difference Factors

In addition to the basic sociodemographic variables discussed earlier, a variety of other individual difference factors were measured in order to assess their relationship to miscomprehension. For the advertisements these included:

- affect (that is, feelings) toward the ad,
- the number of times the ad had been seen in the past,
- the number of times other ads for the same brand had been read,

[9]This was operationally defined in terms of Screener Question 6d; see Appendix G.
[10]This was operationalized in terms of Screener Question 6j; see Appendix G.

- frequency of brand and product usage, and
- perceived importance of the product to the individual's everyday life.

For the editorial communications, these measures included:

- passage interest,
- the number of times the passage had previously been read,
- the number of times similar articles on this topic had been read,
- the frequency of reading similar material, and
- perceived importance of the topic to everyday life.[11]

Two separate regression analyses were performed, one for advertising communications and one for editorial content, to assess the ability of the above variables to account for the Percent Incorrect scores. The individual difference variables just noted, along with the earlier mentioned socio-demographic factors, served as the predictor variables.

For advertising (see Table 4.13), these variables evidenced only a slight relationship to Percent Incorrect responses. The results were equally uneventful in the case of editorial content (see Table 4.14).

A reasonable conclusion is that the miscomprehension of magazine advertising and editorial content occurs across all types of individuals, regardless of sociodemographic factors, usage behavior, previous readership of the communication, interest in the topic, etc.

Measurement Considerations

True vs. False Questions

Because people have a tendency to respond "true" more often than "false," true questions tend to have higher rates of correct responses than do false questions. For this reason, each quiz was designed with an equal number of questions for which true and false were the correct response.

An analysis of the miscomprehension percentages associated with true and false questions revealed that false questions were indeed miscomprehended to a greater degree ($p < .001$) than were true questions (31% vs. 12%, respectively). False questions were also slightly more likely to elicit "don't know" responses (18% vs. 14%; $p < .05$). The findings of this investigation are thus consistent with previous work.

---

[11]It should be emphasized that a number of the indices for both advertising and editorial content assessed the respondent's recall and estimate of events, which may not faithfully correspond with the events themselves.

TABLE 4.13
Correlations Between Individual Difference Variables
and Miscomprehension: Advertising Content

Variable	% Incorrect
Frequency of brand and product usage	− .01
Perceived importance	.02
No. of other ads previously seen for same brand	− .03
Income	− .04
Affect toward ad	.06
Age	.09
Education	− .12
Multiple R =	.16
R squared =	.02

TABLE 4.14
Correlations Between Individual Difference Variables
and Miscomprehension: Editorial Content

Variable	% Incorrect
Number of time similar material on topic had been read	− .02
Income	− .05
Perceived importance of topic	− .05
Age	.06
Passage interest	− .08
Education	− .11
Multiple R =	.17
R squared =	.03

Cross-Question Variations

A final issue concerns the variation in percent Incorrect response across the sample of (108 communications × 6 questions each =) 648 test questions. Each of these questions was answered by approximately 50 respondents participating in the "communication + quiz" condition.

The percent of respondents incorrectly answering a particular question ranged from a high of 96% to a low of 0%. The average (arithmetic mean) was 21%, while the Standard Deviation was 18%.

Of particular interest are the 324 questions used in assessing the advertisements. The vast majority of these questions (n = 300) were associated with some level of incorrect response. Of the remaining 24 questions (or 7.4%), where there was no incorrect response, only two questions had no associated level of Don't Know responses.

TABLE 4.15
Comparing Percent Incorrect and
Percent Don't Know Rates for True
vs. False Questions

	% Incorrect	% DK
True	11.5%	13.5%
False	31.3	17.6

5 Conclusions, Implications, and Future Directions

This concluding chapter has several objectives. The first is to summarize the findings that emerged.

Second, a number of implications are noted for both communication professionals and public policy regulators.

Third, building on the present investigation, we outline several avenues for future research.

BASIC FINDINGS

As assessed using our methodology, the findings described in Chapter 4 lead to the following conclusions.

Comprehension: To what extent do magazine readers understand what they read?

On average, a single reading of a magazine communication is associated with correct answers to 63% of the questions on the material meanings conveyed by that communication. Rates of correct response are higher for advertising content (65%) than for editorial content (61%), and higher for facts (64%) than for inferences (62%). Although statistically significant, these differences are negligible.

Miscomprehension: To what extent do magazine readers misunderstand what they read?

The reading of magazine communications is also associated with substantial levels of *miscomprehension.*

- Every *magazine* can be expected to have at least some readers miscomprehend some of the essential content contained in that magazine.
- Every *magazine communication* can be expected to have at least some readers miscomprehend some of the essential content in that communication.
- A conservative estimate is that 21% of the material *meanings* contained in the typical magazine communication are miscomprehended. The average "don't know" rate is an additional 16%.[1]
- When reading a single magazine communication, 74% of *readers* can be expected to provide at least one incorrect answer to a set of six questions posed on that content; another 16% can be expected to respond with at least one "don't know" response.
- When reading four brief magazine communications, virtually all magazine *readers* (more than 98%) can be expected to exhibit some degree of miscomprehension of at least one of these communications.
- *Inferred meanings* (or implications) are associated with slightly higher levels of miscomprehension (24%) than are the *factual meanings* directly asserted in the literal content (22%).

What is the normative range of miscomprehension of magazine content that might be expected from readers?

The typical range of miscomprehension associated with the meanings contained in mass circulation magazine communications is conservatively estimated at 16–25%.[2]

---

[1]Depending upon how one interprets a "don't know" response, the average amount of miscomprehension may be as low as 21% or as high as 37%.

[2]Depending upon how one interprets a "don't know" response, this range may actually be as high as 30% to 43%.

Do magazine advertisements and editorial communications elicit different levels of miscomprehension?

Editorial content is associated with slightly higher rates of miscomprehension (23%) than is *advertising content* (19%). It is possible that some or all of the superiority of advertisements may be due to the graphics involved, rather than to differences associated with the verbal contents.

Are demographic characteristics of readers related to their miscomprehension of magazine content?

Except for amount of formal education and income, other basic socio-demographic variables appear to be either negligibly related or unrelated to the comprehension or miscomprehension of magazine communications.

Target audience readers, that is, people who claim to be readers of and/or subscribers to a particular magazine, evidence just as much miscomprehension of the contents of that magazine as do members of the magazine-reading public who claim not to read or subscribe to that magazine.

IMPLICATIONS

While the major focus of this investigation was on miscomprehension, our discussion of the implications can begin on a mildly positive note. Although the findings suggest that almost everyone miscomprehends some portion of the magazine communications that they read, and that no type of communication is immune from such miscomprehension, the brighter side of the picture is that the major proportion of most magazine communications seems to be understood correctly, even after only a single reading.

On a less positive note, it is clear that attention to a communication does not automatically translate into comprehension of this communication. Rather, the receiver brings a storehouse of past experience and an ongoing set of expectations to each communication transaction and may interpret, *or misinterpret,* communications in terms of these pre-existing mental phenomena. Given that it is not possible to eliminate either the influence of past experience or the individual's current mental set, it may well be impossible to eliminate miscomprehension. This leads directly to a set of implications for advertisers and advertising researchers, other magazine communicators, and especially public policy makers.

Implications for Public Policy Makers

The present study has substantial implications for regulatory thought and action in regard to deceptive advertising, misleading advertising and the issuance of corrective advertising and affirmative disclosure orders. This study has demonstrated that perfect comprehension is, at best, a very rare phenomenon. One should not assume automatically that an advertisement is itself misleading simply because there is evidence that readers misunderstand some part of it. Just because there is a demonstrable degree of miscomprehension associated with a particular advertisement does not mean that that advertisement is necessarily at fault. A certain proportion of miscomprehension may simply reflect a natural error rate associated with one-way communication in general and/or print communication in particular. If print communications were so easy to understand, then one would expect that high school students taking history, English, political science, home economics, and so forth—the kinds of editorial content found in most mass media magazines—would all be able to achieve 100% correct response when tested on the contents of their textbooks.

As revealed by the present investigation, magazine miscomprehension rates generally are lower for advertising fare than for editorial content. These data also suggest that it would be unreasonable to use "zero miscomprehension" as the standard for evaluating magazine advertising. Perhaps the upper boundary of the interquartile range for advertising (23%)[3] might serve a useful function in this regard. Regulators concerned with misleading and/or deceptive advertising might use this boundary as a triggering mechanism so that advertisements that elicited levels of miscomprehension higher than this range might be considered as possibly warranting further attention.

In this regard, it needs to be noted that each quiz was developed to test the universe of asserted and implied meanings associated with a particular print communication. Hence, the set of six questions comprising any given quiz was usually designed to tap into six different meanings representing that universe. The miscomprehension level obtained for any given communication (such as the 23% figure cited above) thus represents the cumulative percent incorrect answers across a set of six questions.

In contrast, regulator interest is usually directed to a single specific meaning (or claim) rather than to the entire universe of meanings associated with a communication. Although the level of incorrect answers for any question was generally a fraction of that for the entire communication, the

---

[3]All the figures cited in this section refer to Percent Incorrect scores and may need to be adjusted upward to accommodate Don't Know responses.

rates across the 648 individual questions varied widely, from a low of 0% to a high of 96%.

Across the 324 questions used in testing the 54 advertisements, the mean Percent Incorrect score was 18.8%, the median 11.8%, and the interquartile range from 4.1% to 28.0%. The distribution was thus highly skewed, with 25% of the 324 advertising questions scoring below 4.1% incorrect, and 25% scoring above 28.0% incorrect.

When the concern is with specific meanings or claims contained in an advertisement and not with the advertisement as a whole, either the 11.8% median or the 28.0% upper end of the interquartile range for questions may represent the most appropriate comparison figures.

Also note that regulators' attention might vary if it were found that all those who misunderstood a specific claim (say, 20%) did so in a single common way rather than in 20 different and equally frequent ways.[4]

Of course, any attempt to employ a triggering mechanism boundary would have to recognize that, in some instances, even lower-than-average miscomprehension rates might be totally unacceptable. An example would be over-the-counter and prescription pharmaceuticals, where serious health and safety ramifications exist.[5]

It also needs to be remembered that, as described in Chapter 3, the assessment procedures focused on intermediate level material meanings, such as those typically found in general product claims (e.g., "The advertisement claimed that Brand X was low in calories—true or false?"). One might reasonably expect higher levels of comprehension, and correspondingly lower levels of miscomprehension, with assessment procedures that focus on more global meanings (e.g., "The brand being advertised was named Lite—true or false?"). Accordingly, one might argue for lower cut-off threshholds when global meanings are being assessed.

This consideration is relevant in the case of trademark and trade dress matters where the question of concern is not with specific product feature or performance claims, but with more global issues pertaining to source of manufacture, perceptions of "genericness," and brand name identification (e.g., "Was the consumer confused by the advertising or packaging for Brand B so that he thought it was Brand A?").

Implications for Public Health and Safety

A considerable amount of mass media information, especially in the print media, is designed for informative or educational purposes. This study documents the need for great care to insure that these communications are

---

[4]See Jacoby and Small, 1975.
[5]See Jacoby and Small, 1975.

understood correctly. The need increases in direct proportion to the importance of the messages—especially those which involve health and safety consequences.

Although this study dealt with the reading of magazine communications, not instruction sheets or labels, it may be inferred that the latter are also subject to miscomprehension and should therefore be checked for levels of miscomprehension prior to dissemination.

Implications for Advertising Testing

A large proportion of advertising effectiveness research focuses on its persuasive impact, that is, on how advertising purportedly affects consumer attitudes, preferences, purchase intentions, and behavior. As outlined in Chapter 2, most theories and research on the persuasion process assume that satisfactory comprehension necessarily precedes and facilitates attitude and behavior change. This assumption has rarely been examined. Researchers have typically assumed that recall and recognition provide satisfactory indications of comprehension. Yet remembering information and comprehending that information are different and separate processes. We can remember things we don't understand, and understand things we can't remember.

If it cannot be assumed that the essential meaning of the typical communication will be satisfactorily understood, then the implications for attitude- and intentions-oriented advertising research are substantial. When considered in the context of McGuire's[6] thinking, it may be that attitude and intentions measures are being given more weight than is warranted. Alternatively, it may be that the design of research on advertising effects should be expanded so that comprehension is more fully integrated into the assessment.

Implications for Advertisers

There are a number of implications for advertisers. Most basically, the present findings reveal that the comprehension of advertising should be a basic concern of all who develop advertising. Hundreds of millions of dollars are spent annually by advertisers trying to get their messages across to consumers.

While it is comforting to know that readers of print advertising are far more likely to understand than misunderstand their contents, and that magazine advertisements are somewhat better understood than is editorial content, the present data suggest that perhaps 20–25% of the essential

---

[6]As discussed in Chapter 2; also see McGuire, 1972.

contents of an average advertisement are being misunderstood upon first reading.

Both the miscomprehension and "don't know" levels observed in this study suggest a challenge to advertisers to strive for greater clarity of communication.[7] The fact that there is a wide range of miscomprehension across print advertisements suggests that it is possible to improve the level of reader comprehension.

At the very least, the present findings provide a "ceiling level" target at which advertisers can aim. If pretests revealed high rates of miscomprehension (perhaps over 25 or 30%) for a particular advertisement, efforts could then be expended to bring the rates down to acceptable levels before it was released. By lowering the rate of miscomprehension, not only would the advertiser insure that more of his advertising message was being understood accurately, but he would reduce the chances of the advertisement or the campaign becoming the focus of regulatory attention.

Advertisers might even begin to gather miscomprehension data on a regular basis. Perhaps the syndicated advertising evaluation services might be encouraged to devise and routinely provide a "miscomprehension index" along with the other indices they currently do provide.

Implications for General Circulation Magazine Communicators

While it is true that readers are far more apt to understand than misunderstand editorial content, it is discomforting to observe the levels of miscomprehension and non-comprehension obtained in this study. A substantial proportion of editorial content is *not* getting through to the reader or is being misunderstood. The average "don't know" rate for such content was 16% and the average Percent Incorrect rate was 23%.

Is a level of only 61% correct response acceptable, especially when a portion of this may be due to prior knowledge or fortuitous guessing? Perhaps the answer is "yes" in the case of entertainment content. Perhaps the answer is "no" when the consequences of failing to comprehend have health or safety implications, or impinge adversely on the functioning of our democracy. If misunderstanding the content of a communication may have major adverse consequences for the reader, these data suggest that the communication of that information should be checked for levels of

---

[7]According to Ford and Calfee (1986, p. 89), the Federal Trade Commission operates on the assumption "that sellers have an incentive to learn what interpretations consumers take from their ads, since advertising that misses its mark by conveying the wrong impression is likely to be wasted."

miscomprehension prior to that communication being published and circulated.

Implications for Society as a Whole

Finally, the functioning of a democracy is predicated upon and assumes an informed citizenry. Being informed requires acquiring and understanding relevant information concerning the world and events around us. Since the overwhelming majority of information is now communicated through the mass media, it becomes important to know whether—and how well—this information is understood. This knowledge may help the publishers and producers of mass media communications to respond in ways that will ultimately strengthen democracy in the future.

Since the public will not change in the short term, it is incumbent upon communicators to improve their skills and to take all reasonable steps to insure the maximum possible comprehension.

FUTURE DIRECTIONS

This investigation appears to be the first systematic attempt to focus explicitly on the comprehension and especially the *mis*comprehension of authentic magazine communications. In the absence of other investigations, the results represent the "best available empirical estimate" of the level of comprehension/miscomprehension of the content of mass circulation magazines. Moreover, when these findings are integrated with previous work on the miscomprehension of TV communications, a general degree of convergence seems to emerge across mass media communications: after a single exposure, miscomprehension seems to hover somewhere between 20–30%.

Replications

Every investigation has strengths and limitations, advantages and disadvantages. In part, this is because tradeoffs are necessarily made in designing and executing research, and no single investigation is capable of answering all relevant questions. Other investigations are therefore needed to compensate for the limitations inherent in the present study. Some of the factors that warrant further study include the following.

Nature of the Communication Stimuli. The present study examined only full-page ads, and editorial passages of only limited length, appearing in mass circulation magazines. Caution must be exercised in generalizing to stimuli of other sizes and to other types of magazines. Research is clearly needed to address these issues.

Multiple Methods.   Second, it may be argued that the present findings are method-bound: The study utilized only one method from the universe of potentially useful methods. Different levels of comprehension and miscomprehension might have been obtained had other procedures (such as multiple choice formats and "open-book" testing) been used.

This limitation may not be as severe as it first appears. It is not usually possible to apply several assessment procedures to the same respondents, as this is likely to produce a contamination of response. Also note that the single approach that was employed is the kind that is easiest and most likely to be employed in future independent tests. Moreover, as compared to the standard true-false format, the modified true-false format begins to approach the typical multiple-choice format. Further, Gates and Hoyer[8] have provided preliminary evidence to suggest that only minor differences are attributable to multiple choice vs. true-false format. Accordingly, the method selected may not be as limiting as it initially appears.

Claimed vs. Confirmed Readership.   Another potential limitation stems from the reliance on claimed, rather than confirmed, magazine readership. Given the number of magazines involved and the fact that developing and refining the closed-ended quizzes meant that the test occurred approximately a year after the material appeared in print, attempting to use standard industry respondent qualification procedures seemed out of the question. Future research involving fewer magazines and either confirmed subscribers or shorter time spans between publication and test should be able to determine if there were any meaningful differences between claimed and confirmed readers.

Construct and Content Validity.   Also needed is evidence bearing on the psychometric properties of the assessment procedure, especially the construct and content validity of the quizzes. The issue of construct validity may be expressed by the question: "To what extent do scores on the quizzes actually represent the concept of miscomprehension?" Similarly, the issue of content validity may be phrased as: "Given that one can be reasonably certain that incorrect responses to the quiz questions do represent miscomprehension, how well does each set of six quiz questions adequately sample the universe of relevant meanings associated with each communication?" An issue meriting particular attention is question difficulty.

---

[8]Gates and Hoyer, 1986.

Clearly, very difficult questions could shift miscomprehension rates toward 100%, while exceedingly easy questions would have the opposite effect.

As such research is completed, a more refined and accurate description of the degree of miscomprehension associated with magazine communications will begin to emerge. However, it bears repeating that in the absence of such replication research, the findings of the present investigation necessarily stand as the best available empirically derived estimate of the degree of comprehension and miscomprehension associated with mass media magazine communications.

It should also be mentioned that, as discussed in Chapter 1, a variety of different studies employing procedures similar to that used in the present study have produced converging findings regarding the level of miscomprehension.

Extensions

This investigation can be extended meaningfully in several directions.

Multiple Exposures.   At perhaps the most basic level, research needs to address the question: What happens to comprehension/miscomprehension as the respondent experiences multiple exposures to the same test communication? Readers in the real world often end up seeing the same advertisement several times and perhaps reviewing the same article more than once. Does this repeated exposure improve comprehension? Clearly, the impact of multiple exposures on comprehension/miscomprehension is an exceedingly important question that warrants further examination.[9]

Pictorial/Graphic vs. Verbal Content.   For the greater part, the present procedures focused on assessing the meanings associated with the verbal component of the message. Some evidence exists to show that higher levels of miscomprehension are associated with verbal content than with pictorial or graphic content.[10] This would help explain why advertising communications are better comprehended than editorial communications. Greater empirical attention needs to be directed to the question of verbal vs. pictorial comprehension/miscomprehension.

Field tests.   Another extension would involve field tests conducted under more natural conditions, that is, with readers being *unaware* while

---

[9]See Alpert, Golden, and Hoyer, 1983. Relatedly, Mazis (1981) reports that at the end of a 16-month, $10.3 million advertising campaign involving disclosure information on Listerine, 45% of the 7,000 users who were tested still maintained an erroneous referent belief regarding that product. See also Wilkie, McNeill, and Mazis, 1984.

[10]Kuss, 1985; Haedrich, and Kuss, 1986.

they were reading the communication that they would later be participants in a research investigation.

Related Media.   Yet another extension would involve examining the degree of comprehension/miscomprehension associated with other mass media, especially newspapers and radio.

In Chapter 2 we cautioned against extrapolating from the findings on magazine content to other print media. It would be even more unwise to draw direct comparisons between the present data for magazines and the earlier data collected for mass media TV communications,[11] especially given the important dissimilarities involved.[12] However, because we recognize that some readers will be tempted to make such direct comparisons, we shall identify here some procedures that seem advisable.

In terms of the measurement procedure itself, the two most fundamental differences between the present study and the earlier TV investigation are in the use of (1) modified true-false questions, and (2) experimental and control conditions. Probably the fairest way to generate comparison levels from the present data would be to:

1. ignore the data from the quiz only control condition and, confining attention to the experimental condition,
2. allocate a portion of the Don't Know response to "correct" and another portion to "incorrect." Such apportioning can be done using either the second or fourth approach described in the section entitled "Principal Dependent Measures" provided in Chapter 3.

Using this approach, the overall level of miscomprehension in the present study would be estimated as either 29.2% or 25.3%, while that in the TV study was 29.4%. Given the many differences across the two studies, this degree of convergence in findings is particularly noteworthy.

Identifying the Causes of Miscomprehension

A major question remaining to be addressed concerns the *causes* of miscomprehension. A breakdown in the transfer of meaning from one person to another may occur for any of a number of reasons. Perhaps the communication source does a poor job of encoding his meanings into appropriate surface structures. Or perhaps the source is trying to convey an

---

[11]See Jacoby, Hoyer, and Sheluga, 1980.

[12]An important difference not yet mentioned is the fact that the TV study involved non-probability quota sampling of respondents while the present study utilized probability sampling.

idea for which the receiver possesses no relevant prior experience and is therefore incapable of understanding. As an extreme example, imagine trying to convey a complex idea regarding quantum physics to the typical undergraduate English major. Or the meaning may be something that the receiver is capable of understanding, but the source may express that meaning using language beyond the receiver's ken. For example, a reader may clearly understand what is meant by "the Star Wars program proposed by President Reagan," but may fail to understand the same thought when expressed as "the Strategic Defense Initiative proposed by President Reagan."

Or perhaps the medium over which the message was being transmitted contained some imperfection. Examples would be static in a radio transmission, blurred letters in a print message, and so forth. These would produce surface structures that were distorted, indistinct, or completely obliterated.

It is also possible that the environment may contain other stimuli competing for the receiver's attention. As a result, the communication would not be attended to, either in part or in full.

The receiver may himself be the source of communication difficulties. On the one hand, there may be something amiss with either his primary sensory receptors or the neuronal transmission of sensations to the central nervous system. Or the individual may have higher, cortical-level processing difficulties, such as dyslexia. Finally, the individual's prior store of experiences or his current motivational state and expectations might lead him to misinterpret the meanings being transmitted via the incoming stimuli. In any one of these instances, the consequences may be either non- or miscomprehension.

In some instances it is possible to identify the locus of communication breakdown. For example, it may be possible to confirm that problems existed in the quality of physical transmission, or that distractions were present in the external environment.

It may also be possible to rule out some potential causes of breakdown. For instance, it is possible to insure that the linguistic surface structures were indeed adequate representations of the source's intended meaning. (One means of doing so was illustrated in a series of investigations dealing with proposed remedial advertising statements. Although a large proportion of respondents miscomprehended the meanings intended in three different versions of cautionary language carefully developed by the Federal Trade Commission,[13] it was possible, via the application of multidimensional scaling procedures, at least to insure that the three versions were comparable in terms of the meanings that were being conveyed.[14])

---

[13]Jacoby, Nelson, and Hoyer, 1982.
[14]Jacoby, Nelson, Hoyer, and Gueutal, 1984.

Having outlined the general case, let us note that there seem to be two dominant orientations to the question of causation. On the one hand, the arguments of many consumer activists and some regulators suggest that something connected with advertisements, or at least with some advertisements, is the cause of miscomprehension. An opposing perspective is that something associated with the past experience or current mental set and expectations of the reader stimulates miscomprehension.

For example, Preston[15] and Preston and Scharbach[16] interpret their findings of greater miscomprehension for print advertising than for three other forms of print communication in terms of the attributions made by their respondents. According to these authors, people have expectations regarding what they feel an advertiser would like to say and therefore "tend to see the ad actually making such [erroneous] statements even when it does not literally do so."[17]

This interpretation is consistent with findings from the literature on human information processing. Consider, for example, Stevens and Rumelhart's[18] research on "semantic expectations" in which recipients of messages were often found to "jump to conclusions" concerning the content of a message, and to mistake the intended meaning as a result. As Rumelhart emphasizes, "expectations play an important role in perception in general and language understanding in particular."[19] A line of inquiry that applies an attribution theory perspective[20] might also prove extremely useful in addressing the cause-effect question.

The rich literature within cognitive psychology on schema theory[21] provides another solid foundation for investigating the causes of miscomprehension. In particular, to what extent is miscomprehension related to the absence of relevant schema or the presence of erroneous schema?

Finally, inference-making appears to lie at the heart of the comprehension process.[22] A much better understanding is needed of how readers form inferences in response to advertising stimuli. In particular, research is needed to examine the circumstances under which receivers form pragmatic, as opposed to logical, inferences.[23]

As the above discussion suggests, the question of causation could bene-

---

[15]Preston, 1967.
[16]Preston and Scharbach, 1971.
[17]Preston and Scharbach, 1971, p. 24.
[18]Stevens and Rumelhart, 1975.
[19]Rumelhart, 1977, p. 135.
[20]Jones et al., 1971; Shaver, 1975.
[21]See related discussion in Chapter 2.
[22]See Carpenter and Just, 1977; Clark, 1977; Harris, 1977; Ortony, 1978; and the additional sources cited in Chapter 2.
[23]See Harris and Monaco, 1977.

fit from a more systematic exploration of the characteristics of both communications and receivers.

With respect to the communications themselves, what characteristics might be involved? Are certain types of presentation more likely to be miscomprehended? Are communications for certain types of products and product categories differentially linked to miscomprehension? A series of experimental designs in which characteristics of the communication are manipulated could be used to address this issue.

On the other hand, what reader characteristics might be linked with miscomprehension? Several sociodemographic characteristics were considered in this investigation; what other receiver-oriented factors might be more important? A market segmentation approach might be useful here, perhaps involving the use of specially designed activity, interest, and opinion (AIO) scales. Alternatively, the content and organization of knowledge in memory is likely to play an important role.

Another alternative is that miscomprehension represents some type of interaction between communication and reader, so that it is more likely to occur with some types of communication and readers than with others. The characteristics of these specific types of communication and reader are yet to be explored.

Clearly, much additional work remains to be done on the question of causation.

Reducing the Extent of Miscomprehension

Given a satisfactory understanding of the causative factors, we can begin to address the bottom line question: "How can we reduce present levels of miscomprehension to more acceptable levels?" For public policy makers, advertising managers, and mass media communicators, this is the ultimate question of interest. For researchers, it represents a challenge that should not be ignored.

There is reason to believe that research may reveal rules of thumb that writers can use to improve the likelihood of reader comprehension. For example, Carpenter and Just[24] summarize research that suggests the following:

1. Begin sentences with familiar information; place new information at the end of the sentence.
2. It "is easier to comprehend a paragraph that has several references to

---

[24]Carpenter and Just, 1977.

a restricted number of concepts than one that introduces many new, different concepts."[25]

3. Sentences that begin with "intersential connectives"[26] flow more smoothly and are easier to comprehend than those that do not.
4. Sentences that begin with "anaphoric references"[27] are easier to comprehend than those that do not.

A thorough examination of the literature describing fundamental research on reading processes may reveal other useful rules of thumb, and an effort along this line appears well warranted.

However, even after improved communications are developed on the basis of such research, the authors believe it will not be possible to reduce miscomprehension to a zero base level. That is, perfect comprehension will not be generally attainable. Several lines of thought lead to this conclusion.

First, language is an imprecise means of communicating meaning. Many words and phrases have multiple meanings, and the particular meaning extracted by one person is often not the same as that extracted by another. For this and other reasons, some scholars[28] contend that language comprehension is probably the most complex and difficult of all human mental phenomena.

Second, a fundamental tenet underlying behavioral science theory and research is that it is not objective reality, but psychological or "perceived" reality that exerts the greater influence over human thought processes and behavior. The receiver does not approach any communication or event as a tabula rasa. Rather, by virtue of his or her past experiences, each and every human being brings a unique set of values and expectations to a situation, and interprets the objectively presented communication with reference to these subjective factors. Thus, each person's perception and comprehension of a given communication has the potential to differ from any other person's.

---

[25]Carpenter and Just, 1977, pp. 233-234.

[26]An intersential connective establishes the relationship between sentences. Included are such terms as *therefore, because, however,* and *on the other hand.* Consider the following example: "Edgar wanted to go into forestry. Granted, the hours were long and the pay was low. Nevertheless, he wanted to become a forest ranger." As Carpenter and Just point out in regard to this passage, the

... connective *granted* indicates that the second sentence will provide an opposing argument. Without this connective, the second sentence would appear to present a supporting argument, which is contrary to the notion that long hours and low pay are negative attributes of a job (Carpenter and Just, 1977, p. 235).

[27]Anaphoric reference is a device that allows a reader to refer back to a previously mentioned concept by appealing to the previous mention. For example, in the sentences "Edgar certainly loves cars. He dotes on his '56 Chevy," *he* in the second sentence refers back to Edgar (Carpenter and Just, 1977, p. 238).

[28]For example, Rumelhart, 1977.

Much the same process is at work when two or more bystanders witness the same auto accident, yet come away with different understandings of what happened. Their perspectives, past experiences, and expectations will condition what they "see." One person's negative view of business and the capitalistic system may cause him, perhaps unconsciously, to interpret the accident as having been caused by the driver in "the big black limousine." Another witness may, because of a different set of values and expectations, attribute the cause of the same accident to "the hippy driver in the beat-up old red sportscar." In other words, no communication nor event is ever interpreted entirely independently of the past experiences, expectations, and value structures that the perceiver brings to the situation.

Third, one must consider the limitations imposed by the type of communication being employed. In contrast to one-on-one, face-to-face interactions, in which a two-way flow of communication is established, mass media communications are essentially one-way communications. The implications of this are substantial. Perfect comprehension in two-way communication situations is difficult enough. Who among us has not been party to a conversation that ended with one person misunderstanding what the other had said? Consider, then, how much more complex is the problem in one-way communication, where the receiver has no opportunity to ask clarifying questions, and the source of the communication cannot tailor his message to his perceptions of the receiver's needs and intellectual capabilities.

For these reasons, while future research may suggest some ways of reducing the level of miscomprehension with print communications, the pessimistic but realistic prediction is that perfect comprehension (or zero miscomprehension) will not be generally attainable.

A CLOSING OBSERVATION

Some may quarrel with the procedural details of this investigation or with the specific findings obtained, arguing, for example, that the miscomprehension rate is too high to be correct. Some of these arguments may well be valid. No claim is made of providing definitive answers to the research questions that stimulated this investigation. However, given that this appears to be the first broad-scale, systematic investigation of the subject, we do claim that our findings represent the best empirical estimate currently available as to the levels of comprehension and miscomprehension associated with mass media magazine content.

If anything, it is likely that the test procedure produced a lower rate of miscomprehension than would occur under normal reading conditions. The procedure involved uncluttered forced exposure and, because respondents knew they were in a test situation, they were probably more attentive than they would be under normal conditions. Nonetheless, the fact remains that nearly every respondent managed to misunderstand at least some portion of the communications which he or she read. Each and every one of the 108 test communications was misunderstood to some degree. The average amount of miscomprehension is conservatively estimated at 21%. Further, these findings were quite robust, holding true for respondents of different ages, incomes, education levels, sexes, and marital status.

Especially when placed in the context of earlier related investigations, the present study suggests that there is no basis for mass media communicator sanguinity. Too much of the communicator's intended meaning either is not getting through or is misunderstood. On the other hand, there would appear to be natural limits to the amount of improvement that can be expected. Clearly, much research is needed to shed greater light on all aspects of receiver comprehension/miscomprehension.

.

References

Ajzen, I., & Fishbein, M. (1980). *Understanding attitudes and social behavior.* Englewood Cliffs, New Jersey: Prentice-Hall.

Allen, W.H. (1967). Media stimulus and types of learning. *Audio-Visual Instruction, 12,* 27-31.

Alpert, M. I., Golden, L. L., & Hoyer, W. D. (1983). The impact of repetition on advertisement miscomprehension and effectiveness. In R. P. Bagozzi & A. M. Tybout (Eds.), *Advances in Consumer Research, 10.* Ann Arbor, Michigan: Association for Consumer Research, 130-135.

Anderson, R.C. (1972). How to construct achievement tests to assess comprehension. *Review of Educational Research, 42,* 145-170.

Bailey, P., & Pertschuk, M. (1984). The law of deception: The past as prologue. *American University Law Review, 33,* 849-897.

Barrett, M., & Sklar, Z. (1980). *The eye of the storm.* New York: Lippincott and Crowell.

Batra, R., & Ray, M.L. (1983). Advertising situations: The implications of differential involvement and accompanying affect responses. In R.J. Harris (Ed.), *Information processing research in advertising.* Hillsdale, New Jersey: Lawrence Erlbaum Associates, 127-151.

Beighley, K.C. (1952). An experimental study of the effect of four speech variables on listener comprehension. *Speech Monographs, 19,* 249-258.

Bettman, J.R. (1979). *An information processing theory of consumer choice.* Reading, Mass.: Addison-Wesley.

Browne, K. (1978). Comparison of factual recall from film and print stimuli. *Journalism Quarterly, 55,* 350-353.

Brunswik, E. (1956). *Perception and the representative design of psychological experiments.* Berkeley: University of California Press.

Carpenter, P. A., & Just, M. A. (1977). Integrative processes in comprehension. In D. Laberge & S. J. Samuels (Eds.), *Basic process in reading: Perception and comprehension.* Hillsdale, New Jersey: Lawrence Erlbaum Associates, 217-241.

Chaiken, S., & Eagly, A. E. (1976). Communication modality as a determinant of message persuasiveness and message comprehensibility. *Journal of Personality and Social Psychology, 34* (4), 605-614.

Clark, H. H. (1977). Inferences in comprehension. In D. Laberge & S. J. Samuels (Eds.), *Basic processes in reading: Perception and comprehension.* Hillsdale, New Jersey: Lawrence Erlbaum Associates, 243-263.

Cohen, J., & Cohen, P. (1983). *Applied multiple regression correlation: Analysis for the behavioral sciences* (2d ed.). Hillsdale, New Jersey: Lawrence Erlbaum Associates.

Colley, R. (1961). *Defining advertising goals for measuring advertising results.* New York: Association of National Advertisers.

Comstock, G., Chaffee, S., Katzman, N., McCombs, M., & Roberts, D. (1978). *Television and human behavior.* New York: Columbia University Press.

Corey, S. M. (1934). Learning from lectures and learning from reading. *Journal of Educational Psychology, 25,* 459-470.

Cronbach, L. J., Gleser, G., Nanda, H., & Rajaratnam, N. (1972). *The dependability of behavioral measurements: Theory of generalizability for scores and profiles.* New York: Wiley.

Dascal, M. (1981). Strategies of understanding. In H. Parret & J. Bouveresse (Eds.), *Meaning and Understanding.* New York: Walter de Guyter, 327-352.

Deighton, J. (1986). Persuasion as directed inference. In R. J. Lutz (Ed.), *Advances in Consumer Research, 15.* Provo, Utah: Association for Consumer Research, 558-561.

Deming, W. E. (1960). *Sample design in business research.* New York: Wiley.

Dyer, N., & Robinson, J. P. (1980). *News comprehension research in Great Britain.* Paper presented to the International Communication Association, Acapulco, Mexico. May.

Eagly, A.H., & Chaiken, S. (1984). Cognitive theories of persuasion. *Advances in Experimental Social Psychology. 17,* New York: Academic Press, 267-359.

Ebbinghaus, H. (1885). *Memory.* (Reprinted in 1964 by Dover Press, New York.)

Engel, J. F., & Blackwell, R. D. (1982). *Consumer behavior* (4th edition). Chicago: Dryden Press.

Engel, J. F., Blackwell, R. D., & Miniard, P. W. (1986). *Consumer behavior* (5th edition). Chicago: Dryden Press.

Estes, W. K. (1977). On the interaction of perception and memory in reading. In D. Laberge & S. J. Samuels (Eds.), *Basic process in reading: Perception and comprehension.* Hillsdale, N.J.: Lawrence Erlbaum Associates, 1-25.

Federal Trade Commission (1983). Policy statement on deception. 45 *ATRR* 689 (Oct. 27, 1983). Reprinted in In re FTC's enforcement policy against deceptive acts or practices. *Commerce Clearing House, 50* (Nov.), 445.

Fishbein, M., & Ajzen, I. (1975). *Belief, attitude, intention and behavior: An introduction to theory and research.* Reading, Mass.: Addison-Wesley.

Fisher, L. A., Johnson, T. S., Porter, D., Bleich, H. L. & Slack, W. V. (1977). Collection of a clean voided urine specimen: A comparison among spoken, written and computer-based instructions. *American Journal of Public Health, 67* (7), 640-644.

Ford, G. T., & Calfee, J. E. (1986). Recent developments in FTC policy on deception. *Journal of Marketing, 50* (3), 82-103.

Ford, G. T., & Yalch, R. (1982). Viewer miscomprehension of televised communication—A comment. *Journal of Marketing, 46*(4), 27-31.

Frederiksen, C. H. (1975). Representing logical and semantic structure of knowledge acquired from discourse. *Cognitive Psychology, 7,* 371-458.

Gates, F. R., & Hoyer, W. D. (1986). Measuring miscomprehension: A comparison of alternative formats. In R. Lutz (Ed.), *Advances in Consumer Research, 13,* 143-146.

Grass, R. C. & Wallace, W. H. (1973). Advertising communication: Print vs. tv. *Journal of Advertising Research, 14*(5), 19-23.

Gunter, B. (1980a). Remembering the television news: Effects of visual format on information gain. *Journal of Educational Television, 6,* 8–11.

Gunter, B. (1980b). Remembering television news: Effects of picture content. *Journal of General Psychology, 102,* 216–233.

Gunter, B. (1981). Forgetting the news. *Intermedia, 9*(5) (September), 41–43.

Gunter, B., Berry, C., & Clifford, B. R. (1981). Proactive interference effects with television news items: Further evidence. *Journal of Experimental Psychology: Human Learning and Memory,* Vol. 7, No. 6, 480–487.

Gunter, B., Clifford, B.R., & Berry, C. (1980). Release from proactive interference with television news items: Evidence for encoding dimensions within televised news. *Journal of Experimental Psychology: Human Learning and Memory, 6,* 216–223.

Gunter, B., Furnham, A., & Gietson, G. (1984). Memory for the news as a function of the channel of communication. *Human Learning, 3,* 265–271.

Gunter, B., Furnham, A., & Jarrett, J. (1984). Personality, time of day, and delayed memory for tv news. *Personality and Individual Differences, 5*(1), 35–39.

Gunter, B., Jarrett, J., & Furnham, A. (1983). Time of day effects on immediate memory for television news. *Human Learning, 2,* 261–267.

Haedrich, G., & Kuss, A. (1986). Messung des Missverstandnisses von Werbebotschaften bei Kindern und Erwachsenen. In H. Haase & K. Koeppler (Eds.), *Fortschrifte der Markt-psychologie,* Band 4. Frankfurt/M., West Germany.

Harris, R. J. (1977). Comprehension of pragmatic implications in advertising. *Journal of Applied Psychology, 62,* 603–608.

Harris, R. J. (1981). Inferences in information processing. In G. H. Bower (Ed.), *The psychology of learning and motivation.* New York: Academic Press.

Harris, R. J. (Ed.) (1983). *Information processing research in advertising.* Hillsdale, New Jersey: Lawrence Erlbaum Associates.

Harris, R. J., Dubitsky, T. M., & Bruno, K. J. (1983). Psycholinguistic studies of misleading advertising. In R.J. Harris (Ed.), *Information processing research in advertising.* Hillsdale, New Jersey: Lawrence Erlbaum Associates.

Harris, R. J., & Monaco, G. E. (1977). Psychology of pragmatic implication: Information processing between the lines. *Journal of Experimental Psychology: General, 107*(1), 1–22.

Harwood, K. A. (1951). An experimental comparison of listening comprehensibility with reading comprehensibility: Abstract of Ph.D. thesis. *Speech Monographs, 18,* 123–124.

Haugh, O. M. (1952). The relative effectiveness of reading and listening to radio drama as ways of imparting information and shifting attitudes. *Journal of Educational Research, 45,* 489–498.

Honomichl, J. (1986). Special report: Research business review: The nation's top marketing advertising research companies. *Advertising Age, 57* (31), 561. May 19.

Hovland, C. I., Janis, I. L., & Kelley, H. H. (1953). *Communication and persuasion: Psychological studies of persuasion.* New Haven, Connecticut: Yale University Press.

Hoyer, W. D., & Jacoby, J. (1985). The public's miscomprehension of public affairs programming. *Journal of Broadcasting and Electronic Media, 29*(4), 437–443.

Hoyer, W. D., Srivastava, R. K., & Jacoby, J. (1984). Examining the sources of advertising miscomprehension. *Journal of Advertising, 13*(2), 17–26.

Jabine, T. B., Straf, M. L., Tanur, J. M., & Tourangeau, R. (Eds.) (1984). *Cognitive aspects of survey methodology: Building a bridge between disciplines.* Report of the Advanced Research Seminar on Cognitive Aspects of Survey Methodology. Prepared for the Committee on National Statistics, Commission on Behavioral and Social Sciences and Education, the National Research Council. Washington, D.C.: National Academy Press.

Jacoby, J. (1981). Some perspectives on risk acceptance. In K. B. Monroe (Ed.), *Advances in Consumer Research, 8,* 511–516.

Jacoby, J., & Hoyer, W. D. (1981). Reply to Mizerski's criticisms: AAAA's TV miscomprehension researchers say study's flaws aren't serious enough to change major conclusions. *Marketing News 15* (2), July 24, 35-36.

Jacoby, J. and Hoyer, W. D. (1982a). Viewer miscomprehension of televised communication: Selected findings. *Journal of Marketing, 46*(4), 12-26.

Jacoby, J., & Hoyer, W. D. (1982b). On miscomprehending televised communication: A rejoinder. *Journal of Marketing, 46*(4), 35-43.

Jacoby, J., Hoyer, W. D., & Sheluga, D. A. (1980). *Miscomprehension of televised communications.* New York: American Association of Advertising Agencies.

Jacoby, J., Hoyer, W. D., & Sheluga, D. A. (1981). Miscomprehending televised communication: A brief report of findings. In K. Monroe (Ed.), *Advances in Consumer Research, 8,* 410-413.

Jacoby, J., Hoyer, W. D., & Zimmer, M. R. (1983). To read, view or listen? A cross-media comparison of comprehension. In J. H. Leigh & C. R. Martin, Jr. (Eds.), *Current issues and research in advertising.* Ann Arbor: The University of Michigan, 201-218.

Jacoby, J., Nelson, M. C., & Hoyer, W. D. (1982). Corrective advertising and affirmative disclosure statements: Their potential for confusing and misleading the consumer. *Journal of Marketing, 46*(1), 61-72.

Jacoby, J., Nelson, M., Hoyer, W. D., & Gueutal, H. G. (1984). Probing the locus of causation in the miscomprehension of remedial advertising statements. In T. C. Kinnear (Ed.), *Advances in Consumer Research,* Provo, Utah: Association for Consumer Research, *11,* 379-384.

Jacoby, J., & Small, C. B. (1975). The FDA approach to defining misleading advertising. *Journal of Marketing, 39*(4), 65-68.

Jacoby, J., Troutman, T., & Whittler, T. (1986). Viewer miscomprehension of the 1980 presidential debate. *Political Psychology, 7* (2), 297-308.

Jones, E. E., Kanouse, D. E., Kelley, H. H., Nisbett, R. E., Valins, S., & Weiner, B. (1971). *Attribution: Perceiving the causes of behavior.* Hillsdale, New Jersey: Lawrence Erlbaum Associates.

Katz, E., Adoni, H., & Parness, P. (1977). Remembering the news: What the picture adds to recall. *Journalism Quarterly, 54,* 231-239.

Keenan, J. M. (1978). Psychological issues concerning implication: Comments on "Psychology of pragmatic implication: Information processing between the lines" by Harris and Monaco. *Journal of Experimental Psychology: General, 107* (January), 23-27.

King, D. J. (1968). Retention of connected meaningful material as a function of modes of presentation and recall. *Journal of Experimental Psychology, 77* (4), 676-683.

Kintsch, W. (1978). Comprehension and memory of text. In W. K. Estes (Ed.), *Handbook of learning and cognitive processes.* Hillsdale, New Jersey: Lawrence Erlbaum, 57-86.

Krugman, H.E. (1965). The impact of television advertising: Learning without involvement. *Public Opinion Quarterly, 29,* 349-356.

Krugman, H.E. (1966). The measurement of advertising involvement. *Public Opinion Quarterly, 30,* 584-585.

Kuss, A. (1985). Missverstaendnis von Fernsehwerbung. *Werbeforschung und Praxis, 6.*

Laberge, D., & Samuels, S. J. (Eds.) (1977). *Basic processes in reading: Perception and comprehension.* Hillsdale, New Jersey: Lawrence Erlbaum Associates.

Langer, J. L. (1985). Levels of questioning: An alternative view. *Reading Research Quarterly, 20* (May), 586-602.

Langer, J. L. (1986). The construction of meaning and the assessment of comprehension: An analysis of reader performance on standardized test items. In R. Freedle (Ed.), *Cognitive and linguistic analyses of test performance.* New York: Ablex.

Laswell, H. D. (1948). The structure and function of communication in society. In L. Bryson (Ed.), *Communication of ideas.* New York: Harper, 37-51.

Lavidge, R.J., & Steiner, G.A. (1961) A model for predictive measurement of advertising effectiveness. *Journal of Marketing 25* (3), 59-62.

Lindsay, P. H., & Norman, D. A. (1972) *Human information processing: An introduction to psychology.* NY, Academic Press.

Lindsay, P. H., & Norman, D. A. (1977) *Human information processing: An introduction to psychology.* (Second Edition) NY, Academic Press.

Lipstein, B. (1980). Theories of advertising and measurement systems. In *Attitude research enters the 80's.* Chicago: American Marketing Association.

Lipstein, B., & McGuire, W. J. (1978). *Evaluating advertising: A bibliography of the communication process.* New York: Advertising Research Foundation.

Maier, N. R. F., & Thurber, J. A. (1968). Accuracy of judgments of deception when an interview is watched, heard, or read. *Personnel Psychology, 21,* 23-30.

Mazis, M. (1981). The effects of FTC's Listerine corrective advertising order. A report to the FTC. Washington, D.C.

McClelland, L. (1979) On the time relations of mental processes: An examination of systems of processes in cascade. Psychological Review, *86* (4), 287-330.

McClelland, L., & Rumelhart, D. E. (1981) An interactive model of content effects in letter perception: Part 1. An account of basic findings. Psychological Review, *88* (5), 375-407.

McGinnies, E. (1965). A cross-cultural comparison of printed communication in persuasion. *Journal of Psychology, 60,* 1-8.

McGuire, W. J. (1968a). Personality and attitude change: An information-processing theory. In A. G. Greenwald, T. C. Brock, & T. M. Ostrom (Eds.), *Psychological foundations of attitudes.* New York: Academic Press.

McGuire, W. J. (1968b). Personality and susceptibility to social influence. In E. F. Borgatta, & W. W. Lambert (Eds.), *Handbook of personality theory and research.* Chicago: Rand-McNally.

McGuire, W. J. (1969). The nature of attitudes and attitude change. In G. Lindzey & E. Aronson (Eds.), *Handbook of social psychology* (Vol. 3; 2nd ed.). Reading, Mass.: Addison-Wesley.

McGuire, W. J. (1972). Attitude change: The information-processing paradigm. In C. G. McClintock (Ed.), *Experimental social psychology.* New York: Holt, Rinehart, & Winston.

McGuire, W. J. (1973). Persuasion, resistance and attitude change. In I. de Sola Pool, W. Schramm, N. Maccoby, & E. B. Parker (Eds.), *Handbook of communication,* 216-252.

McGuire, W. J. (1976). Some internal psychological factors influencing consumer choice. *Journal of Consumer Research, 2,* 302-319.

McGuire, W. J. (1978). An information processing model of advertising effectiveness. In H. A. Davis & A. J. Silk (Eds.), *Behavioral and management sciences in marketing.* New York: Ronald Press.

McGuire, W. J. (1985). Attitudes and attitude change. In G. Lindzey & E. Aronson (Eds.) *Handbook of Social Psychology* (3rd ed.). Reading, Mass.: Addison-Wesley.

Mitchell, A. A. (1983). Cognitive processes initiated by exposure to advertising. In R. J. Harris (Ed.) *Information processing research in advertising.* Hillsdale, New Jersey: Lawrence Erlbaum Associates, 13-42.

Mizerski, R. W. (1981). Major problems in AAAA's pioneering study of miscomprehension. *Marketing News, 14* (June 12), 7-8.

Mizerski, R. W. (1982). Viewer miscomprehension findings are measurement bound. *Journal of Marketing, 46*(4), 32-34.

Moore, D., & Hutchinson, J. W. (1983). The effects of affect on advertising effectiveness. In R. P. Bagozzi & A. M. Tybout (Eds.), *Advances in Consumer Research, 10.* Ann Arbor, Michigan: Association for Consumer Research, 526-531.

Moriarity, S. E. (1983). Beyond the hierarchy of effects: A conceptual framework. In J. H. Leigh & C. R. Martin, Jr. (Eds.), *Current issues in advertising research.* Ann Arbor: University of Michigan Press, 45–55.

Morris, L. A., Brinberg, D., Klimberg, R., Rivera, C., & Millstein, L. G. (1986). Miscomprehension rates for prescription drug advertisements. In J. H. Leigh & C. R. Martin, Jr. (Eds), *Current issues and research in advertising.* Ann Arbor: University of Michigan Press, 201–218.

Neisser, U. (1976). *Cognition and reality: Principles and implications of cognitive psychology.* San Francisco: W.H. Freeman.

Neisser, U. (1978). Memory: What are the important questions? In M. Gruenberg, P. Morris, & R. Sykes (Eds.), *Practical aspects of memory.* London: Academic Press.

Neisser, U. (1982). Memory: What are the important questions? In U. Neisser (Ed.), *Memory observed.* San Francisco: W. H. Freeman.

Norman, D. T., & Bobrow, D. G. (1975). On the role of active memory processes in perception and cognition. In C. N. Cofer (Ed.), *The structure of human memory.* San Francisco: W. H. Freeman & Company.

Northcutt, N., et al. (1975). *Adult functional competency study: A four-year national investigation.* A summary report provided to the U. S. Office of Education, Department of Health, Education and Welfare. Austin: University of Texas, Division of Extension.

Olson, J.C. (1978). Inferential belief formation in the cue utilization process. In H. K. Hunt (Ed.), *Advances in Consumer Research, 5.* Ann Arbor, Michigan: Association for Consumer Research, 706–713.

Opinion Research Corporation (undated). *A study of media involvement* (4th ed.). New York: Magazine Publisher's Association.

Ortony, A. (1978). Remembering, understanding and representation. *Cognitive Science, 2,* 53–69.

Osgood, C. E. (1959). The representational model and relevant research methods. In I. de Sola Pool (Ed.), *Trends in content analysis.* Urbana: University of Illinois Press.

Osgood, C. E., Suci, G. J., & Tannenbaum, P. (1957). *The measurement of meaning.* Champaign-Urbana: University of Illinois Press.

Peter, J. P., & Olson, J. C. (1987). *Consumer behavior: Marketing strategy perspectives.* Homewood, Illinois: R. D. Irwin.

Petrinovich, L. (1979). Probabilistic functionalism: A conception of research method. *American Psychologist. 34* (5), 373–390.

Petty, R., Caccioppo, J. T., & Goldman, R. (1981). Personal involvement as a determinant of argument-based persuasion. *Journal of Personality and Social Psychology, 40,* 847–855.

Preston, I. L. (1967). Logic and illogic in the advertising process. *Journalism Quarterly, 44*(2), 231–239.

Preston, I. L. (1976). A comment on "Defining misleading advertising" and "Deception in advertising," *Journal of Marketing, 40*(2), 54–57.

Preston, I. L. (1983). Research on deceptive advertising: Commentary. In R. J. Harris (Ed.), *Information processing research in advertising.* Hillsdale, New Jersey: Lawrence Erlbaum Associates, 289–305.

Preston, I. L., & Richards, J. I. (1986a). The relationship of deception to deceptiveness in FTC cases. In R. Lutz (Ed.), *Advances in Consumer Research, 13.* Provo, Utah: Association for Consumer Research, 138–142.

Preston, I. L., & Richards, J. I. (1986b). Consumer miscomprehension as a challenge to FTC prosecutions of deceptive advertising. *John Marshall Law Review, 19*(3), 605–635.

Preston, I. L., & Scharbach, S. E. (1971). Advertising: More than meets the eye? *Journal of Advertising Research, 11*(3), 19–24.

Preston, I. L., & Thorson, E. (1984). The expanded association model: Keeping the hierarchy concept alive. *Journal of Advertising Research, 24* (January), 59–65.

Richgels, D. J. (1982). Schema theory, linguistic theory, and representations of reading comprehension. *Journal of Educational Research, 76*(1), 54-62.

Robinson, J. P., Davis, D. K., Sahin, H., & O'Toole, T. (1980). *Comprehension of television news: How alert is the audience?* Paper presented to the Association for Education in Journalism, Boston.

Robinson, J. P., Levy, M. R., Davis, D. K., Woodall, W. G., Gurevitch, M., & Sahin, H. (1986). *The main source: Learning from television news.* Beverly Hills, Calif.: Sage Publications.

Robinson, J. P., & Sahin, H. (undated draft). *Audience comprehension of television news.* London: British Broadcasting Association.

Rumelhart, D. E. (1977). *Introduction to human information processing.* New York: Wiley.

Russo, J. E., Metcalf, B. L. and Stephens, D. (1981). Identifying misleading advertising. *Journal of Consumer Research, 8*(2), 119-131.

Sahin, H., Davis, D. K., & Robinson, J. P. (1981). Improving the tv news. *Irish Broadcasting Review, 11,* 50-55.

Sales, B. D., Elwork, A., & Alfini, J. J. (1977). Improving comprehension for jury instructions. In B. D. Sales (Ed.), *Perspectives in law and psychology.* New York: Plenum.

Schank, R. C. (1976). The role of memory in language processing. In C. N. Cofer (Ed.), *The structure of human memory.* San Francisco: W. H. Freeman.

Schank, R. C. & Abelson, R. (1977). *Scripts, plans, goals and understanding.* Hillsdale, New Jersey: Lawrence Erlbaum Associates.

Schmittlein, D. C., & Morrison, D. G. (1983). Measuring miscomprehension for televised communication using true-false questions. *Journal of Consumer Research, 10*(2), 147-156.

Schramm, W. S. (1973). Channels and audiences. In I. S. de Sola Pool, W. S. Schramm et al. (Eds.), *Handbook of communication.* Chicago: Rand-McNally, 116-140.

Shaver, K. G. (1975). *An introduction to attribution processes.* Hillsdale, New Jersey: Lawrence Erlbaum Associates.

Simmons 1983 study of media and markets (Publications: Total audiences). New York: Simmons Market Research Bureau, Inc.

de Sola Pool, I., Schramm, W. S., Frey, F. W., Maccoby, N., & Parker, E. B. (Eds.) (1973). *Handbook of communication.* Chicago: Rand-McNally.

Spiro, R. J., Bruce, B. C., & Brewer, W. F. (Eds.) (1980). *Theoretical issues in reading comprehension: Perspectives from cognitive psychology, linguistics, artificial intelligence, and education.* Hillsdale, New Jersey: Lawrence Erlbaum Associates.

Srull, T. K. (1984). The effects of subjective affective states on memory and judgment. In T. C. Kinnear (Ed.), *Advances in Consumer Research, 11.* Ann Arbor: Association for Consumer Research, 530-533.

Stevens, A. L., & Rumelhart, D. E. (1975). Errors in reading: Analysis using an augmented network model of grammar. In D. A. Norman, D. E. Rumelhart, & the LNR Research Group, *Explorations in cognition.* San Francisco: W. H. Freeman.

Stewart, D. W. (1986). The moderating role of recall, comprehension, and brand differentiation on the persuasiveness of television advertising. *Journal of Advertising Research, 25* (March-April), 43-47.

Tierney, R. J., Vaughan, J. L., Jr., & Bridge, C. A. (1979). Toward understanding comprehension: An examination of systems for analyzing inferences. In J. C. Harste & R. F. Carey (Eds.), *New perspectives in comprehension.* Bloomington: Indiana University School of Education, 23-37.

Tourangeau, R. (1984). Cognitive sciences and survey methods. In T. B. Jabine et al. (Eds.), *Cognitive aspects of survey methodology: Building a bridge between disciplines.* Washington, D.C.: National Academy Press, 73-100.

U.S. Department of Education (1986). *Adult illiteracy estimates for the United States* (revised April 14, 1986) and *Update on adult illiteracy* (undated).

Wilkie, W., McNeill, D., & Mazis, M. (1984). Marketing's "Scarlet Letter": The theory and practice of corrective advertising. *Journal of Marketing, 48*(2), 11-31.

Williams, D. C., Paul, J., & Ogilvie, J. C. (1957). Mass media, learning, and retention. *Canadian Journal of Psychology, 11*(3), 157-163.

Wilson, C. E. (1974). The effect of medium on loss of information. *Journalism Quarterly, 51,* 111-115.

Wittrock, M. C. (1981). Reading comprehension. In F. J. Pirozzolo and M. C. Wittrock (Eds.), *Neuropsychological and cognitive processing in reading.* New York: Academic Press, 229-259.

Woodall, W. G., Davis, D. K., & Sahin, H. (1983). From the boob tube to the black box: Television news comprehension from an information processing perspective. *Journal of Broadcasting, 27* (1), 1-23.

Worchel, S., Andreoli, V., & Eason, J. (1975). Is the medium the message? A study of the effects of media, communication, and message characteristics. *Journal of Applied Social Psychology, 5* (2), 157-172.

Young, J. D. (1953). An experimental comparison of vocabulary growth by means of oral reading, silent reading and listening. *Speech Monographs, 20,* 273-276.

Your Opinion Counts. (1986). *Refusal rate study.* Chicago, Illinois: Marketing Research Association.

APPENDIX A

Magazines Covered by Hall's Magazine Reports, 1982

(n = 60)

Editorial Content

I N D E X

Note: Figures in parentheses after magazine names indicate number of agate lines per page.

```
HOUSE BEAUTIFUL (429) ....................................  42
LADIES' HOME JOURNAL (429) ...............................  17
LIFE (680) ...............................................  48
MADEMOISELLE (429) .......................................  32
McCALL'S (429) ...........................................  18
MECHANIX ILLUSTRATED (429) ...............................  58

METROPOLITAN HOME (429) ..................................  43
MODERN MATURITY (420) ....................................  47
NEW SHELTER (420) ........................................  57
NEWSWEEK (420) ...........................................   1
NEW YORK TIMES MAGAZINE (850) ............................   5
OUTDOOR LIFE (429) .......................................  54

PARADE (790) .............................................   7
PARENTS (429) ............................................  22
PEOPLE WEEKLY (420) ......................................   8
POPULAR MECHANICS (429) ..................................  59
POPULAR SCIENCE (429) ....................................  60
PREVENTION (220) .........................................  21

READER'S DIGEST (182) ....................................  49
REDBOOK (429) ............................................  19
SELF (429) ...............................................  23
SEVENTEEN (429) ..........................................  27
SOUTHERN LIVING (420) ....................................  44
SPORTS AFIELD (429) ......................................  55

SPORTS ILLUSTRATED (420) .................................   4
SPRING (429) .............................................  24
SUNSET (420) .............................................  45
'TEEN (420) ..............................................  28
TIME (420) ...............................................   2
TOWN & COUNTRY (429) .....................................  52

U.S. NEWS & WORLD REPORT (420) ...........................   3
VOGUE (429) ..............................................  33
W (1400) .................................................  34
WOMAN'S DAY (429) ........................................  20
WORKING MOTHER (429) .....................................  25
YOUNG MISS (429) .........................................  29
```

Note: Figures in parentheses after magazine names indicate
number of agate lines per page.

APPENDIX B

Magazines Covered by Publishers Information Bureau (PIB) Reports, 1982

(n = 121)

Advertising Content

WEEKLIES & BIWEEKLIES

New York with Cue
New Yorker, The
Newsweek
People Weekly
Rolling Stone—Biweekly
Sporting News
Sports Illustrated
TV Guide
Time
U.S. News & World Report
Us—Biweekly

WOMEN'S

Bride's Magazine— Bimonthly
Cosmopolitan
Essence
Family Circle
Good Housekeeping
Ladies' Home Journal
McCall's Magazine
Modern Bride—Bimonthly
Ms.
Parents'
Redbook Magazine
Self
Seventeen
True Story
Woman's Day
Working Mother
Working Woman

MONTHLIES

A.D.
Atlantic
Bon Appetit
Book Digest
California
Car & Driver
Changing Times
Cuisine
Discover
Ebony
Elks Magazine
Esquire
Families
50 Plus
Food & Wine
Gallery
Games—Bimonthly
Gentlemen's Quarterly
Geo
Golf
Golf Digest
Gourmet
Harper's Magazine
Inside Sports
Life
Metropolitan Home
Modern Maturity—Bimonthly
Money
Mother Earth News— Bimonthly
National Geographic Magazine
National Lampoon
Natural History
New West—See California
Omni
Oui
Penthouse
Playboy
Psychology Today

MONTHLIES (cont.)

Reader's Digest
Road & Track
Saturday Review
Science Digest
Science 82
Scientific American
Signature
Ski
Skin Diver
Smithsonian
Sport
Tennis
Texas Monthly
Town & Country
Travel/Holiday
Travel & Leisure
World Press Review
World Tennis

HOME

Architectural Digest
Better Homes & Gardens
Colonial Homes—Bimonthly
Country Living
Country Journal
Family Handyman, The
Home
House Beautiful
House & Garden
New Shelter
Organic Gardening
Southern Living
Sunset Magazine

FASHION & SERVICE

Glamour
Harper's Bazaar
Mademoiselle
Vogue

BUSINESS

Black Enterprise
Business Week
Dun's Business Month
Forbes—Biweekly
Fortune—Biweekly
Harvard Business Review—
   Bimonthly
Inc.
Industry Week—Biweekly
Nation's Business
Venture

YOUTH

Boy's Life

OUTDOORS & SPORTS

Field & Stream
Outdoor Life
Sports Afield

MECHANICS & SCIENCE

Mechanix Illustrated
Popular Mechanics Magazine
Popular Science

NEWSPAPER SUPPLEMENTS &
                SECTIONS

Family Weekly
New York Times Magazine
Parade

APPENDIX C

Magazines Covered in
Simmons Market Research Bureau
(SMRB) 1982 Study of Media and Markets

(n = 122)

	AUDIENCE (000)			AVG CIRC (000)	READERS PER COPY·		
	TOTAL				TOTAL		
	ADULTS	MEN	WOMEN		ADULTS	MEN	WOMEN
TOTAL	161656	76155	85500	·	·	·	·
BARRON'S	874	635	239	266	3.28	2.39	0.90
BETTER HOMES & GARDENS	21045	4819	16226	8053	2.61	0.60	2.01
BON APPETIT	2987	789	2199	1261	2.37	0.63	1.74
BUSINESS WEEK	4173	3139	1034	775	5.39	4.05	1.33
CAR AND DRIVER	2658	2359	299	686	3.88	3.44	0.44
CBS MAGAZINE NTWK. (NET)	5946	4798	1148	1629	3.65	2.94	0.70
CBS MAGAZINE NTWK. (GROSS)	6865	5616	1249	1629	4.21	3.45	0.77
CHANGING TIMES	2741	1653	1089	1479	1.85	1.12	0.74
CONDE NAST MAG. PKG(NET)	12039	1350	10688	5174	2.33	0.26	2.07
CONDE NAST MAG. PKG(GROSS)	16653	1624	15029	5174	3.22	0.31	2.90
COSMOPOLITAN	9596	1559	8036	2586	3.71	0.60	3.11
COUNTRY LIVING	1854	526	1328	658	2.82	0.80	2.02
CUISINE	1726	570	1156	754	2.29	0.76	1.53
CYCLE WORLD	2228	1899	329	331	6.72	5.73	0.99
DECORATING & CRAFT IDEAS	2410	279	2131	734	3.28	0.38	2.90
DEC CRFT ID/SO. LIV(NET)	7085	1675	5410	2800	2.53	0.60	1.93
DEC CRFT ID/SO. LIV(GROSS)	7366	1712	5654	2800	2.63	0.61	2.02
DISCOVER	1624	1077	547	808	2.01	1.33	0.68
EBONY	6851	2972	3879	1251	5.48	2.38	3.10
ESQUIRE	2345	1537	809	672	3.49	2.29	1.20
ESSENCE	2697	721	1976	693	3.89	1.04	2.85
FAMILY CIRCLE	18033	2359	15673	6911	2.61	0.34	2.27
THE FAMILY HANDYMAN	3134	2169	966	1114	2.81	1.95	0.87
FAMILY WEEKLY	25520	12157	13363	12305	2.07	0.99	1.09
FIELD & STREAM	8023	6391	1632	2036	3.94	3.14	0.80
FORBES	2123	1603	519	733	2.89	2.19	0.71
FORTUNE	2666	1903	763	616	4.33	3.09	1.24
GENTLEMEN'S QUARTERLY	2093	1410	684	477	4.39	2.96	1.43
GLAMOUR	5794	419	5376	1934	3.00	0.22	2.78
GOLF DIGEST	2157	1463	694	979	2.20	1.49	0.71
GOLF DIGEST/TENNIS (NET)	3195	2031	1164	1437	2.22	1.41	0.81
GOLF DIGEST/TENNIS (GROSS)	3228	2062	1166	1437	2.25	1.44	0.81
GOLF MAGAZINE	1833	1379	454	692	2.65	1.99	0.66
GOLF MAGAZINE/SKI (NET)	3621	2787	833	1077	3.36	2.59	0.77
GOLF MAGAZINE/SKI (GROSS)	3727	2862	865	1077	3.46	2.66	0.80
GOOD HOUSEKEEPING	17765	2562	15203	5115	3.47	0.50	2.97
HARPER'S BAZAAR	3150	281	2869	634	4.97	0.44	4.53
HEALTH	2321	611	1710	863	2.69	0.71	1.98
HEARST MAG CORP BUY(NET)	41275	12738	28537	17164	2.40	0.74	1.66
HEARST MAG CORP BUY(GROSS)	58306	16747	41559	17164	3.40	0.98	2.42
HEARST MEN'S PKG. (NET)	9944	8078	1866	2554	3.89	3.16	0.73
HEARST MEN'S PKG. (GROSS)	10977	8950	2027	2554	4.30	3.50	0.79
HOUSE BEAUTIFUL	4492	965	3526	855	5.25	1.13	4.13
INDUSTRY WEEK	714	649	65	299	2.39	2.17	0.22
INSIDE SPORTS	3292	2931	361	547	6.02	5.36	0.66
JET	6057	2902	3155	670	9.04	4.33	4.71
LADIES HOME JOURNAL	13961	1571	12390	5284	2.64	0.30	2.34
LHJ FAM GRP COMBO (NET)	17441	2640	14801	7290	2.39	0.36	2.03
LHJ FAM GRP COMBO (GROSS)	19054	2870	16184	7290	2.61	0.39	2.22
LIFE	9402	4865	4537	1347	6.98	3.61	3.37
L. A TIMES HOME MAGAZINE	2893	1436	1457	1318	2.20	1.09	1.11
MADEMOISELLE	3690	283	3407	1102	3.35	0.26	3.09
MCCALL'S	15142	1784	13359	6373	2.38	0.28	2.10
MECHANIX ILLUSTRATED	4661	3932	729	1607	2.90	2.45	0.45
METROPOLITAN HOME	1120	383	737	737	1.52	0.52	1.00

	AUDIENCE (000)			AVG CIRC (000)	READERS PER COPY·		
	TOTAL				TOTAL		
	ADULTS	MEN	WOMEN		ADULTS	MEN	WOMEN
TOTAL	161656	76155	85500	·	·	·	·
MONEY	3646	2214	1433	1090	3.34	2.03	1.31
MONTHLY MAG OF FOOD & WINE	769	374	395	356	2 16	1.05	1 11
MS.	1306	143	1162	472	2 77	0.30	2 46
NATIONAL ENQUIRER	15623	5852	9771	4516	3.46	1.30	2 16
NATIONAL GEOGRAPHIC	20566	10861	9705	8555	2.40	1.27	1.13
NAT'L SUPPLEMENT PK(NET)	98145	46871	51275	52581	1.87	0.89	0 98
NAT'L SUPPLEMENT PK(GROSS)	110281	53021	57260	52581	2.10	1.01	1.09
NATURAL HISTORY	1116	539	577	463	2.41	1.17	1.25
NEWSWEEK	16345	9927	6418	2987	5 47	3.32	2.15
NEW YORK INCLUDING CUE	1198	570	627	440	2.72	1.30	1.43
THE NY TIMES DAILY EDITION	3035	1661	1375	922	3.29	1.80	1 49
THE NY TIMES MAGAZINE	3944	2000	1944	1499	2.63	1.33	1.30
THE NEW YORKER	2344	1228	1116	480	4.88	2.56	2.32
OMNI	2833	1772	1061	622	4.56	2.85	1.71
1001 HOME IDEAS	2772	688	2084	1144	2.42	0.60	1 82
ORGANIC GARDENING	2911	1331	1580	1286	2.26	1.03	1.23
OUI	1705	1447	258	551	3 10	2.63	0 47
OUTDOOR LIFE	5047	3979	1068	1486	3.40	2.68	0.72
PARADE	43573	20456	23116	22008	1.98	0.93	1.05
PARENTS	3938	821	3117	1635	2.41	0.50	1.91
PENTHOUSE	6587	5399	1188	3317	1.99	1.63	0 36
PEOPLE	19403	7443	11960	2349	8.26	3.17	5.09
PLAYBOY	11134	9109	2026	4471	2.49	2.04	0.45
POPULAR HOT RODDING	2373	2144	229	241	9.86	8 91	0.95
POPULAR MECHANICS	6197	5194	1004	1543	4.02	3.37	0.65
POPULAR SCIENCE	4585	3870	715	1653	2.77	2.34	0.43
PREVENTION	4114	945	3169	2419	1 70	0.39	1.31
PSYCHOLOGY TODAY	AUDIENCE DATA NOT SHOWN BECAUSE OF CHANGE IN RATE BASE CIRCULATION						
READER'S DIGEST	39066	16528	22538	18517	2.11	0.89	1.22
REDBOOK	8679	1088	7590	4334	2.00	0.25	1.75
ROAD & TRACK	2666	2419	246	588	4.53	4.11	0.42
ROLLING STONE	4021	2729	1292	736	5.47	3.71	1.76
RUNNER'S WORLD	986	657	329	331	2 98	1.98	0.99
SATURDAY EVENING POST	2209	829	1380	607	3.64	1.37	2.27
SCIENCE DIGEST	1291	783	508	479	2.69	1.63	1.06
SCIENCE 82	1451	827	624	754	1.92	1.10	0.83
SCIENTIFIC AMERICAN	1883	1404	479	562	3.35	2.50	0.85
SELF	2310	326	1984	1023	2.26	0.32	1.94
SEVENTEEN	3110	334	2776	1384	2.25	0.24	2.01
SKI	1894	1483	411	385	4.92	3.85	1.07
SMITHSONIAN	4520	2263	2256	1955	2.31	1.16	1 15
SOAP OPERA DIGEST	3372	399	2973	582	5.79	0.69	5.11
SOUTHERN LIVING	4956	1433	3523	2065	2.40	0.69	1.71
SPORT	3734	3167	567	939	3.98	3.37	0.60
THE SPORTING NEWS	1848	1612	236	465	3 97	3.46	0.51
SPORTS AFIELD	3489	2974	515	532	6 56	5.59	0.97
SPORTS ILLUSTRATED	13248	10668	2581	2419	5.48	4.41	1.07
STAR	10348	3562	6785	3385	3.06	1.05	2.00
SUNDAY (NET)	47382	23027	24355	22723	2.09	1.01	1.07
SUNDAY (GROSS)	49300	24010	25290	22723	2.17	1.06	1.11
SUNSET	3464	1213	2251	1408	2.46	0.86	1.60
TENNIS	1071	599	472	457	2.34	1.31	1.03
TIME	20699	11806	8894	4561	4.54	2.59	1.95
TOWN & COUNTRY	1203	309	894	296	4.07	1.04	3.02
TRAVEL & LEISURE	1863	972	891	899	2.07	1.08	0.99
TRUE STORY	3732	433	3299	1446	2.58	0.30	2.28
TV GUIDE	36334	16702	19631	17782	2.04	0.94	1.10
US	3582	1334	2248	1022	3.50	1.31	2.20
U.S. NEWS & WORLD REPORT	9259	5885	3374	2109	4.39	2.79	1.60
VOGUE	4858	596	4262	1115	4.36	0.53	3.82
WALL STREET JOURNAL	6291	4253	2038	2035	3.09	2.09	1.00
WOMAN'S DAY	15825	998	14627	6705	2.36	0.15	2.21
WORKING MOTHER	875	70	806	371	2.36	0.19	2.17
WORKING WOMAN	1088	79	1009	487	2.23	0.16	2.07
WORLD TENNIS	614	306	308	365	1.68	0.84	0.84
ZIFF-DAVIS MAG NTWK(NET)	9767	7548	2219	3319	2.94	2.27	0.67
ZIFF-DAVIS MAG NTWK(GROSS)	12156	9618	2538	3319	3.66	2.90	0.76

· READERS PER COPY BASED ON 48 STATES.
SOURCE: ABC PUBLISHERS' STATEMENTS; PUBLISHERS' QUOTATIONS.

APPENDIX D

The 36 Qualifying Magazines

Rank	Magazine*	Audience (in thousands)
1.	Reader's Digest	39,066
2.	Better Homes & Gardens	21,045
3.	Time - W**	20,699
4.	People - W	19,403
5.	Ladies' Home Journal	19,045
6.	Family Circle	18,033
7.	Good Housekeeping	17,765
8.	Newsweek - W	16,345
9.	Woman's Day	15,825
10.	McCall's	15,142
11.	Sports Illustrated - W	13,248
12.	Cosmopolitan	9,596
13.	Life	9,402
14.	U.S. News & World Report - W	9,259
15.	Redbook	8,679
16.	Field & Stream	8,023
17.	Popular Mechanics	6,197
18.	Glamour	5,794
19.	Outdoor Life	5,047
20.	Vogue	4,858
21.	Mechanix Illustrated	4,661
22.	Popular Science	4,585
23.	House Beautiful	4,492
24.	Parents	3,938
25.	Mademoiselle	3,690
26.	Harper's Bazaar	3,150
27.	Family Handyman	3,134
28.	Seventeen	3,110
29.	Bon Appetit	2,987
30.	Self	2,310
31.	G.Q.	2,093
32.	Country Living	1,854
33.	Cuisine	1,726
34.	Town & Country	1,203
35.	Metropolitan Home	1,220
36.	Working Woman	1,088

---

* The odd-ranked magazines were selected for use in the miscomprehension study.
** W = weekly magazine.

APPENDIX E

Hall's Reports 18 Major Categories
For Sorting Magazine Editorial Content

100	National Affairs
200	Foreign/International
300	Amusements
400	Beauty and Grooming
500	Building
600	Business and Industry
700	Children
800	Gardening and Farming
900	Food and Nutrition
1000	Health/Medical Science
1100	Home Furnishings
1200	Sports/Recreation/Hobby
1300	Travel/Transportation
1400	Wearing Apparel
1500	Culture/Humanities
1600	General Interest
1700	Miscellaneous
1800	Fiction, Stories

APPENDIX F

The PIB Reports 29 Major Categories For Sorting Magazine Advertising Content

APPAREL SECTION

A100   Apparel, Footwear, Accessories

BUSINESS—FINANCIAL SECTION

B100   Business & Consumer Services
B200   Insurance
B300   Office Equipment, Stationary & Writing Supplies
B400   Publishing & Media
B500   Industrial Materials
B600   Freight, Industrial & Agricultural Development

DRUGS—TOILETRIES SECTION

D100   Toiletries & Cosmetics
D200   Drugs & Remedies

FOODS—BEVERAGE SECTION

F100   Food & Food Products
F200   Confectionery, Snacks & Soft Drinks
F300   Beer, Wine & Liquor

GENERAL— RETAIL SECTION

G100   Cigarettes, Tobacco & Accessories
G200   Jewelry, Optical Goods & Cameras
G300   Entertainment & Amusement
G400   Sporting Goods & Toys
G500   Miscellaneous
G600   Retail &/or Direct By Mail

HOME—BUILDING SECTION

H100   Household Furnishings
H200   Household Equipment & Supplies
H300   Home Entertainment Equipment
H400   Soaps, Cleansers & Polishes
H500   Building Materials, Equipment & Fixtures

TRANSPORTATION—AGRICULTURAL SECTION

T100   Automotive, Automotive Accessories & Equipment
T200   Gasoline, Lubricants & Fuels
T300   Aviation, Aviation Accessories & Equipment
T400   Travel, Hotels & Resorts
T500   Agriculture & Farming
T600   Horticulture

APPENDIX G

Main Study

Screener Questionnaire
and
Main Questionnaire
(for female respondents)

GUIDELINE RESEARCH CORPORATION
3 West 35th Street
New York, New York 10001

Job #Q01-013
February, 1985

MAGAZINE STUDY
- Screener -
Females

NAME:_____

ADDRESS: _____

CITY:_____ STATE: _____ ZIP:_____

TELEPHONE NUMBER: (   ) _____

INTERVIEWER:_____ DATE: _____

SAMPLE CLUSTER #: _____
(6)(7)(8)   (9)(10)

Hello, my name is _____ of Guideline Research Corporation, a nationwide market research organization. We're conducting a survey and we'd like to ask you a few questions about some of the things that appear on television and in magazines.

1. To begin with, could you please tell me how many females, 18 years of age and over, live in this household?

    RECORD #: _____ (IF "O" TERMINATE)   11-

2. In order for me to determine whom to interview, please give me the first name of those female family members who are 18 years of age and over. Let's start with the oldest and work down to the youngest. (RECORD NAMES BELOW).

3. (FOR EACH PERSON LISTED, ASK:)
    What is (NAME)'S age? (RECORD BELOW NEXT TO APPROPRIATE NAME.)

PERSON INTERVIEWED	NAME	AGE	
1	_____	_____	12-
2	_____	_____	13-
3	_____	_____	
4	_____	_____	
5	_____	_____	
6	_____	_____	
7	_____	_____	
8	_____	_____	

INTERVIEWER: REFER TO FIRST NUMBER ON STRIP (IN UPPER RIGHT CORNER). NOW REFER TO NUMBER TO THE LEFT OF NAMES YOU LISTED. INTERVIEW THE PERSON WHOSE NAME APPEARS ON THE LINE THAT HAS THE SAME NUMBER AS THE FIRST NUMBER ON THE STRIP. IF THERE IS NO NAME ON THAT LINE, CONTINUE IN THIS MANNER UNTIL YOU LOCATE A NUMBER/ LINE WITH A NAME ON IT. THIS IS THE ONLY PERSON ELIGIBLE TO BE INTERVIEWED IN THIS HOUSEHOLD. CIRCLE THE NUMBER TO THE LEFT OF THIS PERSON'S NAME.

IF DESIGNATED RESPONDENT IS NOT AT HOME, SET-UP APPOINTMENT FOR CALLBACK INTERVIEW.

DAY: _____ DATE: _____ TIME: _____

RESULTS OF CALLBACK ATTEMPTS

	NOT AT HOME	REFUSED INTERVIEW	INTERVIEWED
Callback #1	[ ]	[ ]	[ ]
Callback #2			

IF NECESSARY, INTRODUCE YOURSELF TO DESIGNATED RESPONDENT.

CONTINUE WITH Q. 4a ON SCREENER

165

-2-

4a. Do you usually watch some television at least once a week?
                    (14)
             Yes 1
             No .... 2 ___ (SKIP TO Q. 5a)

4b. On average, about how many hours of television would you say you watch <u>during a typical seven day week</u>? (RECORD NUMBER OF HOURS)
                              15-
           # HOURS: _____16-

5a. (ASK EVERYONE)
    Now thinking about magazines, do you <u>usually read</u> or <u>look through</u> some portion of a magazine at least once a month?
                         (17)
             Yes .... 1___ (CONTINUE WITH Q. 5b)
             No .... 2___ (TERMINATE, SAVE SCREENER. THIS <u>DOES NOT</u>
                                  COUNT TOWARDS YOUR QUOTA OF COMPLETED
                                  INTERVIEWS)

5b. <u>During a typical seven day week</u>, on average, about how many different magazines do you usually read or look through? (RECORD NUMBER OF MAGAZINES)
                                           18-
                  # MAGAZINES: _____19-

5c. What is the name of the magazine you read most often? (DO NOT READ LIST) (CIRCLE AS MANY AS MENTIONED.)

(20)	(21)	(22)
Bon Appetit 1	House Beautiful 1	Popular Science 1
Better Homes & Gardens 2	Ladies Home Journal .. 2	Readers Digest 2
Cosmopolitan 3	Life 3	Redbook 3
Country Living 4	Mademoiselle 4	Seventeen 4
Cuisine 5	McCalls 5	Self 5
Family Circle 6	Mechanix Illustrated . 6	Sports Illustrated .. 6
Family Handyman 7	Metropolitan Home 7	Time 7
Field & Stream 8	Newsweek 8	Town & Country 8
Gentlemen's Quarterly 9	Outdoor Life 9	U.S. News &
Glamour 0	Parents 0	World Report 9
Good Housekeeping X	People X	Vogue 0
Harper's Bazaar .... Y	Popular Mechanics .... Y	Woman's Day X
		Working Woman .... Y
		Other (SPECIFY:)
		_____ 23-
		_____ 24-
		_____
		_____
		_____

6a. (HAND CARD 6 AND LEAVE IN VIEW THROUGH Q. 61.) Here are the names of just a few of the hundreds of different magazines that are available in most parts of the United States. Please take a moment to look at this list. (WHEN RESPONDENT HAS FINISHED READING, CONTINUE.) Are there any magazines on this list that have you never heard of before today? (25)

       Yes .... 1 _____ (ASK Q. 6b)   No .... 2 ____ (SKIP TO Q. 6c)

6b. Which of these magazines have you never heard of before today? (RECORD ON GRID BELOW UNDER COL. Q.6b "NEVER HEARD OF")

6c. (ASK EVERYONE) Are you a regular reader of any magazines on this list? That is, do you read or look through at least one out of two issues of any of these magazines? (26)

       Yes .... 1 _____ (ASK Q. 6d)   No .... 2 ____ (TERMINATE. SAVE SCREENER.)

6d. Which magazines are they? (RECORD ON GRID BELOW UNDER COL. Q. 6d. "READ/LOOK AT") (IF ANY BOXED MAGAZINES CIRCLED, TERMINATE AND SAVE SCREENER.)

6e. (ASK EVERYONE) Have you, yourself, ever subscribed to any of these magazines? (27)

       Yes .... 1 _____ (ASK Q. 6f)   No .... 2 ____ (SKIP TO Q. 6g)

6f. Which magazines are they? (RECORD ON GRID BELOW UNDER COL. Q. 6f - "RESP. EVER SUBS.") (IF ANY BOXED MAGAZINES CIRCLED, TERMINATE AND SAVE SCREENER.)

6g. (ASK EVERYONE) To the best of your knowledge, has anyone else in this household ever subscribed to any of these magazines? (28)

       Yes .... 1 _____ (ASK Q. 6h)   No .... 2 ____ (SKIP TO Q. 6i)

6h. Which magazines are they? (RECORD ON GRID BELOW UNDER COL. Q.6h-"OTHER EVER SUBS")

6i. (ASK EVERYONE) Thinking about the present time, do you yourself currently subscribe to any of the magazines on this list? (29)

       Yes .... 1 _____ (ASK Q. 6j)   No .... 2 ____ (SKIP TO Q. 6k)

6j. To which of these magazines do you now subscribe? (RECORD ON GRID BELOW UNDER COL. Q. 6j - "RESP. NOW SUBS.) (IF ANY BOXED MAGAZINES CIRCLED, TERMINATE AND SAVE SCREENER.)

6k. (ASK EVERYONE) As best you know, does anyone else in this household currently subscribe to any other magazines on this list? (30)

       Yes .... 1 _____ (ASK Q. 61)   No .... 2 ____ (CONTINUE WITH MAIN QUESTIONNAIRE)

61. To which of these magazines do they subscribe? (RECORD ON GRID BELOW UNDER COL. Q. 61 - "OTHER NOW SUBS."). (THEN CONTINUE WITH MAIN QUESTIONNAIRE.)

	Q. 6b Never Heard Of (31)	Q. 6d Read/ Look At (33)	Q. 6f Resp. Ever Subs. (35)	Q. 6h Other Ever Subs. (37)	Q. 6j Resp. Now Subs. (39)	Q. 61 Other Now Subs. (41)
American Unicorn	1	1	1	1	1	1
Bon Appetit	2	2	2	2	2	2
Cuisine	3	3	3	3	3	3
Good Housekeeping	4	4	4	4	4	4
House Beautiful	5	5	5	5	5	5
Ladies Home Journal	6	6	6	6	6	6
Life	7	7	7	7	7	7
Mademoiselle	8	8	8	8	8	8
Metropolitan Home	9	9	9	9	9	9
News of the Globe	0	0	0	0	0	0
	(32)	(34)	(36)	(38)	(40)	(42)
Readers Digest	1	1	1	1	1	1
Redbook	2	2	2	2	2	2
Time	3	3	3	3	3	3
Woman's Day	4	4	4	4	4	4
No one else in household				Y		Y

TERMINATE AND SAVE SCREENER

REMOVE CARD 6. CONTINUE WITH MAIN QUESTIONNAIRE.

GUIDELINE RESEARCH CORPORATION
3 West 35th Street
New York, New York 10001

Job #Q01-013
February, 1985

MAGAZINE STUDY
- Main Questionnaire -
(FEMALES)

43-1

NAME: _____

TIME STARTED: _____ TIME ENDED: _____ TOTAL TIME: _____

1.   The next questions have to do with articles and ads that appear in the magazines
     that you just saw listed. I'm going to show you four different items taken from
     those magazines. Some of these are ads while others are brief passages taken from
     articles. After you've had a chance to read each, I'm going to ask you a few
     questions about it.

-2-

2. | HAND RESPONDENT [C2] AND SAY: | 6-
7- | | CARD II |

Here is the first item. Please read what it says, and tell me when you're finished.

| RECORD AMOUNT OF TIME RESPONDENT TAKES TO READ ITEM. | 8- |
| _____ MINUTES _____ SECONDS | 9-
10- |

3a. | REMOVE [C2] FROM VIEW AND ASK: |

What was the main message of the ad you just read? (IF RESPONDENT IS UNSURE, SAY: "What was the main point that was discussed in the ad you just read?")

_____ 11-
_____ 12-
_____ 13-
_____ 14-
_____ 15-
_____ 16-

3b. What other points were in the ad you just read? (IF RESPONDENT IS UNSURE, SAY: "What other things were discussed in the ad you just read?")

_____ 17-
_____ 18-
_____ 19-
_____ 20-
_____ 21-
_____ 22-

4. I'm going to give you a page listing six statements about the ad you just read. The purpose of these statements is to find out how well this ad did in getting its message across. Please answer these questions based only on what you just read and not on anything else you might have known about the subject before now. Just read each statement and circle whether you think it is true or false. (TURN TO STATEMENTS ON NEXT PAGE. HAND QUESTIONNAIRE AND PENCIL TO RESPONDENT.)

-3-

C 2

Based upon the ad you just read, which of the following statements is True and which is False?

Remember: Base your answers only upon what you think the ad said or implied.

	CIRCLE ONE ANSWER		
	True	False	Don't Know
1. The production line for the is automated with computers and robots	1	2	3 (23)
2. The is the fastest selling Chevrolet ..	1	2	3 (24)
3. The on-board computer allows the car to give better performance	1	2	3 (25)
4. The is a low-priced, yet high-quality automobile	1	2	3 (26)
5. The has a 3.0 liter engine	1	2	3 (27)
6. The has more horsepower than the 6 top selling imports	1	2	3 (28)

5. PLACE |C2| IN FRONT OF RESPONDENT ONCE AGAIN AND SAY:

How did you feel about this ad? Would you say you .. (READ LIST)
(29)

    Liked it very much 5
    Liked it 4
    Neither liked nor disliked it 3
    Disliked it, or 2
    Disliked it very much 1

6a. To the best of your knowledge, have you ever seen this particular ad before?
(30)

    Yes .... 1—— (ASK Q. 6b)
    No .... 2——
    Don't know .... 3—┘ (SKIP TO Q. 6c)

6b. Approximately how many times before today had you seen this particular ad? (DO NOT ACCEPT A RANGE. PROBE FOR A SPECFIC NUMBER)
31-
TIMES: _____32-

6c. (ASK EVERYONE)
Other than this particular ad, approximately how many times have you seen other ads for this very same brand? (DO NOT ACCEPT A RANGE. PROBE FOR A SPECIFIC NUMBER)
33-
TIMES: _____34-

7a. Before today, had you yourself ever bought or used _____?
. (CATEGORY)
(35)

    Yes 1
    No .... 2—— (SKIP TO Q. 8)

7b. And would that have been ... (READ LIST)
(36)

    Very frequently 4
    Frequently 3
    Sometimes, or 2
    Rarely 1

7c. Have you yourself, ever bought or used _____?
(37)   (BRAND)

    Yes 1
    No .... 2—— (SKIP TO Q. 8)

7d. And, would that have been ... (READ LIST)
(38)

    Very frequently 4
    Frequently 3
    Sometimes, or 2
    Rarely 1

8. Thinking about how _____ relates to you in your everyday life, would you say it is ... (CATEGORY) (READ LIST)
(39)

    Very important 5
    Important 4
    Neither important nor unimportant 3
    Unimportant, or 2
    Very unimportant 1

REMOVE |C2| FROM VIEW. CONTINUE WITH NEXT PAGE.

40-79 REJ

80-2

-2-

2. | HAND RESPONDENT $E5$ AND SAY: | 6-
7- | | CARD III |

Here is another item. Please read what it says, and tell me when you're finished.

| RECORD AMOUNT OF TIME RESPONDENT TAKES TO READ ITEM. | 8-
9-
_____ MINUTES _____ SECONDS | 10- |

3a. | REMOVE $E5$ FROM VIEW AND ASK: |

What was the main message of the ad you just read? (IF RESPONDENT IS UNSURE, SAY: "What was the main point that was discussed in the ad you just read?")

_____ 11-
_____ 12-
_____ 13-
_____ 14-
_____ 15-
_____ 16-

3b. What other points were in the ad you just read? (IF RESPONDENT IS UNSURE, SAY: "What other things were discussed in the ad you just read?")

_____ 17-
_____ 18-
_____ 19-
_____ 20-
_____ 21-
_____ 22-

4. I'm going to give you a page listing six statements about the ad you just read. The purpose of these statements is to find out how well this ad did in getting its message across. Please answer these questions based only on what you just read and not on anything else you might have known about the subject before now. Just read each statement and circle whether you think it is true or false. (TURN TO STATEMENTS ON NEXT PAGE. HAND QUESTIONNAIRE AND PENCIL TO RESPONDENT.)

-3-

E 5

Based upon the passage you just read, which of the following statements is True and which is False?

Remember: Base your answers only upon what you think the passage said or implied.

	CIRCLE ONE ANSWER		
	True	False	Don't Know
1. You should not take medications	1	2	3 (23)
2. Commonly used medications can cause a loss of hearing	1	2	3 (24)
3. The dosage plays a role in determining side effects	1	2	3 (25)
4. In most cases, side effects cause permanent damage	1	2	3 (26)
5. Almost all medications have dangerous side effects	1	2	3 (27)
6. People who have used medications for a long time are more likely to have side effects than those who have used them for a short time	1	2	3 (28)

-4-

WHEN RESPONDENT HAS FINISHED, CHECK TO MAKE CERTAIN EACH STATEMENT HAS BEEN ANSWERED. IF ANY ARE NOT ANSWERED, HAND BACK TO RESPONDENT. POINT TO STATEMENTS NOT ANSWERED & SAY: "WOULD YOU PLEASE PUT DOWN ANSWERS TO THESE STATEMENTS."

5. PLACE $E5$ IN FRONT OF RESPONDENT ONCE AGAIN AND SAY:

How did you feel about this ad? Would you say you .. (READ LIST)
(29)
Liked it very much 5
Liked it 4
Neither liked nor disliked it 3
Disliked it, or 2
Disliked it very much 1

6a. To the best of your knowledge, have you ever seen this particular ad before?
(30)
Yes .... 1— (ASK Q. 6b)
No 2
Don't know .... 3⌐ (SKIP TO Q. 6c)

6b. Approximately how many times before today had you seen this particular ad? (DO NOT ACCEPT A RANGE. PROBE FOR A SPECFIC NUMBER)
31-
TIMES: _____ 32-

6c. (ASK EVERYONE)
Other than this particular ad, approximately how many times have you seen other ads for this very same brand? (DO NOT ACCEPT A RANGE. PROBE FOR A SPECIFIC NUMBER)
33-
TIMES: _____ 34-

7a. Before today, had you yourself ever bought or used _____?
(CATEGORY)
(35)
Yes 1
No .... 2— (SKIP TO Q. 8)

7b. And would that have been ... (READ LIST)
(36)
Very frequently 4
Frequently 3
Sometimes, or 2
Rarely 1

7c. Have you yourself, ever bought or used _____?
(37) (BRAND)
Yes 1
No .... 2— (SKIP TO Q. 8)

7d. And, would that have been ... (READ LIST)
(38)
Very frequently 4
Frequently 3
Sometimes, or 2
Rarely 1

8. Thinking about how _____ relates to you in your everyday life, would you say it is ... (CATEGORY) (READ LIST)
(39)
Very important 5
Important 4
Neither important nor unimportant 3
Unimportant, or 2
Very unimportant 1

40-79 REJ
80-3

REMOVE $E5$ FROM VIEW. CONTINUE WITH NEXT PAGE.

-2-

2. | HAND RESPONDENT $\boxed{L3}$ AND SAY: | 6-
7- | | | | $\boxed{\text{CARD IV}}$ |

Here is another item. Please read what it says, and tell me when you're finished.

| RECORD AMOUNT OF TIME RESPONDENT TAKES TO READ ITEM. | 8- |
| _____ MINUTES _____ SECONDS | 9-
10- |

3a. | REMOVE $\boxed{L3}$ FROM VIEW AND ASK: |

What was the main message of the passage you just read? (IF RESPONDENT IS UNSURE, SAY: "What was the main point that was discussed in the passage you just read?")

_____ 11-
_____ 12-
_____ 13-
_____ 14-
_____ 15-
_____ 16-

3b. What other points were in the passage you just read? (IF RESPONDENT IS UNSURE, SAY: "What other things were discussed in the passage you just read?")

_____ 17-
_____ 18-
_____ 19-
_____ 20-
_____ 21-
_____ 22-

4. I'm going to give you a page listing six statements about the passage you just read. The purpose of these statements is to find out how well this passage did in getting its message across. Please answer these questions based only on what you just read and not on anything else you might have known about the subject before now. Just read each statement and circle whether you think it is true or false. (TURN TO STATEMENTS ON NEXT PAGE. HAND QUESTIONNAIRE AND PENCIL TO RESPONDENT.)

-3-

L 3

Based upon the ad you just read, which of the following statements is True and which is False?

<u>Remember</u>: Base your answers <u>only</u> upon what you think the ad said or implied.

	CIRCLE ONE ANSWER		
	True	False	Don't Know
1. A "peppermint twist" is mixed with ice and water	1	2	3	(23)
2. One can obtain a free recipe booklet merely by writing to	1	2	3	(24)
3. has existed since 1858	1	2	3	(25)
4. does not want you to drink alone ..	1	2	3	(26)
5. The only way to drink peppermint schnapps is over ice	1	2	3	(27)
6. Peppermint Schnapps tastes better than "no-name" brands	1	2	3	(28)

-4-

WHEN RESPONDENT HAS FINISHED, CHECK TO MAKE CERTAIN EACH STATEMENT HAS BEEN
ANSWERED. IF ANY ARE NOT ANSWERED, HAND BACK TO RESPONDENT. POINT TO
STATEMENTS NOT ANSWERED & SAY: "WOULD YOU PLEASE PUT DOWN ANSWERS FOR THESE
STATEMENTS."

---

5.   PLACE $\boxed{L3}$ IN FRONT OF RESPONDENT ONCE AGAIN AND SAY:

How did you feel about this passage? Would you say it was .. (READ LIST)
(29)
```
Very interesting ..................... 5
Interesting .......................... 4
Neither interesting nor boring ...... 3
Boring, or ........................... 2
Very boring .......................... 1
```

6a.   To the best of your knowledge, have you ever seen this particular passage before?
(30)
```
Yes .............. 1 ──→ (ASK Q. 6b)
No ............... 2 ┐
Don't know ....... 3 ┘──→(SKIP TO Q. 6c)
```

6b.   Approximately how many times before today had you seen this particular passage?
(DO NOT ACCEPT A RANGE. PROBE FOR A SPECIFIC NUMBER)
31-
TIMES: _____ 32-

6c.   (ASK EVERYONE)
What about other magazines or newspaper stories dealing with the very same topic?
Before today, approximately how many other articles have you looked at or read
about this very same topic? (DO NOT ACCEPT A RANGE. PROBE FOR A SPECIFIC NUMBER)
33-
ARTICLES _____ 34-

7.   Would you say that you read similar material on this topic ... (READ LIST)
(35)
```
Very frequently ........ 4
Frequently ............. 3
Sometimes, or .......... 2
Rarely ................. 1
```

8.   Thinking about how this topic relates to you in your everyday life, would you say
it was ... (READ LIST)
(36)
```
Very important ........................ 5
Important ............................. 4
Neither important nor unimportant .... 3
Unimportant, or ....................... 2
Very unimportant ...................... 1
```

REMOVE $\boxed{L3}$ FROM VIEW.
CONTINUE WITH NEXT PAGE.

37-79 REJ
80-4

-2-

2. | HAND RESPONDENT $F6$ AND SAY: | 6-
7- | CARD V |

Here is another item. Please read what it says, and tell me when you're finished.

| RECORD AMOUNT OF TIME RESPONDENT TAKES TO READ ITEM. | 8-
9-
_____ MINUTES _____ SECONDS | 10-

3a. | REMOVE $F6$ FROM VIEW AND ASK: |

What was the main message of the passage you just read? (IF RESPONDENT IS UNSURE,
SAY: "What was the main point that was discussed in the passage you just read?")

_____ 11-
_____ 12-
_____ 13-
_____ 14-
_____ 15-
_____ 16-

3b. What other points were in the passage you just read? (IF RESPONDENT IS UNSURE,
SAY: "What other things were discussed in the passage you just read?")

_____ 17-
_____ 18-
_____ 19-
_____ 20-
_____ 21-
_____ 22-

4.   I'm going to give you a page listing six statements about the passage you just
read. The purpose of these statements is to find out how well this passage did in
getting its message across. Please answer these questions based only on what you
just read and not on anything else you might have known about the subject before
now. Just read each statement and circle whether you think it is true or false.
(TURN TO STATEMENTS ON NEXT PAGE. HAND QUESTIONNAIRE AND PENCIL TO RESPONDENT.)

-3-

F 6

Based upon the passage you just read, which of the following statements is True and which is False?

Remember: Base your answers only upon what you think the passage said or implied.

	CIRCLE ONE ANSWER		
	True	False	Don't Know
1. The drop waist dress is ideal for thin people .. 1		2	3	(23)
2. The collarless style makes a thick neck less obvious 1		2	3	(24)
3. The drop waist dress can be worn by women with heavy thighs 1		2	3	(25)
4. This dress is perfect for maternity wear 1		2	3	(26)
5. The drop waist dress should fit loosely 1		2	3	(27)
6. The drop waist dress is of good quality 1		2	3	(28)

-4-

> WHEN RESPONDENT HAS FINISHED, CHECK TO MAKE CERTAIN EACH STATEMENT HAS BEEN
> ANSWERED. IF ANY ARE NOT ANSWERED, HAND BACK TO RESPONDENT. POINT TO
> STATEMENTS NOT ANSWERED & SAY: "WOULD YOU PLEASE PUT DOWN ANSWERS FOR THESE
> STATEMENTS."

5. PLACE F6 IN FRONT OF RESPONDENT ONCE AGAIN AND SAY:

How did you feel about this passage? Would you say it was .. (READ LIST)
(29)
Very interesting 5
Interesting 4
Neither interesting nor boring 3
Boring, or 2
Very boring 1

6a. To the best of your knowledge, have you ever seen this particular passage before?
(30)
Yes .... 1 ──→ (ASK Q. 6b)
No 2
Don't know .... 3 ──→(SKIP TO Q. 6c)

6b. Approximately how many times before today had you seen this particular passage?
(DO NOT ACCEPT A RANGE. PROBE FOR A SPECIFIC NUMBER)
31-
TIMES: _____ 32-

6c. (ASK EVERYONE)
What about other magazines or newspaper stories dealing with the very same topic?
Before today, approximately how many other articles have you looked at or read
about this very same topic? (DO NOT ACCEPT A RANGE. PROBE FOR A SPECIFIC NUMBER)
33-
ARTICLES _____ 34-

7. Would you say that you read similar material on this topic ... (READ LIST)
(35)
Very frequently 4
Frequently 3
Sometimes, or 2
Rarely 1

8. Thinking about how this topic relates to you in your everyday life, would you say
it was ... (READ LIST)
(36)
Very important 5
Important 4
Neither important nor unimportant 3
Unimportant, or 2
Very unimportant 1

REMOVE F6 FROM VIEW.
CONTINUE WITH NEXT PAGE.

37-79 REJ
80-5

-5-

9. I have just a few final questions which are used for statistical classification
    purposes only. Are you ... (READ LIST)
                                          (44)
                              Single 1
                              Married 2
                              Widowed 3
                              Divorced, or 4
                              Separated 5
        (DO NOT READ)———▶Refused .... Y

10. What was the last grade of school that you completed? (DO NOT READ)
                                                                    (45)
                      Eighth grade or less 1
                      1-3 years high school 2
                      High school graduate 3
                      Attended college/did not graduate .. 4
                      Graduated 2 year college 5
                      Graduated 4 year college 6
                      Attended graduate school 7
                      Advanced (graduate school) degree .. 8
        (DO NOT READ)———▶Refused .... Y

11a. Are you currently employed?
                                    (46)
                      Yes 1
                      No 2
        (DO NOT READ)———▶Refused .... 3———▶(SKIP TO Q. 12)

11b. Are you employed ... (READ LIST)
                                                            (47)
                Full-time -- that is 30 hours a week or more, or 1
                Part-time -- less than 30 hours a week 2

12. (ASK EVERYONE) (SHOW CARD 12)
    Finally, we classify people into broad income groups. Please read me the letter
    which corresponds to your total annual family income before taxes.
                                          (48)
                      A. Under $10,000 1
                      B. $10,000 - $14,999 2
                      C. $15,000 - $19,999 3
                      D. $20,000 - $24,999 4
                      E. $25,000 - $34,999 5
                      F. $35,000 - $49,999 6
                      G. $50,000 - $74,999 7
                      H. $75,000 and over 8
        (DO NOT READ)———▶Refused 0

            ┌───┐
            │ THANK YOU VERY MUCH FOR YOUR COOPERATION! │
            └───┘

                                          ┌──────────────┐
                                          │ 44-79 REJ   │
                                          ├──────────────┤
                                          │   80-1   │
                                          └──────────────┘

APPENDIX H

Pre-test Questionnaire

GUIDELINE RESEARCH CORPORATION   Q01-013A
3 West 35th Street
New York, New York   10001   January, 1985

<u>MAGAZINE STUDY</u>
- Main Questionnaire -

FEMALES

RESPONDENT'S NAME: _____

1.   Next month, we'll be starting a survey, all around the country, on how well people
      understand the material that appears in national magazines. Before that survey can
      begin, we need to make certain that the questions we ask are easily understood.
      That is what we are doing now.

2.   HAND RESPONDENT $L3$

      First, please take time to read this. Please tell me when you're finished reading
      it. (WHEN RESPONDENT HAS FINISHED, CONTINUE:)
      I'm going to hand you a page that contains six statements that we're thinking of
      using next month. As I mentioned, we'd like to make certain that they are easily
      understood.

      We don't need your answers. All you have to do is simply indicate if each of the
      statements is clear to you. Please read the first statement. If the entire
      statement is clear to you, simply write "OK" next to it. If certain portions of
      the statement are not clear to you, or if you don't understand it, simply circle
      those words or phrases which are not clear.

      HAND RESPONDENT QUIZ LABELLED $L3$

      (ALLOW RESPONDENT SUFFICIENT TIME TO FINISH ALL 6 STATEMENTS.)

3.   HAND RESPONDENT $A3$

      Now, please take time to read this. Please tell me when you're finished reading
      it.
      (WHEN RESPONDENT HAS FINISHED, HAND QUIZ LABELLED $A3$ AND REPEAT DIRECTIONS
      ABOVE.)

4.   REPEAT FOR $B4$

5.   REPEAT FOR $H6$

6.   Finally, please tell me what was the last grade of school you completed? (DO NOT
      READ LIST)

                        Eighth grade or less 1
                        1-3 years high school 2
                        High school graduate 3
                        Attended college/did not graduate 4
                        Graduated 2 year college 5
                        Graduated 4 year college 6
                        Attended graduate school 7
                        Advanced (graduate school) degree 8
              (DO NOT READ) Refused .... Y

APPENDIX I

Communications and Quizzes for many of the 54 Editorial Stimuli

Note: An attempt was made to include all 54 non-advertising test communications and their corresponding quizzes in this Appendix. As a number of authors and/or publications denied our request for permission to reproduce, only about half of these communications are included here.

The communications that are included are presented in alphabetical order by name of the magazines in which they appeared. Further, it should be pointed out that in some cases the communications have been photographically reduced to fit on the pages of this volume.

LIGHT AND REFRESHING LEMON DESSERTS

BY OLIVIA ERSCHEN
PHOTOGRAPHS BY VICTOR SCOCOZZA

DESSERTS ARE MY SPECIALTY, so naturally I tend to view the seasons in terms of the pastry cart: Berries and ice creams are great in summer, earthy tarts and robust steamed puddings help me through the fall and winter. But when it comes to springtime, I want something lighter and more refreshing—and sometimes just a little bit glamorous. In my opinion, nothing satisfies as perfectly as the tang of lemon.

Actually, I have been equating lemon with this time of year ever since I took the first bite of my grandmother's lemon meringue pie. For years, no matter what kind of pastry I was eating, I imagined how it could be transformed into something with lemon. And when I began to travel extensively and study food, my list of favorite lemon desserts grew to include a *tarte au citron* I learned while working as a pastry chef, a *vacherin* I enjoyed at a popular restaurant and the *miroir* cakes I saw in Paris. Now my repertoire includes everything from an easy lemon and berry "parfait" to an elaborate Frozen Lemon and Meringue Cake.

J 4

Based upon the passage you just read, which of the following statements is True and which is False?

Remember: Base your answers only upon what you think the passage said or implied.

	CIRCLE ONE ANSWER		
	True	False	Don't Know
1. The author thinks that tarts and puddings are best in the fall 1		2	3 (23)
2. The author once worked as a pastry chef 1		2	3 (24)
3. The author's favorite springtime desserts involve the taste of lemon 1		2	3 (25)
4. Lemon desserts are the only type of desserts the author likes to make 1		2	3 (26)
5. Ms. Erschen has a variety of recipes from around the world 1		2	3 (27)
6. The author's grandmother taught her how to make lemon desserts 1		2	3 (28)

Ravioli, those tasty little packets that most often contain some variation of a veal and cheese filling, are ideal containers for any number of stuffings. The combination of chicken livers braised in Marsala and mixed with toasted chopped walnuts is a particularly delicious one. We like to wrap this mixture in spinach pasta and then top it with a light *besciamella* sauce.

J 5

Based upon the passage you just read, which of the following statements is True and which is False?

Remember: Base your answers only upon what you think the passage said or implied.

| | CIRCLE ONE ANSWER | | |
	True	False	Don't Know
1. Veal and cheese variations are common fillings for ravioli 1		2	3 (23) T\F
2. The authors recommend using a spinach pasta for a specific dish 1		2	3 (24) T\F
3. Ravioli are bland tasting no matter what they are stuffed with 1		2	3 (25) F\F
4. The authors probably do not have a good deal of experience in making ravioli dishes 1		2	3 (26) F\I
5. It is better to stick with the same recipe and make only slight variations when it comes to making a ravioli dish 1		2	3 (27) F\I
6. The authors enjoy creating different combinations for ravioli fillings 1		2	3 (28) T\I

Cruises and Crossings

Travel narrows the mind, a friend once said. He meant of course that the more we journey, the more we judge. But it is difficult for even the most seasoned traveler to contemplate a sea voyage with anything less than the highest expectations. And Cunard's *Queen Elizabeth II* doesn't disappoint.

Cruises and ocean trips should be about luxury, courtesy and romance, and these elements are always on hand. Cunard is justly proud of the spacious accommodations it has to offer. Whether in transatlantic or first class, the cabins have good creature comforts, ample closets and private baths. Passengers are attended by a room steward and stewardess who cater to any wish throughout the trip.

There is a nonstop program of activities: The dance floors and gaming rooms are favored spots for many. And there are unexpected events such as Grandparents' Get Together (an exchange of photographs and stories), spelling bees, chess tournaments, and lectures on a variety of topics from financial management to art. For the relentlessly athletic, there are indoor and outdoor swimming pools, trapshooting and a well-equipped gymnasium. Hearty types can even have a run around the deck.

But the main activity during most passages is eating. Executive chef John Bainbridge, who has been with the *QE II* since she was commissioned in 1969, supervises a kitchen that can produce 10,000 abundant meals a day. The handsome, well-upholstered chef says, "We will prepare anything for our passengers if we have advance notice. We can do Pritikin diet meals, Live Longer diets, you name it. We never like to say 'no.' " But his heart is with those who look forward to a cruise as a time to indulge, and for them he offers a new menu at every meal, a wide variety of choices and classic dishes beautifully presented.

Despite the temptations of the table—both dining and gambling—there is time to sit alone in a deck chair and watch the water, whales and an occasional supertanker. For many of us in these hurried times, this kind of privacy is really the greatest luxury.

J 6

Based upon the passage you just read, which of the following statements is True and which is False?

Remember: Base your answers only upon what you think the passage said or implied.

CIRCLE ONE ANSWER

	True	False	Don't Know	
1. The Cunard's Queen Elizabeth II is very concerned about keeping its passengers happy .	1	2	3	(23)
2. Passengers on the Queen Elizabeth II can expect to find luxury, romance, and courtesy .	1	2	3	(24)
3. The Queen Elizabeth II is mainly a seagoing health club	1	2	3	(25)
4. The executive chef on the Queen Elizabeth II claims that there are seldom any requests for special diet meals to be prepared	1	2	3	(26)
5. The Queen Elizabeth II has special spelling bees for grandparents	1	2	3	(27)
6. Even someone with discriminating tastes would be satisfied with the Queen Elizabeth II	1	2	3	(28)

Corfu Town's Citadel, a fortress and lighthouse built on a promontory, mixes Byzantine and Venetian architecture.

CORFU

GREECE WITH A DIFFERENT FLAVOR

BY WILLIAM BAYER AND PAULA WOLFERT

One travels the Mediterranean in search of paradise: those timeless places where trees are laden with fruit, the earth is pungent with wild herbs, fish are freshly caught, vegetables taste the way they should, light glitters off white houses, water is sweet, wine is good, and the sand is clean.

This is the Mediterranean myth of a robust, simple life: perfect lunches, long siestas, moonlight swims, a friendly village café. We think of Robert Graves in Majorca; the Gerald Murphys in Cap d'Antibes; Delacroix in Tangier; Byron, Henry Miller, and Lawrence Durrell in Greece; as well as the scores of artists for whom "living well was the best revenge" and who understood the sophistication of simplicity, the taste of bread and cheese, the feel of the sun upon one's skin, the sight of sheep grazing on a hillside, and the sound of water gently lapping against sea-carved rocks.

K 4

Based upon the passage you just read, which of the following statements is True and which is False?

Remember: Base your answers only upon what you think the passage said or implied.

CIRCLE ONE ANSWER

	True	False	Don't Know
1. The Mediterranean myth includes visions of people leading a simple life	1	2	3 (23)
2. Corfu is actually part of Italy	1	2	3 (24)
3. Both Byzantine and Venetian architecture are reflected in Corfu Town's Citadel	1	2	3 (25)
4. The authors think that Corfu is a great place to live	1	2	3 (26)
5. The main occupations of Corfu are fishing and growing fruit	1	2	3 (27)
6. The authors think that artists could be too sophisticated to enjoy life in Corfu	1	2	3 (28)

JACQUES PEPIN ON TECHNIQUE

Preparing Asparagus

Perhaps more than any other vegetable, asparagus conveys the coming of spring. Both the thin, mild green asparagus commonly found in our markets and its larger white European counterpart are sprouts growing from subterranean roots called crowns. The white asparagus is kept underground as it grows, to ensure its whiteness and endow it with a specific taste, while our common green variety is allowed to mature aboveground, where it develops a beautiful green color with touches of purple.

Whichever asparagus you choose, be sure to select tight, firm spears, identifying features of young and tender specimens. As asparagus gets older, the tips of its spears—the "flowers"—will open and crumble and the stems will wrinkle. This indicates a tougher and drier asparagus, past its prime.

K 6

Based upon the passage you just read, which of the following statements is True and which is False?

Remember: Base your answers only upon what you think the passage said or implied.

| | CIRCLE ONE ANSWER | | |
	True	False	Don't Know
1. The asparagus sold in American supermarkets and grocery stores is a sprout that grows from underground roots called crowns	1	2	3 (23) T\F
2. The asparagus found in Europe is typically green	1	2	3 (24) F\F
3. One can tell that asparagus is young if it has a tight stem	1	2	3 (25) T\F
4. Fresh asparagus can only be bought in the spring	1	2	3 (26) F\I
5. Asparagus should only be eaten if it is young ..	1	2	3 (27) T\I
6. It is better to eat white asparagus than green asparagus	1	2	3 (28) F\I

BLUEPRINTS

BUILD YOUR OWN TIMBERLINE RETREAT

E ach spring, I dust off the old plans for the vacation retreat I've planned to build some day when funds permit. If you, too, have a "dream house," or if your ship has finally come in and a second home is now financially possible, consider this all-cedar beauty. Whether your ideal vacation is to ski in the "high lonesome" country of the Sierras, where this home is located, or to dig clams on the Maine seashore, this Timberline model by Justus Homes will make a perfect retreat for your family.

The big bay windows bring all the outdoors into both the first floor and loft, whatever the view from your site. The dining and living areas combine into a great room, and the loft can be finished with plenty of storage and sleeping space for times when you get the whole gang together.

Testimonials from past customers attest that the design and manufacturer's instructions make the home easy for even an amateur to assemble. The basic wall components are 4-in. x 8-in., kiln-dried, double tongue and groove cedar timbers. The corners are dovetailed rather than overlapped in conventional log style. Heavy-duty "Arctic" insulation packages are available where required.

Other options include cedar decks and rails, garages, all-weather wood foundations, kits for finishing basements, and interior finish kits that include kitchen cabinets, electrical hardware, plumbing and appliances.

Prices vary by model (300 standard plans are offered), size and options chosen. For a contractor-built, "turnkey" complete house, figure between $45 and $75 per square foot. If you do all the work yourself estimate a cost between $35 and $45 per sq. ft. With the owner-builder approach (hiring some subcontract help) estimate somewhere between these two ranges.

For more information, send $5 for a 64-page portfolio to Justus Co., Inc., Dept. FH, P.O. Box 98300, Tacoma, WA 98499. — **Gary Branson**

In 1981, Justus Homes won the "Best in the West" Gold Nugget Award from Builder magazine and the Pacific Coast Builders Conference for the best manufactured home. Justus offers 300 stock designs to choose from, but will produce your own plans from their custom design service.

The interiors (right) suggest the aroma of fresh-sawn cedar. All-cedar construction promises low maintenance inside and out; the exterior can be left unfinished to weather to a soft gray. The loft plan below is one option for an interior arrangement.

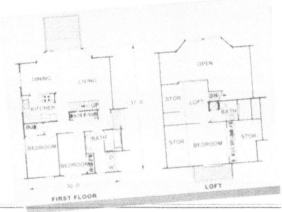

FIRST FLOOR

LOFT

Q 4

Ba d upon the passage you just read, which of the following statements is True and
wh: h is False?

Remember: Base your answers only upon what you think the passage said or implied.

	CIRCLE ONE ANSWER		
	True	False	Don't Know
1. This home would be easy for an amateur to assemble	1	2	3
2. This home is made of oak	1	2	3
3. This home should be built for use only as a vacation retreat	1	2	3
4. This home has plenty of storage and sleeping space	1	2	3
5. This home would not be difficult to keep warm in the winter	1	2	3
6. This home is constructed with pre-assembled sections	1	2	3

Please don't eat the tulips

Flower gardens are enjoyable for young and old alike, but keep an eye on young children playing in the garden. The National Safety Council warns that some spring-blossoming plants are poisonous. Also, U.S. Poison Control Centers say plants have become the most frequent cause of child poisonings.

Tulips and Lily-of-the-Valley, among the first to bloom in the spring, can cause extreme discomfort, though they are not deadly. Philodendrons cause swelling and irritation of the mouth and throat when eaten, and can be deadly.

The NSC recommends that you keep these points in mind to prevent nibbling of plants and to treat symptoms if plants have been ingested:

- Learn the scientific name of any indoor plant you buy and label it on the planter, or stick a label marker in the soil. If your child eats the plant, you can identify it when you contact your doctor, nearest poison control center or hospital emergency room. For outside gardens, keep a file book of scientific names. For instance, Lily-of-the-Valley is *Convallaria majalis.*

- Keep houseplants out of reach of young children. Use shelves or hanging pots. Never put a plant in a child's bedroom.

- When gardening outside, keep unplanted bulbs and seeds out of your children's reach.

- If a child eats a plant, call your poison control center or doctor immediately. Do not induce vomiting unless a physician recommends it.

For more information, write to the National Safety Council, Dept. FH, 444 N. Michigan Ave., Chicago, IL 60611. — **Ray Lorenz**

Q 5

Based upon the passage you just read, which of the following statements is True and which is False?

Remember: Base your answers only upon what you think the passage said or implied.

	CIRCLE ONE ANSWER		
	True	False	Don't Know
1. If a child were to eat a philodendron, he could die	1	2	3 (23)
2. You should not grow spring flowers if children will be around	1	2	3 (24)
3. If a child eats a plant, you should immediately induce vomiting	1	2	3 (25)
4. By taking simple precautions, you can reduce the dangers associated with spring flowers	1	2	3 (26)
5. Plants have become the most frequent cause of child poisonings	1	2	3 (27)
6. If a child eats a tulip, there is little cause for concern	1	2	3 (28)

THOMSON'S TOMATO PICKS FOR 1984

Dozens of tomato varieties are available on the market, and all gardeners have their personal favorites, but I think that you should grow more than one type. One may be better suited than another for your climate and soil conditions. By growing several different varieties you won't be putting all your eggs into one basket.

I suggest that you plant nothing but hybrid varieties, such as **Better Boy, Champion, Jetstar, Supersonic** or **Celebrity.** Hybrids are highly disease resistant and have terrific growth characteristics.

If you're planning to grow tomatoes in wire cages, consider a determinate variety such as **Celebrity,** a new hybrid. Celebrity grows to a height of about 5 ft. and stops. Its energy is then concentrated into developing the fruit. A determinate tomato's terminal buds set fruit and stop stem growth, so it is self-topping and doesn't require staking.

Celebrity is my top choice for 1984. In addition to being ideal for cage growth, it has a perfect fruit form, a wonderful flavor, grows to 7 oz. or more, and is disease resistant. I've already tested it, and I think it's a super tomato for America's gardens.

I recommend **Floramerica** for southern gardens. Very popular in Alabama, Georgia and Louisiana, it's a hybrid determinate, highly disease resistant, and grows large, handsome fruits.

Beefmaster is ideal for the south and west, but it will grow anywhere. It's disease resistant, a hybrid indeterminate, and produces 2-lb. tomatoes on fast-growing vines.

Better Boy is an indeterminate hybrid that is grown nationwide. Its fruits weigh up to 16 oz., are perfect for slicing, and the plant is disease resistant. It can be caged, but should be staked for best results. Better Boy is known for its vigorous vine growth.

Champion, a hybrid indeterminate, is an early maturing variety, highly disease resistant, weighs about 7 oz., and is fine tasting.

Jetstar is a more compact-growing hybrid indeterminate that is ideal for caging or staking. Fruits grow to 7 oz. to 8 oz. This plant also has a high disease resistance. It's popular in southern and western states.

Photo: Gardens for All

```
┌──────────┐
│   0 6    │
└──────────┘
```

Based upon the passage you just read, which of the following statements is True and which is False?

Remember: Base your answers only upon what you think the passage said or implied.

	True	False	Don't Know
		CIRCLE ONE ANSWER	

	True	False	Don't Know	
1. Thomson's top pick for 1984 is the Champion tomato	1	2	3	(23)
2. Thomson suggests that you should only plant hybrid tomatoes	1	2	3	(24)
3. Hybrid tomatoes are not as being as regular tomatoes	1	2	3	(25)
4. There is one type of tomato that is best for each area of the country	1	2	3	(26)
5. Hybrid tomatoes taste as good as regular tomatoes	1	2	3	(27)
6. If you grow several different varieties of tomatoes, the chances of having a good yield are greater	1	2	3	(28)

The tragic leading ladies

From the famous daily, *The Hollywood Reporter*, comes this inside account of two consummate stars who *almost* had everything.

By Tichi Wilkerson and Marcia Borie

In the early fall of 1930, twenty-four-year-old producer and director Howard Hughes plucked lovely Jean Harlow from the ranks of Hollywood extras. He started her on the road to stardom in his \$4-million production of *Hell's Angels*. After his press agent, Linc Quarberg, dubbed Jean "the platinum blonde," the nationwide hype swung into full gear. When early photographs of Jean were released, every newspaper in the country picked them up, and she became famous before anyone had even seen her on screen.

Then, when *Hell's Angels* was released, stardom was stamped indelibly on Jean Harlow. Hughes could not readily find a follow-up film for her, so he loaned her out to Columbia for her next film, *Platinum Blonde*. That sent her stock soaring. But when Harlow began to make salary demands, Hughes considered her ungrateful and sold her contract to MGM.

H Jean arlow

She was the beautiful and witty "platinum blonde." But her stardom was poignantly brief.

C Joan rawfor

Even her stunning success was no substitute for the love and admiration she craved.

D 6

Based upon the passage you just read, which of the following statements is True and which is False?

Remember: Base your answers only upon what you think the passage said or implied.

	True	False	Don't Know	
		CIRCLE ONE ANSWER		
1. Howard Hughes discovered Jean Harlow	1	2	3	(23)
2. Harlow's first film was Platinum Blonde	1	2	3	(24)
3. Jean Harlow became famous before any one had seen her in a movie	1	2	3	(25)
4. Once discovered, Jean Harlow immediately became a star	1	2	3	(26)
5. Jean Harlow was one of the most talented actresses of the 1930's	1	2	3	(27)
6. Jean Harlow did not like Howard Hughes	1	2	3	(28)

THE ELEMENTS OF COMFORT

THE BEDROOM

Y our hideaway, the one room just for the two of you, deserves to have inviting touches— the choicest comforters, most versatile lighting, sweetest scents.

Down-filled pillows are pricey, but worth every penny. Sweet dreams!

Best beds

Whether you have a vintage brass bed, a cherry four-poster or a no-nonsense modern frame, your mattress and box spring are what make you comfortable. Invest in the best mattress you can afford and replace it every ten years. Most people opt for innerspring, which affords the most support, but soft (lots of padding over coils) or firm (less cushioning) is up to you. Don't be timid about testing: Stretch out on floor models for at least five minutes each.

The ultimate sheets: no-iron 200+ count cotton.

104

F 5

Based upon the passage you just read, which of the following statements is True and which is False?

Remember: Base your answers only upon what you think the passage said or implied.

	CIRCLE ONE ANSWER		
	True	False	Don't Know
1. When it comes to comfort, the bed frame is the most important element 1		2	3	(23)
2. When choosing a box spring, most people prefer outer spring because of its support for the back 1		2	3	(24)
3. You should choose your bed very carefully 1		2	3	(25)
4. People have very individual preferences regarding what type of bed is best for them 1		2	3	(26)
5. You should invest in the best mattress affordable and replace it every 10 years 1		2	3	(27)
6. For the best night's sleep, this article suggests picking a no-nonsense modern frame 1		2	3	(28)

Q *I'd like to plant a small cutting garden in my backyard, which has good direct sunlight. What particular types of flowers would you recommend for a beginning gardener?*

A Some easy-to-grow flowers I think you'd enjoy are zinnias, marigolds, daisies, cosmos, asters, sunflowers, snapdragons, alyssum, chrysanthemums and dianthus—all of which are annuals easily grown from seed. To make your garden pretty, I suggest putting strawberry plants, which have small leaves and little white flowers, around the border. You can buy them at your local garden center, and you won't need many because the plants multiply. Eight plants would probably do— one in each corner and one in the middle of each row. Strawberry plants send out runners with a little plant at the end of each. In the fall, you can dig up these little plants and transplant them next to their parents. In a year, the perimeter of your garden will be overflowing with strawberry plants, and you'll have the added pleasure of fresh strawberries for summer meals.

N 4

Based upon the passage you just read, which of the following statements is True and which is False?

Remember: Base your answers only upon what you think the passage said or implied.

	CIRCLE ONE ANSWER		
	True	False	Don't Know
1. The person writing the question asked for advice on growing strawberries	1	2	3 (23)
2. Strawberry plants multiply so you don't need to buy enough to fill your whole garden	1	2	3 (24)
3. Strawberry plants must be dug up in the fall ...	1	2	3 (25)
4. Strawberry plants are easy to take care of	1	2	3 (26)
5. Daisies and marigolds grow easily from seed	1	2	3 (27)
6. To have a successful garden, the flowers should be grown from seed	1	2	3 (28)

BEHIND THE WHEEL

By Don Chaikin

SAFE DRIVING STARTS IN THE DRIVER'S SEAT

CLIP-ON WIDE-ANGLE REARVIEW MIRROR   ITEM ON DASHBOARD REFLECTING OFF WINDSHIELD

THREE-SPOKE STEERING WHEEL   PASSENGER-SIDE REARVIEW MIRROR

Equipping your car for safety can mean ordering tilt steering and outside mirrors on both sides. You can add a wide-angle rearview mirror. Be sure to keep dash top clear.

Ever since the first cars took to the road, the major cause of automobile accidents has remained the same: the driver.

Being at the controls of a 2,000-plus-pound projectile that's moving along at highway speeds of 50 mph or more, is a serious responsibility—one that's taken too lightly, unfortunately. Each time you slip behind the wheel you must *think safety.*

Last month in this column, we discussed predrive safety habits. Now we'll see how to develop another important yet simple safety habit.

First, make sure the driver's seat is properly adjusted for you. Someone else may have driven since you last did; or perhaps the seat was moved to make room for someone in the back. Rear-seat passengers may have to sacrifice a few inches of legroom for driver comfort.

Adjust the seat fore and aft and the seat-back angle (if possible) so that with both hands on the wheel (as they should be when you drive) your elbows will be slightly bent. For optimum control, position your hands on the wheel at the 9- and 3-o'clock or 10- and 2-o'clock positions. If your car has a tilt steering wheel, adjust it, too. *Tip:* If your car doesn't have a three-spoke steering wheel, consider installing one for better control and easier wheel handling. To correctly position the seat, sit in it with your shoulders snugly against the seat back. Then fully extend your arm straight out over the steering wheel. The wheel's rim should touch your wrist as you lower your arm.

You'll find that your legs, too, will be comfortably bent, resulting in good pedal control. Use your left foot to balance your body by resting it on the floorboard or wheel arch when not clutching.

Now, with the seat properly positioned, adjust all the mirrors to provide as large a rear view as possible. You also want to be able to quickly glance at your mirrors, taking your eyes off the road for a minimal amount of time. *Tip:* If your car isn't factory-equipped with a passenger's side mirror, install one.

Next, clear the dashboard of any objects, such as paper, that might reflect off the windshield and inhibit vision. Place them instead in a nondistracting but accessible place, like the glove compartment, door pocket or center console. Make sure that the seats and floor are free of objects that could fly about the interior during a sudden maneuver or get wedged under the pedals.

Once comfortably settled in the car with coat and gloves off buckle your seat belt. Make sure adult passengers buckle theirs, too. Children should be properly restrained in safety or booster seats.

New next month
Now that we've covered the basics, we will focus on specific situations in this column. Starting next month you'll find a driver-safety quiz on this page. Find out how *you* would react to emergency driving situations—and compare your response to the advice of our nationally recognized experts. **MI**

Sitting too close to the steering wheel is a poor technique. Sharply bent elbows and knees indicate poor driver control

To determine proper distance from the steering wheel, extend your arm, with shoulder against seat back, and lower it Wheel rim should meet your wrist

P 4

Based upon the passage you just read, which of the following statements is True and which is False?

Remember: Base your answers only upon what you think the passage said or implied.

	CIRCLE ONE ANSWER		
	True	False	Don't Know
1. The major cause of automobile accidents is poorly constructed cars	1	2	3 (23)
2. If the seat is not adjusted properly, the driver is not as safe	1	2	3 (24)
3. The only acceptable position for the driver's hands on the steering wheel is the ten and two o'clock position	1	2	3 (25)
4. A three-spoke steering wheel gives the driver better control	1	2	3 (26)
5. Loose objects placed on the dashboard could cause an accident	1	2	3 (27)
6. Following the tips in the article will insure that you don't get into an accident	1	2	3 (28)

Cabinetmaker Robert Phipps likes to point out that trends toward downsize houses put as much pressure on him to design space-saving furniture as they do on architects to come up with efficient floor plans.

Building furniture that fits into his small Connecticut house led Phipps to focus on designing multifunctional pieces. "For me, the design comes from thinking about how the piece will be used day to day and how it will fit into the surrounding space," he says.

An example of his approach to multipurpose design is a kitchen island he built for his own use. It solves the problem of providing multiple work surfaces needed for various food preparation tasks—and yet is compact.

The island's three work tops are interchangeable. It has a butcher-block cutting board, a pastry surface made of Du Pont's Corian (Phipps chose this marble look-alike over traditional marble to keep the weight of the removable pastry board to a minimum), and a large bowl for mixing salads. All three work surfaces are stored inside the island. A standard-size, built-in waste receptacle makes kitchen litter disposal easy. And, an attached wooden rack holds knives and other utensils.

P 5

Based upon the passage you just read, which of the following statements is True and which is False?

Remember: Base your answers only upon what you think the passage said or implied.

<u>CIRCLE ONE ANSWER</u>

	True	False	Don't Know
1. This article focuses on the design of space-saving furniture	1	2	3 (23)
2. Robert Phipps developed some of his ideas from the experience of furnishing his own house	1	2	3 (24)
3. Robert Phipps emphasizes usefulness when designing pieces of furniture or cabinetry	1	2	3 (25)
4. Phipps built his own kitchen island with interchangeable surfaces	1	2	3 (26)
5. Phipps believes that each item in a home should have one unique function	1	2	3 (27)
6. Phipps designs items mainly for the kitchen	1	2	3 (28)

INCREASE YOUR CAR'S CARGO CAPACITY

By Slaton L. White

When you replace your large car with a smaller, more fuel-efficient one, expect to forfeit a lot of storage space. Many of the newer cars have sacrificed trunk space for less weight—all in the name of fuel economy. Short of jettisoning one of the kids, leaving your luggage behind or buying a mini pickup instead of a car, what options does the owner of a downsize automobile have when he wants to head out on vacation or carry large, bulky cargo?

Basically, there are two options: Tow the gear in a trailer or tote it on the roof. Both choices involve trade-offs, most noticeably a measurable decrease in fuel economy as well as a marked change in the car's handling characteristics. However, many manufacturers offer a broad range of products designed to minimize the trade-offs.

P 6

Based upon the passage you just read, which of the following statements is True and which is False?

Remember: Base your answers only upon what you think the passage said or implied.

	True	False	Don't Know
		CIRCLE ONE ANSWER	
1. To increase space for a downsize automobile, there are three main options	1	2	3
2. When a trailer is added, a subcompact has all the advantages of a larger car	1	2	3
3. Toting gear on a roof will decrease fuel economy	1	2	3
4. In general, you should not buy a subcompact if you have a family unless you have to	1	2	3
5. Manufacturers offer products which are designed to minimize problems with towing	1	2	3
6. You should not give in to a lack of space if you own a subcompact car	1	2	3

In the guest room, the severe architecture of the new wing is enriched by furniture with a past, though not necessarily fine antiques.

The twin beds are newish French, crafted of satinwood, and outfitted in down-filled satin comforters, all estate sale purchases.

L 4

Based upon the passage you just read, which of the following statements is True and which is False?

Remember: Base your answers only upon what you think the passage said or implied.

	CIRCLE ONE ANSWER		
	True	False	Don't Know
1. Furniture with a past complements the severe architecture of the new wing 1		2	3	(23)
2. The guest room contains twin beds that are of 17th century French design 1		2	3	(24)
3. The twin beds and comforters were purchased from expensive furniture 1		2	3	(25)
4. The guest room reflects a distaste for contemporary furniture 1		2	3	(26)
5. The guest room does not contain any antiques ... 1		2	3	(27)
6. Careful thought went into decorating the guest room 1		2	3	(28)

THE NEW AMERICAN CUISINE

There are other food writers in America—some more renowned, many
more pretentious—but none as influential or as down-home charming as Claiborne

Craig Claiborne:
The Typewriter Chef

Cottage industry: Claiborne's kitchen is his office. From here come *The Times* articles that influence millions.

By Robert Sam Anson

Ten a.m., at Ray and Peachy Halsey's food stand in Water Mill, Long Island, and as usual at this time of the morning, the place is nearly deserted. There is, in fact, only one customer: a balding, slightly overweight, middle-aged man, patrolling the aisles with what appears to be special urgency.

The shopper is in a dither. He has invited a few friends over for lunch, and though the centerpiece of the main course—four fat, boned squabs, which he will stuff with a mixture of wild rice, cognac and foie gras—is already in hand, there are a hundred other details to attend to, and time is ticking by.

Craig Claiborne glances at his watch and the smile that usually crosses his lips momentarily disappears. The guests he has summoned to sample the untested menu he is preparing for a benefit later in the month for The New York Public Library are arriving at 1 p.m., and he still has two more stops to make: the first, down the road at the fish market in Wainscott; the second, even farther down the road, will be in East Hampton at Dean & DeLuca. All that before he even begins to think about switching on the gas of his Garland range at his home in The Springs.

METROPOLITAN HOME APRIL 1984

| L 5 |

Based upon the passage you just read, which of the following statements is True and which is False?

Remember: Base your answers only upon what you think the passage said or implied.

CIRCLE ONE ANSWER

	True	False	Don't Know	
1. Mr. Claiborne planned to serve squabs stuffed with a rice mixture 1		2	3	(23)
2. Mr. Claiborne had two more stops to make before he could begin preparing his menu 1		2	3	(24)
3. Mr. Claiborne invited guests from the New York Public Library to sample the untested menu ... 1		2	3	(25)
4. Mr. Claiborne wanted to show off his cooking abilities 1		2	3	(26)
5. Mr. Claiborne was very concerned with pleasing his guests 1		2	3	(27)
6. Mr. Claiborne planned poorly for his grocery purchase 1		2	3	(28)

METROPOLITAN HOME OF THE MONTH

A Suburban House You Can Love

Things are not always what they seem and, though this sprawling white house is just the sort of sage Colonial you'd expect in the environs of D.C., it has surprises. It does, in fact, incorporate a small George Washington-era structure. But the main house was built in the 1930s of materials salvaged from 18th century town houses demolished to make way for the Federal Triangle downtown. The big news now, however, is behind this shy

facade: It's a contemporary wing, a second house almost, conceived like the first as a series of cottages. Of course, it's always risky to add a footnote to history, particularly a second one, but all the newness here is carefully applied and has the same deep comfort, charm and richness of the originals.

Produced by Steven Wagner
with Patsy Rogers
Written by Donald Vining
Design by Dorothy Slover
Photographs: Jacques Dirand
Resources, page 90

37

L 6

Based upon the passage you just read, which of the following statements is True and which is False?

Remember: Base your answers only upon what you think the passage said or implied.

	CIRCLE ONE ANSWER		
	True	False	Don't Know
1. The main house was built during the 1930's	1	2	3 (23)
2. This house does not bear any resemblance to a George Washington-era structure	1	2	3 (24)
3. The materials used in building the house were obtained from demolished 18th century town homes	1	2	3 (25)
4. The new house has very different qualities than the original portion of the house	1	2	3 (26)
5. The most recent addition reflects a preference for a mixture of architectural styles	1	2	3 (27)
6. The house described in the article is actually several dwelling units	1	2	3 (28)

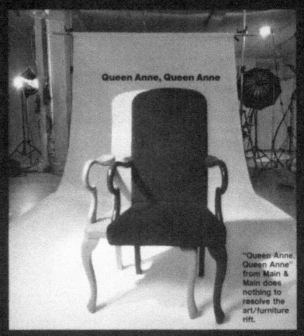

DESIGN PORTFOLIO

IS IT FURNITURE OR IS IT ART?

Queen Anne, Queen Anne

"Queen Anne, Queen Anne" from Main & Main does nothing to resolve the art/furniture rift.

By Denise Domergue

New ideas in American furniture design in the 1980s seem to be emerging fast and furiously from, of all places, the art world. Galleries of art, not design showrooms, are introducing the most appealing and innovative furniture to be seen in decades. The phenomenon is springing up all across the country and quite independently, as though some muse from the nation's collective unconscious suddenly fed a healthy sprinkling of artists the impulse to make art that functions.

Los Angeles writer DENISE DOMERGUE wrote Artists Design Furniture, *to be published this month by Harry N. Abrams.*

Produced by Steven Wagner; Photograph by Joseph Standart
Resources, page 90

K 5

Based upon the passage you just read, which of the following statements is True and which is False?

Remember: Base your answers only upon what you think the passage said or implied.

	True	False	Don't Know
	CIRCLE ONE ANSWER		
1. There have been few dramatic changes in furniture design in the 1980's 1		2	3
2. The furniture design trends discussed in this article involve bright colors and unusual shapes 1		2	3
3. The 1980's design trends discussed in this article are forecasted to be short-lived 1		2	3
4. The art world is responsible for many of the new ideas in furniture design 1		2	3
5. The furniture in the article was designed mainly to be used by artists 1		2	3
6. This furniture is more likely to be attractive to those who like modern furniture 1		2	3

(23) F|F
(24) T|I
(25) F|F
(26) T|F
(27) F|I
(28) T|I

$$\boxed{\text{BOATING}}$$

New Aids For Fitting Out

Spring launching time used to be a lot more complicated. Mostly it was a matter of keeping even with the advancing age of a hull—leaks and loose fittings, dry rot and peeling paint, stains under the varnish and growth over the bottom paint, plus rust and corrosion afflicting the engine.

The maintenance-free boat still hasn't arrived —and isn't likely to—but now we can play fix up instead of catch up. This is the time of year when today's boatmen improve their rigs instead of struggling to keep them from getting worse.

Of course, if you enjoy tinkering and have spare time (the secret to saving money is doing it yourself), you can find bargain boats that someone doesn't feel like repairing this month. For any used boat more than 20 feet long, the first step is to check phone books and boat yards for the name of a marine surveyor. His fee will include a report on what kind of shape the hull and engine are actually in and what repairs are necessary. Usually, he can also estimate the cost of these repairs. He can't tell you if you should attempt the work yourself and won't tell you if the asking price for the boat is a bargain. But a professional survey is worth its weight in the money that it saves, and the disappointments and headaches that it prevents.

```
0 4
```

Based upon the passage you just read, which of the following statements is True and which is False?

Remember: Base your answers only upon what you think the passage said or implied.

	CIRCLE ONE ANSWER		
	True	False	Don't Know
1. For boats over 20 feet, it would be unwise to buy one without first checking with a marine surveyor	1	2	3 (23)
2. The maintenance-free boat will be here soon	1	2	3 (24)
3. A marine surveyor will tell you if you should attempt to make repairs yourself	1	2	3 (25)
4. For boats under 20 feet, marine surveyors' fees make it impractical to get an estimate ..	1	2	3 (26)
5. A marine surveyor will make the needed repairs on a boat	1	2	3 (27)
6. The major problem associated with a boat involves an aging hull	1	2	3 (28)

EDITORIAL TRAILS

The Threatening Indian Problem

I have been warned by friends to lay off the Indian problem. They have cautioned me that the Indian lobby in Congress is too strong to fight, and that "The Great American Guilty Conscience," actively kept alive by the Indians, has stripped the American people of their ability to deal logically with the rampant Indian excesses that are becoming more flagrant every day. Make no mistake. The tribes are on the move. They aim to lay claim to as much land—your land—as they can get, and they plan to commercialize our fish and game resources. **Sixty million outdoor sportspeople, countless nature lovers, and the American people in general can go to hell.**

0 5

Based upon the passage you just read, which of the following statements is True and which is False?

Remember: Base your answers only upon what you think the passage said or implied.

<table>
<tr><td></td><td colspan="3">CIRCLE ONE ANSWER</td></tr>
<tr><td></td><td>True</td><td>False</td><td>Don't Know</td></tr>
<tr><td>1. The Indian lobby in Congress is very strong .....</td><td>1</td><td>2</td><td>3</td><td>(23)</td></tr>
<tr><td>2. The author is angry with the Indians ....</td><td>1</td><td>2</td><td>3</td><td>(24)</td></tr>
<tr><td>3. The author believes that the Indians are trying to get more land and resources than they have a right to ....</td><td>1</td><td>2</td><td>3</td><td>(25)</td></tr>
<tr><td>4. The American people are dealing logically with the Indian problem ....</td><td>1</td><td>2</td><td>3</td><td>(26)</td></tr>
<tr><td>5. The Indians are planning to prevent Americans from fishing ....</td><td>1</td><td>2</td><td>3</td><td>(27)</td></tr>
<tr><td>6. The author estimates that there are 30 million nature lovers affected by the Indians' desires ....</td><td>1</td><td>2</td><td>3</td><td>(28)</td></tr>
</table>

South-Central Alaska's Spectacular Scenery
The Wrangell-St. Elias National Park and Preserve, 200 miles south of Anchorage, is on the World Heritage list as an outstanding natural area. Many people say the 12.3-million-acre park where the Wrangell, St. Elias, and Chugach mountains converge is the most beautiful part of Alaska. This region, so rugged that even Indians have avoided it, abounds in natural wonders. The park has more mountains higher than 16,000 feet and more glaciers—more than five million acres of snow and ice—than any other spot in North America. In the southern tip of the park is Malaspina, a glacier bigger than the state of Rhode Island. People wanting to make the record books by scaling an unclimbed mountain can find several in this national park. The park is a prime area for river running with all classes of water.

```
0 6
```

Based upon the passage you just read, which of the following statements is True and which is False?

Remember: Base your answers only upon what you think the passage said or implied.

	CIRCLE ONE ANSWER		
	True	False	Don't Know
1. Many people say that Wrangell-St. Elias National Park is the most beautiful part of Alaska	1	2	3 (23)
2. In the southern tip of the park, there is a glacier bigger than the State of Rhode Island	1	2	3 (24)
3. The park is so rugged that only Indians have lived there	1	2	3 (25)
4. Wrangell-St. Elias National Park is an ideal place for mountain climbers	1	2	3 (26)
5. Very few mountains in the park have been climbed	1	2	3 (27)
6. Wrangell-St. Elias National Park is the only place to mountain climb in Alaska	1	2	3 (28)

WE LIVE at a moment of apparent despair. Many conservatives tell us mournfully that our values are eroding. Many liberals maintain that the quality of life is eroding. And almost everyone—from socialist to supply-sider—seems to agree that our economy, and the economies of much of the rest of the world, have been in a chaotic mess for a dozen years or so.

This, at least, is the story that seems to come at us through the flow of modern communications. It is a story often primed by intellectual panic-mongering; it is connected to overheated political rhetoric; it is sparked by the printed word; and it is puffed up and ultimately dominated by television.

My view is that this picture of despair and failure is wrong. More than that, it is dangerous. My own sense of the matter is that we live in a nation and a world that in most respects—excuse the expression—never had it so good.

Excerpted with permission from "The Good News Is That the Bad News is Wrong" by Ben J. Wattenberg, Reader's Digest, April 1984.

A 4

Based upon the passage you just read, which of the following statements is True and which is False?

Remember: Base your answers only upon what you think the passage said or implied.

	CIRCLE ONE ANSWER		
	True	False	Don't Know
1. According to liberals, the quality of life is eroding	1	2	3 (23) T|F
2. Non-liberals and non-conservatives believe the world is in great shape	1	2	3 (24) F|I
3. The author believes that the liberals and conservatives are wrong	1	2	3 (25) T|F
4. According to the author, we should be more optimistic about the quality of life	1	2	3 (26) T|I
5. Tne liberals and conservatives are endagering our way of life	1	2	3 (27) F|I
6. The negative views are dominated by the printed word	1	2	3 (28) F|F

Some 80 million Americans—almost 40 percent of us—are overweight by 20 pounds or more. Many of us try fad diets and reducing drugs that nearly always fail in the long run and doom their devotees to a health-damaging loss-gain seesaw. To make weight loss last, you must adopt nutritionally sound eating habits and make other simple life-style changes.

Exercise is an all-around tonic for body and mind. It can go a long way toward reducing the need for medical care and improving the quality of your life. To get your quota, incorporate more activity into your daily routines. For example, walk instead of driving short distances; take the stairs instead of an elevator. Set aside time each day for concentrated exercise. Brisk walking is possible for nearly everyone and is a very effective calorie consumer and total body conditioner.

A 5

Based upon the passage you just read, which of the following statements is True and which is False?

Remember: Base your answers only upon what you think the passage said or implied.

	CIRCLE ONE ANSWER		
	True	False	Don't Know
1. Twenty percent of Americans are overweight	1	2	3 (23)
2. Exercise will keep you from having to see the doctor	1	2	3 (24)
3. In order to be healthy, you should try to exercise every day	1	2	3 (25)
4. Fad diets nearly always fail	1	2	3 (26)
5. A great number of Americans need to be more concerned about their health	1	2	3 (27)
6. The key to healthy exercise is brisk walking	1	2	3 (28)

MIDDLE EAST
His Majesty Is Not Pleased

From King Hussein, an election-year setback for U.S. policy

If there was any doubt about the magnitude of the Reagan Administration's recent diplomatic failures in the Middle East, it has now been dispelled by one of Washington's best Arab friends, King Hussein of Jordan. The Administration had been hoping that despite the collapse of its policy in Lebanon, the U.S. might be able to encourage a round of peace negotiations between Israel and such moderate Arab states as Jordan and Egypt, and perhaps the wing of the Palestine Liberation Organization led by P.L.O. Chairman Yasser Arafat. Last week, however, King Hussein turned thumbs down on any such initiative. In a stinging rebuke to Washington, the King told the New York *Times:* "I now realize that principles mean nothing to the U.S. Short-term issues, especially in election years, prevail."

At the heart of Hussein's concern, as always, was the continuing Israeli occupation of the West Bank. Said the King: "We see things in the following way. Israel is on our land. It is there by virtue of American military and economic aid that translates into aid for Israeli settlements. Israel is there by virtue of American moral and political support to the point where the U.S. is succumbing to Israeli dictates. You obviously have made your choice, and your choice is Israel. Therefore, there is no hope of achieving anything."

B 4

Based upon the passage you just read, which of the following statements is True and which is False?

Remember: Base your answers only upon what you think the passaqe said or implied.

	CIRCLE ONE ANSWER		
	True	False	Don't Know
1. King Hussein has been one of the United States' best Arab friends	1	2	3 (23)
2. King Hussein wishes to initiate a round of talks between the P.L.O. and Israel	1	2	3 (24)
3. King Hussein does not believe that the U.S. wants to make a long term settlement in the Middle East	1	2	3 (25)
4. Israel's occupation of the West Bank is a major cause of the current problem	1	2	3 (26)
5. King Hussein will no longer negotiate with the United States	1	2	3 (27)
6. According to Hussein, the United States is entirely to blame for the problem	1	2	3 (28)

Manufacturing Is in Flower

After years of neglect, America's factories are taking on a fresh allure

"Nothing runs like a Deere," goes the slogan of the world's largest maker of farm equipment. These days, industrial engineers are changing that to "Nothing runs like a Deere factory." In its new plant on the northeast edge of Waterloo, Iowa, Deere is using computer-controlled assembly techniques to turn out a score of tractor models, bearing as many as 3,000 options, without costly plant shutdowns for retooling. The factory seems to be making a difference in Deere's profits. While sales rose slightly because of a strengthening farm economy, earnings during the last three months of 1983 were $2 million, *vs.* a loss of $28.5 million a year earlier. The company credited the improvement largely to "increased efficiency and cost reductions in North American manufacturing operations."

As modern as it is, though, the Deere factory can hardly compare with the frontier-breaching printed-circuit-board plant of A T & T Technologies in Richmond, Va. There computers receive complex instructions from a dozen Bell Laboratories design centers scattered throughout the U.S. The instructions are then used to turn out on demand a limitless variety of circuit boards containing hundreds of parts. The operation is so smooth that A T & T can change designs overnight without interrupting production.

The Deere and A T & T plants represent the new pizazz in American manufacturing. Long U.S. industry's neglected stepchild, subordinated to finance and marketing, the process of making products is suddenly coming into its own, commanding more and more attention from company executives. Firms are pouring money into new manufacturing facilities and stocking them with such advanced equipment as computer-driven robots, lasers and ultrasonic probes. Last week the Commerce Department reported that U.S. business plans to spend $344 billion on new plant and equipment this year, up 12% from 1983. That is the biggest annual increase in 17 years.

B 5

Based upon the passage you just read, which of the following statements is True and which is False?

Remember: Base your answers only upon what you think the passage said or implied.

	CIRCLE ONE ANSWER		
	True	False	Don't Know
1. Bell has centered its computer-controlled technology in one location	1	2	3 (23)
2. Deere's computer-controlled assembly has reduced plant shutdowns	1	2	3 (24)
3. AT&T and Deere were the first computer-controlled plants	1	2	3 (25)
4. U.S. businesses increased their spending on new plants and equipment in 1984 by approximately 12 percent over 1983	1	2	3 (26)
5. Computer-controlled manufacturing can make companies more successful	1	2	3 (27)
6. Manufacturing has now become more important than marketing and finance	1	2	3 (28)

The Downhill Road from Troy

THE MARCH OF FOLLY *by Barbara W. Tuchman; Knopf; 447 pages; $18.95*

The thread of folly that runs through Barbara Tuchman's books is a filament of doom. In *The Guns of August*, a wrongheaded French strategy in the first days of World War I leads inexorably to the deadlock of the trenches. The tensions and energies of *fin-de-siècle* Europe and America in *The Proud Tower* are primed to explode in that same war. And the chaos of the 14th century becomes *A Distant Mirror* of the modern distemper.

In her latest work, this fatal thread becomes the whole cloth, as Tuchman explores the nature of governmental folly and dissects some choice examples: the Renaissance papacy, 18th century England, the 20th century U.S. Folly, as Tuchman defines it, is not simply incompetence or tyranny or hubris, but rather "the pursuit of policy contrary to self-interest." She requires that the policy was perceived as folly in its own time, that a sensible alternative was available, and that the policy nonetheless was carried out by a group over more than one political lifetime. She makes one exception to that last criterion, the brief episode of the wooden horse at Troy.

Tuchman seizes on the legend as evidence that such folly "is an old and inherent human habit." But her purpose seems deeper. The tale, told most memorably by Vergil in the *Aeneid*, portrays the Trojans as victims of fate. Despite the urgings of citizens that the Greek gift be destroyed or at least broken open, Troy's leaders take it in, hidden Greeks and all, because the gods have so ordained. That excuse will not do for Tuchman. "The gods (or God, for that matter) are a concept of the human mind," she writes. "The gods' interference ... is man's device for transferring the responsibility of folly."

A 6

Based upon the passage you just read, which of the following statements is True and which is False?

Remember: Base your answers only upon what you think the passage said or implied.

	CIRCLE ONE ANSWER		
	True	False	Don't Know
1. Barbara Tuchman is the author of the book, The Downhill Road from Troy	1	2	3 (23)
2. In Tuchman's latest work, the use of folly is identical to using humor to make a point	1	2	3 (24)
3. Tuchman's latest work is about governmental folly	1	2	3 (25)
4. It would be Tuchman's opinion that governments have made a number of bad decisions down through the ages	1	2	3 (26)
5. Tuchman does not believe in God	1	2	3 (27)
6. According to Tuchman, when a policy was perceived as folly, there was usually no other alternative	1	2	3 (28)

All the elements of a familiar scenario were back on center stage of U.S. foreign policy. Not long ago, the setting was Lebanon. This time it was the scarred landscape of El Salvador. As it has so often before, the Reagan Administration was rattling sabers as a means of drawing the line against Communist expansion in Central America. The Administration's aim, paradoxically enough, was to focus attention on a supposedly peaceable watershed: the March 25 presidential election in El Salvador, a long-awaited contest in which the outcome is uncertain and the stakes are considerable. With the balloting only a few days away, the Administration was making martial noises in a number of ways:

C 4

Based upon the passage you just read, which of the following statements is True and which is False?

Remember: Base your answers only upon what you think the passage said or implied.

	CIRCLE ONE ANSWER		
	True	False	Don't Know
1. The Reagan administration has been involved in the affairs of only two countries	1	2	3	(23)
2. The outcome of the El Salvadorian presidential election has already been decided	1	2	3	(24)
3. The Reagan administration tried to influence elections in El Salvador	1	2	3	(25)
4. El Salvador is an important country to American interests	1	2	3	(26)
5. Just before El Salvador, the U.S. was involved in Lebanon	1	2	3	(27)
6. The administration wanted to draw attention away from the Presidential election	1	2	3	(28)

LOOKING SNAZZY

WHEN YOU HAVE THE SNIFFLES

If ever makeup should come to a woman's rescue, it's when the miseries of a cold turn nose and eyes red and puffy.

BY BARBARA BERNAL

Cosmetics can do a fine job of disguising the ravages of sneezing and blowing. But don't go overboard, cautions Beauty Editor Karlys Daly Brown. Dramatic makeup, bold colors, will only call attention to a face that's truly not at its best. Instead, aim for a softly pretty look with a delicate palette. (Avoid strong shades in dress too.) Keep hair soft and full. A slicked-back do is too stark.

F 4

Based upon the passage you just read, which of the following statements is True and which is False?

Remember: Base your answers only upon what you think the passage said or implied.

	CIRCLE ONE ANSWER		
	True	False	Don't Know
1. Bold colors should be used for a face that is not at its best 1		2	3 (23)
2. Make-up is even more important to a woman's looks when she has a cold 1		2	3 (24)
3. Hair should be soft and full when you have a cold 1		2	3 (25)
4. When you have a cold, you should not go out in public without make-up 1		2	3 (26)
5. You can still look pretty when you have a cold . 1		2	3 (27)
6. When you use make-up as the author suggests, others will neve be able to tell that you have a cold 1		2	3 (28)

The drop waist, near right, beautifully hides a thick waist, big seat, protruding tummy or large hips. The full skirt masks heavy thighs, and the collarless neckline is just right for a short neck. *Don't wear this* if you're very thin (it's too loose) or have short legs. By Liz Claiborne in cotton poly, sizes 4–14, $76. TIP: No-waist styles shouldn't fit closely.

F 6

Based upon the passage you just read, which of the following statements is True and which is False?

Remember: Base your answers only upon what you think the passage said or implied.

CIRCLE ONE ANSWER

	True	False	Don't Know	
1. The drop waist dress is ideal for thin people ..	1	2	3	(23)
2. The collarless style makes a thick neck less obvious	1	2	3	(24)
3. The drop waist dress can be worn by women with heavy thighs	1	2	3	(25)
4. This dress is perfect for maternity wear	1	2	3	(26)
5. The drop waist dress should fit loosely	1	2	3	(27)
6. The drop waist dress is of good quality	1	2	3	(28)

APPENDIX J

Supervisor and Interviewer Instructions

Research Corporation   3 West 35th Street, New York, N.Y. 10001, (212) 947-5140

JOB #Q01-013
Magazine
May, 1985

Dear Supervisor:

Enclosed are the following materials for the "Magazine Study", a door-to-door probability study to begin on Wednesday, May 1.

- Practice Interview Set (Yellow)
- Pink Female Screeners
- Blue Male Screeners
- Card 6, Card 12
- Numbered Female Interviewing Packets
- Numbered Male Interviewing Packets
- Interviewing Instructions
- Cluster Map
- Household Listing Booklet
- Phone Report Sheets
- Validation Sheets

ASSIGNMENT:

You are to complete <u>15</u> interviews <u>per cluster</u> as indicated on the front page of your Household Listing Booklet.

SCHEDULE:

Brief and Begin: - - - - - - - - Wednesday, May 1
Interim Phone Reports: - - - - - See Schedule on Page 3
End: - - - - - - - - - - - - - - On or before Wednesday, May 8
Final Phone Report: - - - - - - Thursday, May 9
Ship Back: - - - - - - - - - - - Thursday, May 9
(see "Returning Work")

STUDY DESIGN:

1. This is a door-to-door probability study.

2. Each Cluster point is identified by a two-digit number. This Cluster # appears in the Yellow Circle on your Cluster Map as well as on your Household Listing Booklet.

3. Each cluster is assigned <u>15</u> completions.

4. Each cluster is to be assigned to one top-notch interviewer.

PRACTICE INTERVIEWS:

Every interviewer must do a <u>practice interview</u>. A special Practice Interview Set has been provided.

-2-

TYPE OF SAMPLE:

This is a Probability Study. You will be working in assigned areas which have been selected on a random basis. Within the specific areas the interviewer will be prelisting household addresses, and then attempting to complete interviews at each prelisted address. Respondent selection will be determined by a special numbering pattern which appears on each screener. SEE INTERVIEWER INSTRUCTIONS FOR DETAILS.

NOTE: Phone Reports are due as per your schedule. (Use the "Phone Reports" for further details.)

BRIEFING:

1. The briefing must be conducted by you or a Senior Staff member.

2. Your briefing should be held at a time when you can reach our office if necessary. Our hours are 9:00 AM to 5:00 PM New York (Eastern) time. If you will be briefing at a time which precludes your reaching our office, call me immediately. You will be given a phone number to call in case of any questions.

3. Every interviewer must complete a practice interview.

4. At your briefing, you must stress the following:

        - Use of all materials
        - Information needed for Phone Reports
        - Sampling instructions
        - Every item in the Interviewing Instructions

5. If you must replace an interviewer, the replacement interviewer must be rebriefed in the exact manner in which you briefed the other interviewer.

    In order to avoid having to brief any new interiviewers, it is to your advantage to retain interviewers who indicate that they will be available for the span of the study.

PHONE REPORTING:

Accurate reports are essential to this study. Use the Phone Report Sheet when making reports. Supply each of your interviewers with one of these forms so that reports to you are accurate.

Receiving reports and being prepared to give reports is part of your supervisory responsibility. Adjustments in bills will be made if reporting is not timely and accurate.

Reporting hours and mileage is extremely important. We will not pay for hours which have not been reported.

All reports must be cumulative.

-3-

Outlined below is a schedule of when you are to call Guideline. Please be aware that this schedule is <u>Eastern time</u>. Adjust as necessarsy so that <u>you</u> call <u>us</u> on time.

If your reporting time is early in the day, it may be best for you to have your interviewer contact you at the end of the previous interviewing day so that your report will be ready in the morning.

When you call us, please refer to your Cluster number. Note <u>that each Cluster</u> <u>point has been assigned a number and reports are to be given separately for</u> <u>each Cluster point.</u>

> YOU ARE TO MMAKE THREE PHONE REPORTS; ONE ONE FRIDAY - MAY 3,
> ONE ON MONDAY - MAY 6, AND ONE ON THURSDAY, MAY 9.

Outlined below is your report schedule of your three report days. REMEMBER: THESE TIMES ARE <u>EASTERN</u> TIMES. Adjust to your time zone!

TIME TO CALL	10-11AM	11-12PM	12- 1PM	2 - 3PM	3 - 4PM	4 - 5PM
	CLUSTERS	CLUSTERS	CLUSTERS	CLUSTERS	CLUSTERS	CLUSTERS
	1	8	24	36	58	68
	2	9	25	38	59	69
	3	14	28	40	60	73
	4	15	29	41	61	74
	5	16	30	42	62	76
	6	17	31	45	63	77
	7	18	32	48	64	78
	10	19	33	51	65	79
	11	20	35	52	66	80
	12	21	37	53	67	81
	13	22	47	55	70	82
	34	23	49	56	71	83
	39	26	50	87	72	84
	44	27	54	88	75	85
	46	43	57	89	90	86

-4-

VALIDATION SHEETS:

Every completed interview must be legibly listed on a Validation Sheet. Each sheet has room for the 15 completes to be listed.

EDITING:

You must thoroughly edit all questionnaires. You must also check to be sure that the Household Listing Sheet verifies against the assigned maps and the addresses listed on completes.

VALIDATING:

WE WILL BE VERIFYING LISTED HOUSEHOLDS AND COMPLETES.

You are to validate a minimum of 2 interviews. In order that we avoid harassing respondents, you are to indicate validated work directly on the Validation Sheet.

IF YOU DETECT A DISCREPENCY, YOU ARE TO CALL THIS OFFICE IMMEDIATELY.

RETURNING WORK/MATERIALS:

- When you ship back to us, send us the completed qusetionnaries in two bundles -- one male, one female. Send the magazine material back in its packets.

On or Before Thursday, May 9

I. You will be returning the following:

1. Practice Interview

2. Completed work, bundled by male and female completes

3. All magazine material, each in its appropriate envelope.

4. All maps stapled to the back of the Household Listing Booklet.

5. All terminated screeners.

II. Ship back via Federal Express - Standard Air

- Charge to our account # (100-0112-9)
- DO NOT INSURE
- MARK THE JOB # (Q01-013) on the waybill

-5-

> NOW, IF YOU HAVE NOT DONE SO ALREADY, PLEASE READ THE
> INTERVIWER INSTRUCTIONS AND EXAMINE THE MATERIALS.

BILLING:

Hours and mileage billed must correspond to hours and mileage reported.

YOUR BILL MUST HAVE YOUR CLUSTER NUMBER(S) ON THEM, AS WELL AS THE JOB NUMBER.
If your company has done more than one cluster submit a separate bill for each
cluster.

You are to submit an itemized bill on typed or printed letterhead. Any "out
of pocket" expenses listed on your bill must be accompanied by appropriate
receipts.

You must provide receipts for:

- Tolls
- Parking
- Public Transportation/cabs
- Postage over $10.00
- Telephone charges

You need not receipt:

- Charges for materials taken out of your office stock
- Postage under $10.00

Receipts help to speed your bill through. Therefore, IF IN DOUBT, PROVIDE A
RECIEPT!

If you have any questions, call me at 800-223-5306 (NY State: 212-947-5140).

Thank you for your help with this study.

Very truly yours,

Elyse Gammer
Field Director

GUIDELINE RESEARCH CORPORATION
3 West 35th Street
New York, New York   10001

JOB #Q01-013
Magazine
April, 1985

INTERVIEWER INSTRUCTIONS

PURPOSE:
To interview either a male or female over 18 years of age in each selected household. As described below, this person will be chosen in a specific manner. Once chosen, this person must meet other eligibility requirements.

DESIGN:
This is a Probability study for which you will be working with specifically prescribed sampling areas. Each area was selected on a random basis to ensure equal representation of the country's population. To further ensure such representation within a household, there will be but one household member selected for this study from among all eligible household members.

MATERIALS:
You will be working with the following materials:

- Yellow Practice Interviews
- Pink Female Screeners
- Blue Male Screeners
- Card 6, Card 12
- Numbered Female Interviewing Packets
- Numbered Male Interviewing Packets
- Household Listing Booklets
- Area map with Cluster #
- Phone Report Sheets
- Several sharpened pencils
- Stapler

ASSIGNMENT:
You will complete 15 interviews in your cluster.

CALLBACKS:
There are to be up to 3 calls to reach the designated respondent at a household; the original contact and up to two callbacks. It is imperative that you follow Callback Instructions accurately. Details are within this set of instructions.

PHONE REPORTS:
Your supervisor will give you a schedule as to when to call in reports. You will be calling in reports using the Phone Report Sheet which your Supervisor will give to you.

DELIVERING WORK:
Your supervisor will give you a schedule as to when to deliver work.

AREA MAPS:
You will be given one map. Your area is outlined in Green. Your starting point is a red "X".

LISTING BOOKLET:
You have been given one Household Listing Booklet. The first page of this booklet is where you will list households. The next 4 pages will be used only if necessary. See "Use of Household/Listing Booklet" section for more details.

CONFI-DENTIALITY:
This survey is confidential. All materials are the property of Guideline Research Corporation and our client. You are not to discuss this study with anyone.

ELIGIBILITY:
A qualified respondent is a male or female who:

- Is the designated respondent in his/her household
- Usually read or looks through magazines at least once a month (Q.5a)
- Is a regular reader of at least one of the listed magazines (Q.6c)
- Does not mention either of the boxed magazines in Q's 6d, 6f, or 6j.
- Is willing to be interviewed for about 15 minutes.

Additionally, the respondent may not be known personally by you.

STUDY
OVERVIEW: This study is being done to determine whether what people read is
              perceived correctly. We will be obtaining this information by exposing
              respondents to material taken from several popular magazines. Once
              exposed to this material, the respondent will be asked a short (six
              question) true/false quiz. Each respondent will be exposed to four
              different items of magazine material, two "ads" and two "text".
              Additionally, each respondent will be asked to fill out two quizzes which
              refer to magazine material which was not shown.

              In order to simplify this procedure, we have prepared interviewing
              "packets" -- one for each respondent -- which contain the necessary
              magazine material items as well as the questionnaire for each interview
              you must do.

THE INTERVIEWING
PACKETS: There are 15 interviewing packets, one for each respondent in your
              Cluster. Each packet is marked on the front with the respondent number
              and sex (example: Female #1, Female #2, Male #1, Male #2, etc.). Your
              15 packets will consist of either 9 females and 6 males OR 8 females and
              7 males. For your first female respondent, you will use the packet
              marked "Female #1". For your first male respondent you will use the
              packet marked "Male #1". For your second female respondent your will use
              the packet marked "Female #2", and so on.

              Each packet contains a Main Questionnaire and the appropriate magazine
              material. The questionnaire will indicate when to show which magazine
              item. The magazine items are in acetate sleeves and are coded by a
              letter/number combination such as "A6" or "D3". This code appears on the
              back of the acetate on a white dot.

              BE VERY CAREFUL THAT YOU USE THE CORRECT PACKET, BOTH NUMBER AND SEX.

SOME PROCEDURAL
POINTS: 1. Use a new Screener at every household.

              2. When you complete an interview, staple the screener to the front of
                 the main questionnaire.

              3. Phone Reports are very important. Be sure to follow the call-in
                 schedule set by your supervisor.

AIDS IN OBTAINING INTERVIEWS

1. The questionnaire itself requires about 15 minutes. Feel free to tell your
    prospective respondent that the interview will only take about 15 minutes of his or
    her time.

2. If you are asked, you may tell respondents that every individual response will be
    combined together in a computerized total. We are not interested in keeping
    information about what any one individual thinks.

SPECIAL NOTES

1. For this study, you must use your full name (first and last name) wherever your
    name is required. (Front of the Screener; front of the Household Listing Booklet;
    Phone Report Sheets; top of your area map. Write legibly.) If your name is "Mary
    Smith," it must appear as such. "Mrs. M. Smith" or "M. Smith" or "M.S." or "Mary
    S." are not acceptable.

2. Your briefing is a learning experience. Do not hesitate to ask any questions. Be
    sure you are fully comfortable with and understand what you are doing.

3. You will complete at least one Practice Interview provided especially for this
    purpose.

4. Once you arrive at your assigned area starting point, if you have any questions or
    problems, CALL YOUR SUPERVISOR IMMEDIATELY! DO NOT TAKE IT UPON YOURSELF TO CHANGE
    YOUR AREA IN ANY WAY!

5. Take these instructions with you when you go out to interview. Use them as a
    reference for any problems you might encounter. Feel free to write on these
    instructions; highlighting areas, etc. We have found that almost always, the
    answer to your question was with you all the time -- right in your instructions.

-3-

6. Your question-by-question instructions will explain how to use the Screener and Questionnaire. It is very important that you read the Screener/Questionnaire <u>exactly</u> as it is written! If a respondent has trouble understanding, simply re-read the question slowly and clearly. Do not "re-write" the question!

USE OF HOUSEHOLD LISTING BOOKLET

The Household Listing Booklet "sets up" your sampling area and provides you with an "at a glance" record of what has been done/must be done at each household in your sample.

Your Household Listing Booklet consists of five pages: <u>Page 1</u> contains room for 20 households to be listed; <u>Pages 2-5</u> each contain room for 6 households to be listed.

Your procedure is as follows:

1. Complete Page 1 (details follow).

2. You must exhaust all possibilities of Page 1 (Original Contact plus up to 2 Callbacks) before you can go on.

3. If you complete your assigned quota within the 20 households listed on Page 1 you will <u>not</u> use any more pages. If you do <u>not</u> complete your assigned quota within the 20 households listed you will go on to Page 2 of the Household Listing Booklet.

4. Page 2 provides room for 6 households. Start listing with the next household after the last household you listed. List six households, then proceed.

5. You must exhaust all possibilities of Page 2 before you would go on to Page 3, etc.

Let's take a closer look at the Household Listing Booklet.

-4-

Section A: This is your Cluster #. The Cluster # is a two-digit number which also appears in the yellow circle on your map.

Section B: Print in your first and last name.

Section C: This is the assigned quota for your cluster. The total number of interviews is 15.

Section D: This is where you will print in the street addresses of your sample. Include house number/building #, street name and -- if applicable, apartment #.

Section E: This indicates the sex designation of the household. THIS NEVER CHANGES. Once a household is designated "F" (female) or "M" (male), that is the screener you will use for that household. Look at the example below. 75 Overhill Drive can be screened only for a female (Pink Screener) because the household Sex Designation is "F". 77 Overhill Drive can be screened only for a male (Blue Screener) because the Household Sex Designation is "M".

Section F: Using the codes in Section G, indicate what happened at each household for each attempt. If it is your 1st or 2nd contact, but you will not be going back to that household (because of a refusal, complete, or terminate) DRAW A LINE THROUGH the remaining disposition boxes for that household. See example below.

Section G: These are the letter codes you will use in Section F. PLEASE PRINT LEGIBLY!

-5-

USE OF THE PHONE REPORT SHEET

The Phone Report Sheet, if filled out properly, will give us an accurate reflection of what has been happening in your cluster point. The information for your Phone Report Sheet is gathered from your Household Listing Booklet.

SECTION I - COMPLETES

o   Enter your "total" last.

o   First, look down the "1st Contact" column. Count the "X"'s. This amount indicates how many completes you obtained at the 1st contact. Enter this number on the appropriate line.

o   Repeat for "2nd Contact" and "3rd Contact" columns.

o   Add these three lines together to get your total. Enter total in box marked "I".

SECTION II AND III - "TERMINATES" AND "ALIVES"

o   Enter your "total" last.

o   ALWAYS REFER TO THE LAST "DISPOSITION" COLUMN USED FOR EACH HOUSEHOLD TO OBTAIN YOUR TALLIES.

For example, for listing #1, look across the Disposition boxes. If only a 1st Contact has been made, the outcome of that contact is what you tally. If a 2nd contact has been made, the outcome of that contact is what you tally. If a 3rd contact has been made, the outcome of that contact is what you tally.

Enter the results of the appropriate lines of the Phone Report Sheet and then do your totals.

SECTION IV

Your Grand Total should equal the total number of households listed. If not, go back and re-tally.

SECTIONS V AND VI ARE SELF-EXPLANATORY.

> DO NOT BEGIN LISTING WITH THE FIRST HOUSEHOLD AT YOUR STARTING POINT. SKIP THE FIRST HOUSEHOLD. LIST THE SECOND HOUSEHOLD AS #1 ON PAGE 1 OF YOUR HOUSEHOLD LISTING BOOKLET. CONTINUE UNTIL 20 HOUSEHOLDS ARE LISTED.

1.   The maps used are the most up-to-date that are available. However, sometimes they become a bit out-dated and do not show all the side streets. If, in your location, there are urban blocks or side roads in rural areas which do not appear on the map, you must go into these side streets and side roads and interview those households which normally would come into the sample had the map been correct.

For example, if your map shows the drawing on the left, but your location is actually the drawing on the right, follow the route shown in the drawing on the right.

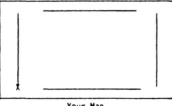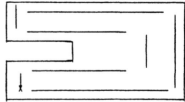

Your Map | The Actual Location

2.   After you have listed 20 households on Page 1, you are to stop listing. Go back to the Household listed as #1 and make your first attempt to screen and complete an interview with a designated respondent in that household.

-6-

3. Record the results of this attempt on the line for listing #1 in your Household #1 in your Household Listing Booklet. Then go on to Listing #2.

4. Continue contacting households until you have made at least an attempt at each of the 20 households on Page 1.

5. At any household, once you have a designated respondent, this is the only person in that household with whom you are to conduct the interview; no one else is considered eligible. If the designated respondent is not at home, set up a callback appointment.

6. You are to make two callbacks in your attempt to interview the designated respondent. Unless an appointment has been made, these callbacks are to be reasonably spaced apart so that your likelihood of interviewing the designated respondent is increased. As a rule of thumb, at least two hours should have elapsed between callbacks in a "Not At Home" situation. This two hour rule can be waived, however, if you see that a "Not At Home" household has become occupied in less than the two hour span. If the person answering the door is busy or the designated respondent is busy, set up a callback appointment.

7. When an appointment has been made with a designated respondent, if you wish you may telephone that person to confirm your appointment in advance of going. However, a telephone confirmation does not count as a callback.

8. If you have not reached your assigned quota once you have exhausted all possibilities for the 20 households listed on Page 1 of your booklet, you will go on to Page 2 of your booklet. Page 2 has room for six more listings.

9. After you have listed 6 households on Page 2 you are to stop listing. Go back to the household listed as number 21 and proceed.

10. If you have not reached your assigned quota once you have exhausted all possibilities for the 6 households listed on Page 2 of your booklet, you will go on to Page 3. Proceed as in Steps 10 and 11.

ADDRESS IDENTIFICATION

When you list a household on your listing sheet, write the house number of the building, the street name and, if an apartment, the apartment number (and/or letter).

Never list more than one household on a single line of your listing sheets. Households in multiple dwellings, even though they have the same street number, must be identified and listed separately.

Where there are no street address numbers or, in multiple households, no apartment numbers, you must still provide some positive identifications of the household's location.

For example, a home with no visible street number can be described as "next to 150 Elm Street", or "between 50 and 52 Maple Street", or "in rear of 17 Walnut Avenue".

In rural areas, or other places where no street numbering system exists, it is still necessary to provide some exact identification of the housing unit that begins a segment.

You may find a RFD Mail Box name or number that will identify the housing unit. Or in some cases, you will need to enter some brief but definite description, such as "2-story house with blue roof on Old Army Road south of intersection with U.S. Highway 77" or "old farm house, with old-fashioned well in front yard, one-half mile beyond Spring Creek Bridge on Horseshoe Road near Blue Rapids Dam".

In apartment buildings without apartment identifications, you can describe locations as "basement front", or "first floor, second apartment right", etc.

DEFINITIONS

To be sure that we understand each other as these instructions continue, we would like to define the terms that we shall be using, in the exact sense in which they will be employed.

Cluster: The work area assigned to you. In cities, a cluster may consist of a single block or a group of blocks. Outside of cities, a cluster may consist of more or less open country, within clearly defined limits or borders.

-7-

SAMPLING INSTRUCTIONS

INTERVIEW

Since it is impossible to interview every person in a given area, a cross-section of those persons living in the area must be chosen. The results of a study conducted in a probability sample should reflect the overall activities of all people living within that area. As a result, it is essential that interviews be completed with those hard to reach respondents as well as those easy to obtain. This is the reason for evening, Saturday and Sunday interviewing hours and up to 2 callbacks. Instructions on how to select the person you are to interview in a household are discussed in the Questionnaire Instructions. It is also important that you keep refusals to a minimum. As an interviewer, it is up to you to use your expertise to gain cooperation.

CLUSTER AND CLUSTER MAP

Your cluster map indicates the area in which you are to work. It is possible that in some cases, the map may be incorrect or the street names may have been changed. Make corrections or draw a new map, if necessary. Under no circumstances are you to change areas or interview on any but the streets indicated on your Cluster Map. You are to proceed in the direction indicated by the arrows. A red "X" indicates where you are to start.

THE HOUSEHOLD

You will note that we have referred to conducting interviews in households. A household is a place where one or more people live together. Each household will usually have:

        a. A separate entrance into a main hallway or street.
        b. A separate mailing address.
        c. Separate cooking facilities.

However, the presence of any of these (a, b or c) is actually sufficient to consider them a separate household.

The actual survey is to be conducted only in households or occupied dwelling units. Therefore, DO NOT include hospitals, businesses, schools, hotels and other institutions. Tenants or apartment hotels, however, are to be interviewed. Boarding houses and rooming houses with less than five lodgers are to be considered as one household only. If there are five or more lodgers, they are to be treated like hotels and you are NOT to interview them. Trailers count as households if they are the family's REGULAR home -- otherwise, do not include them.

Stores, funeral parlors and other places of business are NOT households and should NOT be included UNLESS the family also lives there. If, for example, a man operates a store in the front of the building but lives in the back with his family, then you must include them as a household.

DWELLING UNITS

In general, a dwelling unit is a group of rooms, or a single room occupied or intended for occupancy as separate living quarters by a family or other group of persons living together or by a person living alone.

A house, apartment or other group of rooms, or a single room is regarded as a dwelling unit when it is occupied or intended for occupancy as separate living quarters, that is, when the occupants do not live and eat with any other persons in the structure and when there is either (1) direct access from the outside or through a common hall or (2) a kitchen or cooking equipment for the exclusive use of the occupants. In hotels, a single room qualifies as a dwelling unit if occupied by a person whose usual residence is the hotel or a person who has no usual residence elsewhere.

Living quarters of the following types are not included in the housing unit inventory: rooming houses with five lodgers or more, transient accomodations (tourist courts, hotels, etc., which are predominantly for transients) and barracks for workers (railroad construction, or other migratory groups).

APARTMENT BUILDINGS

An apartment building contains a number of households (as does an apartment hotel). Each individual apartment counts as a separate household.

1. Work from the bottom up to the top floor -- basement, the first floor, then the second floor, etc.

2. On each floor, take the apartments in order of their number or letters -- Apartment #1, #2, #3, etc. or Apartment A, B, C etc.

3. If the apartments have no numbers or letters, take them in the following order on each floor: Left front, then left rear, then right rear, then right front. In other words, take the apartments in clockwise order around each floor, starting with the apartment just to the left of the front door or stairway as you come in.

4. Always remember to include the apartment letter or number in the household address. If there is no letter or number, record "left front", "left rear", etc. Don't forget that a superintendent's or janitor's apartment is to be included as one of the household in an apartment building.

5. Some apartments have electric locks on the front doors. In this case, try to get in by "buzzing" one of the apartments in the building. Remember that mailboxes and bells give you a good idea of the number of apartments on each floor.

VACANT HOMES:

A home is considered vacant if it is obvious no one lives there (i.e., boarded up). DO NOT LIST VACANT HOMES. If a family is on vacation or temporarily out of town, this is not considered a vacant home; it would be a "not at home". Such a household must receive an original call plus one callback.

HOUSEHOLDS ON VACATION:

As stated above, these are considered occupied dwellings, although they are temporarily unoccupied. You must make your original contact plus up to two callbacks. Even if you are told by a neighbor that the residents of a household will not be back for some time, you must make your contacts.

QUESTIONNAIRE ADMINISTRATION

1. Instructions

    Questionnaire instructions, including all skip instructions, are printed all in caps. Where necessary, they are underlined or offset in boxes to better catch your attention. Before beginning any interviewing, it is important that you completely familiarize yourself with the various skip instructions. By doing so, you will be better able to keep a continuous flow during the interview and not have to fumble or hesitate.

    DO NOT READ ANY CHOICES (LIST) UNLESS SPECIFICALLY TOLD TO DO SO! Only read choices where it is indicated on the questionnaire. (For this study, there are very few instances where you will be reading the list.)

2. "D.K." and "REF"

    If a respondent says that he does not know the answer to any question, indicate this by putting "D.K." (standing for "Don't Know") in the area where the answer is to be recorded. On the other hand, if the respondent refuses to answer a question despite your attempts to get him to answer, indicate this by writing "REF" (standing for "Refused") in the area where the answer is to be recorded. By following this procedure, you are assuring us that you have asked all required questions of the respondent.

3. General Interviewing Techniques

    You should be familiar with these basic interviewing techniques which you must follow on our studies.

    a. Ask questions for word-for-word, exactly as they are printed on the questionnaire.

    b. Ask questions in the order they appear on the questionnaire.

    c. When a word or a phrase is underlined, emphasize it.

9

c. DO NOT explain, interpret, or add to a question. If a respondent does not understand a question, merely re-read it. DO NOT EXPLAIN IT.

e. Record answers to open-end questions word-for-word. Never abbreviate or summarize an answer.

f. Never erase anything on the questionnaire. If it is necessary to make a correction, cross out the original answer and then circle the correct number or box. In the case of open-end questions, write in the correct answer.

g. In the few instances where indicated, be sure to read all of the pre-listed answers to a question. Please read all of the alternatives before accepting the respondent's answer. By the same token, never read where you are told to "DO NOT READ".

h. In questions where there are pre-listed answers, if a respondent gives you an answer which does not appear on the questionnaire, write it out on the "other" lines provided.

i. Use a pencil. DO NOT USE INK.

j. Write legibly. If we cannot read your writing, your work is meaningless.

k. Immediately after the close of the interview, check through the entire questionnaire for completeness, legibility, etc. If you come across any omissions or incomplete questions while checking the interview, ask the respondent for his/her assistance.

QUESTION-BY-QUESTION INSTRUCTIONS

SCREENER

o   The following instructions apply to both the male and female screener versions as the procedures are the same. However, for the sake of brevity, we will use the pronoun "he".

o   Use a new screener at every household.

o   Read introduction.

Q. 1:   Print in the number. If "0", terminate.

Q. 2:   Stress that you want to start with the oldest male. If there is only one male in the household who is 18 or over, simply write in this person's name.

Q. 3:   Print in age of each person.

- If any age given is under 18, erase that person from the listing and re-list the others properly.
- Is any males are out of age order, erase and re-list.

-10-

SELECTING THE DESIGNATED RESPONDENT

As we have told you, random selections are a very important part of this study. Your
sampling area was selected randomly; the respondent you will interview will also be
selected randomly.

We have referred to this respondent as the "designated" respondent. This is because
once the appropriate names are listed, the only person eligible for this interview must
be "designated" by some means.

For this study, the designated respondent is designated by means of an easy-to-use
number system.

1. Each screener has a label strip attached to the top right corner.

2. The strip has the numbers 1 to 8 printed on it, but the numbers can be in any
    order.

    EXAMPLE:
        A strip on one screener may look like ...

3	5	7	1	8	6	4	2

        While another screener may have the numbers in the following order ...

2	4	6	8	7	5	3	1

        Or still another screener may have the numbers as follows ...

8	1	3	6	7	5	2	4

        ETCETERA

3. On the grid for Question 3, to the left of the lines for the name of each
    person, you will see the numbers 1 to 8 in order.

PERSON INTERVIEWED	NAME	AGE
1	_____	___
2	_____	___
3	_____	___
4	_____	___
5	_____	___
6	_____	___
7	_____	___
8	_____	___

EXAMPLE: (for rows 4)

4. To determine who is the designated respondent ...

    a. Refer to the numbered label strip.

    b. Look at the first number listed.

    c. Now look at the grid.

    d. Interview the person with that number to the left of his name.

    e. If there is no name on that line, refer to the second number on the strip.

    f. Interview the person with that number to the left of his name.

    And so on until you locate a number/line with the name on it. THIS IS THE ONLY
    PERSON ELIGIBLE TO BE INTERVIEWED IN THIS DWELLING UNIT. THIS IS YOUR
    DESIGNATED RESPONDENT.

5. Circle the number to the left of this person's name.

5. Circle the number to the left of this person's name.

   EXAMPLE:

   LABEL STRIP ——— | 4 5 7 1 8 6 3 2 |

PERSON INTERVIEWED	NAME	AGE
1	_____	___
2	_____	___
3	_____	___
4	_____	___
5	_____	___
6	_____	___
7	_____	___
8	_____	___

In the above example, the interviewer listed the three eligible household members 18 years of age and over. The interviewer then referred to her label strip. Since Lee was listed on line 1, Lee is the designated respondent in that household.

Now, what if Lee's nephew Robert lived with them? Let's take a look.

   LABEL STRIP ——— | 4 5 7 1 8 6 3 2 |

PERSON INTERVIEWED	NAME	AGE
1	_____	___
2	_____	___
3	_____	___
4	_____	___
5	_____	___
6	_____	___
7	_____	___
8	_____	___

Robert would be the designated respondent. The interviewer looked at the label strip. The first number is 4. Robert's name appears on line 4 so he is the designated respondent.

Here's still another example:

   LABEL STRIP ——— | 8 6 7 2 5 3 4 1 |

PERSON INTERVIEWED	NAME	AGE
1	_____	___
2	_____	___
3	_____	___
4	_____	___
5	_____	___
6	_____	___
7	_____	___
8	_____	___

In this example, Jeff is the person whose name was on the first line that matched a number on the label strip. (There was no one on lines 8, 6, or 7.)

Now, try this one yourself.

LABEL STRIP ———— | 8 2 3 5 4 7 1 6 |

PERSON INTERVIEWED	NAME	AGE
1		
2		
3		
4		
5		
6		
7		
8		

You should have selected TOMMY as your designated respondent.

IF AT THIS POINT YOU DO NOT UNDERSTAND THIS PROCEDURE, GO OVER IT ONCE MORE
WITH YOUR SUPERVISOR.

/3-

QUESTION - BY - QUESTION INSTRUCTIONS

Q. 4a: Record one answer. If "yes", ask Q. 4b. If "no", skip to Q. 5a.

Q. 4b: Print in average number of hours. Do not accept a "range" - such as "8 - 10 hours". If the respondent gives a range, ask for a best estimate of one amount of hours.

Q. 5a: Ask everyone. Record one answer. If "yes", go on to Q. 5b. If "no", TERMINATE AND SAVE SCREENER. THIS DOES NOT COUNT TOWARD YOUR COMPLETION QUOTA.

Q. 5b: Print in one amount of magazines. Do not accept a "range", but if respondent reads more than one magazine equally and most often, you may circle them both/all. For example, someone may read "Time" and "Newsweek" every week and consider them both as the magazines they read most often.

           o Hand Card 6. Card 6 stays in front of the respondent through Question 61.

           o Be careful to keep your place while using this grid as only every other response is circled on the grid (6b, 6d, 6f, 6h, 6j, 6i) while the other questions are "yes/no" questions to be recorded in the question area above the grid.

Q. 6a: Allow respondent ample time to read the card. Then, ask question and record a "yes" or "no" answer. If "yes", ask Q. 6b. If "no", skip to Q. 6c.

Q. 6b: In column Q. 6b, record as many as mentioned.

Q. 6c: If "yes" ask Q. 6d. If "no" TERMINATE AND SAVE SCREENER.

Q. 6d: In column Q. 6d, record as many as mentioned. If either of the boxed magazines ("American Unicorn" or "News of the Globe") TERMINATE AND SAVE SCREENER. DO NOT COUNT TOWARD COMPLETION QUOTA.

Q. 6e: If "yes", ask Q. 6f. If "no" skip to Q. 6g.

Q. 6f: In column Q. 6f, record as many as mentioned. If either of the boxed magazines, TERMINATE AND SAVE SCREENER. DO NOT COUNT TOWARD COMPLETION QUOTA.

Q. 6g: If "yes" ask Q. 6h. If "no", skip to Q. 6i.

Q. 6h: In column Q. 6h, record as many as mentioned.

Q. 6i: If "yes", ask Q. 6j. If "no", skip to Q. 6k.

Q. 6j: In column Q. 6j, record as many as mentioned. If either boxed magazine mentioned, TERMINATE AND SAVE SCREENER. DO NOT COUNT TOWARD COMPLETION QUOTA.

Q. 6k: If "yes", ask Q. 6l. If "no", take back Card 6 and go on to Main Questionnaire.

Q. 6l: In column Q. 6l, record as many as mentioned.

           o Take back Card 6. Continue with Main Questionnaire.

MAIN QUESTIONNAIRE

           o The following instructions apply to both the male and female Main Questionnaires as the procedures are the same. However, for the sake of brevity, we will use the pronoun "he".

           o Select appropriate (male or female) interview packet. (Packet contains main questionnaire with quizzes attached and magazine material.)

               - Place magazine material face down in one pile (code dots facing up toward you)

           o At no time is the respondent to be exposed to any magazine material until indicated in the Main Questionnaire.

-14-

Q. 1:   Read to respondent.

Q. 2:   By examining code dots, select the appropriate item from the magazine material
          pile and hand to respondent. Keep track of how long it takes respondent to
          read item. Record time in area provided.

          NOTE: If "zero" minutes (it took only seconds to read the item) or "zero"
                  seconds (it took an even number of minutes to read the item) be sure to
                  put a "0" on the appropriate line.

Q. 3a: Once the respondent finishes reading, remove the item and put aside.

          Write in response of _main_ message. (Other points go on the line provided for
          Q. 3b)

Q. 3b: Write in other points.

Q. 4:   Be sure respondent understands. Turn to next page, but before handing to
          respondent DOUBLE CHECK, that the code in the upper right hand corner of the
          quiz matches the code of the magazine material first read. IF THE CODES DO NOT
          MATCH, STOP! Put all materials back into the packet. TERMINATE THIS
          INTERVIEW. Return the incorrect packet to your supervisor. This does _not_
          count as a complete. Otherwise, hand respondent questionnaire opened to quiz.
          Allow respondent as much time as needed. Check for completion. If any
          questions are not answered, hand the quiz back to the respondent for
          completion.

Q. 5:   Place indicated magazine item back in front of respondent and proceed.

          Read list and record one answer.

Q. 6a: If "yes", ask Q. 6b. If "no" or "don't know" skip to Q. 6c.

Q. 6b/6c: Print in one amount. Do not accept a range. If respondent is unsure, ask for
          a "best estimate".

	FOR ITEMS WITH A DIGIT ENDING "1", "2" or "3"	FOR ITEMS WITH A DIGIT ENDING "4", "5" or "6"
Q. 7a:	If "yes" ask Q.7b. If "no", skip to Q. 8	Q.7/8: Read list and record one answer.
Q. 7b:	Read list. Record one answer.	
Q. 7c:	If "yes" ask Q.7d. If "no", skip to Q. 8	
Q.7/8:	Read list. Record one answer	

                    REMOVE INDICATED ITEM FROM VIEW.

          o Continue until all administer items/quizzes are done. Then administer the
             last page of the Main Questionnaire (classification)

CLASSIFICATION

Q. 9:   Read list (except "refused"). Record one answer.

Q.10:   Do not read list. Record one answer.

Q. 11a: If "yes", ask Q. 11b. If "no" or "refused", skip to Q. 12.

Q. 11b: READ LIST and record one answer.

Q. 12:   SHOW CARD 12. Record one answer.

          o Obtain respondent information
          o Staple Screener to Main Questionnaire
          o Clip all magazine material together
          o Indicate as completed on the appropriate tally sheet.

APPENDIX K

Validation Questionnaire

GUIDELINE RESEARCH CORPORATION
3 West 35th Street
New York, New York 10001

Job # 001-013

Magazine Study

May, 1985

VALIDATION QUESTIONNAIRE

- ASK TO SPEAK TO THE PERSON WHOSE NAME IS LISTED ON VALIDATION SHEET
- CORRECT ANSWERS ARE CIRCLED
- PROBE WHERE INDICATED

Hello (Mr./Miss/Mrs./Ms./)_____, I'm_____from Guideline Research in New York. Recently a study was done in your area and we're calling to thank you for your participation, and to confirm a few points.

1. Recently, did you take part in a survey where an interviewer asked you some questions about magazines?   ?

                    YES.....(1)

                    NO.......2 ➤ BEFORE TERMINATING, BE SURE NO ONE ELSE
                                 IN HOUSEHOLD WAS INTERVIEWED.

2. Do you usually read or look through at least some portion of a magazine at least once a month:

                    YES......(1)

                    NO........2 ➤WHAT DID YOU TELL THE INTERVIEWER?

3. Please tell me, where did the interview take place:

                    MUST BE RESPONDENT'S HOME

4. Finally, prior to the interview, did you know the interviewer personally?

                    YES.......1 ➤PROBE TO DETERMINE EXACT RELATIONSHIP

                    NO.......(2)

        THANK YOU FOR YOUR HELP WITH OUR STUDY!!!

266

Author Index

Subject Index

B

Beliefs
  brand, 31, 45
  communication, 17, 45–48, 88
  material, 23–24
  message, 31
  referent, 17, 46, 88

C

Communication
  beliefs, 45–48
  components of, 2
  effects, 28–54
    comprehension (see Comprehension)
    post-comprehension, 36–37, 48
    pre-comprehension, 36–37
  importance of, 2
  media, 15, 25–26
    interpersonal, 25
    mass, 25–26
  messages, 15, 22, 36
    content vs. structure, 22
    comprehension of, 22
    editorial vs. advertising content, 22
    factual vs. inferential content, 23
    graphic features, 82
    linguistic features, 82–83

material vs. immaterial content, 23–24
  receivers, 26–28, 36
    literacy of, 15, 27, 55–57
    target audience, 76–77
    sources, 21, 36
Comprehension
  definition, 2
  involvement and, 38, 90
  importance of, 5–6
  of molar vs. molecular meanings, 24
  necessary prior stages, 36–37
    attention, 37
    central cortical representation, 37
    exposure, 36–37
    peripheral sensory reception, 37
  outcomes of, 17, 48–54
    comprehension, 17, 49–51
    miscomprehension, 17, 51
    non-comprehension, 17, 48–49
  process of, 38–48
    belief formation, 45–48
    bottom-up processing, 16, 38–39
    inference making, 44
    inputs to, 33–34
    meanings (implied), 43
    meanings (asserted), 43
    morphemic representation, 41–42
    schema and schemata, 16, 39, 42
    semantic analysis, 16, 41
    sensory analysis, 16, 39

271

For Product Safety Concerns and Information please contact our EU
representative GPSR@taylorandfrancis.com
Taylor & Francis Verlag GmbH, Kaufingerstraße 24, 80331 München, Germany

www.ingramcontent.com/pod-product-compliance
Ingram Content Group UK Ltd.
Pitfield, Milton Keynes, MK11 3LW, UK
UKHW021442080625

459435UK00011B/349